W9-BBG-248

282   DALLY, Mary Vincent
DAL   Married to a Catholic
      priest

Married to a Catholic Priest

Married to a Catholic Priest

A Journey in Faith

Mary Vincent Dally

Loyola University Press • Chicago

Loyola University Press
3441 North Ashland Avenue
Chicago, Illinois 60657

LIBRARY OF CONGRESS CATALOGING IN PUBLICATION DATA

Dally, Mary Vincent.
    Married to a Catholic priest : a journey in faith / Mary Vincent Dally.
      p. cm.
    ISBN 0-8294-0599-2
    1. Dally, Peter, 1928– . 2. Catholic Church—United States—
Clergy—Biography. 3. Converts, Catholic—United States—
Biography. 4. Episcopal Church—Clergy—Biography. 5. Anglican
Communion—United States—Clergy—Biography. 6. Dally, Mary
Vincent. I. Title.
    BX4668.D25D34   1988
    282'.092'2—dc19
    [B]   88-17511
                                                                 CIP

Designed by C. L. Tornatore

To Peter, with all my love.
And to the courageous men and women
of the Pastoral Provision

FOREWORD

At the moment of baptism, Christians begin a life-long pilgrimage of faith. It becomes the responsibility of the newly baptized to walk with the Lord toward the ultimate goal of full union with God. Along this pilgrim journey there are hills and valleys which can traversed only by faith. Particular moments and unexpected events become the occasions of success or failure depending on the way they are faced.

When Pope John Paul II issued The Pastoral Provisions allowing former ministers of other beliefs who had become Catholic to also be ordained priests even though they were married, he created exactly such an occasion. That this is a unique challenge for the men in question goes without saying. Thus we often overlook the unique struggles and opportunities of the wives of these men.

As I finish my second reading of Mary Dally's work, I am impressed, inspired, and amazed at how well she used the occasion offered by The Pastoral Provisions as a source of tremendous spiritual growth and positive movement on her own pilgrim journey.

In *Married To A Catholic Priest—A Journey In Faith*, Mary Dally opens her heart to express the fears and frustrations, the sorrows and hurts which she experienced at that particular moment of her life. She shares her dreams and her hopes, her joys and successes all in an open, authentic way. This is no novel. It is the real life story and experiences of a real woman of faith.

In her writings, Mary clearly evidences that she believes in God, she loves Him, and she works daily to follow Him. She displays a tender love for her own namesake, Mary, the Mother of Jesus. She expresses a true belief in The Catholic Church. She is indeed a woman of great faith.

Although I had the opportunity of sharing somewhat in Mary's pilgrimage, I never fully recognized the depth and intensity of her own experience until I read this, her own account. Until then, The Pastoral Provisions pointed merely to the men who were to be ordained. Now I see them encompassing the wives and families, indeed, the whole Church. Above all, I see our good and gracious God working in and through His Church, loving each of us and guiding us safely on our pilgrim journey.

Most Reverend Eusebius J. Beltran
Bishop of Tulsa

May 12, 1988
Feast of the Ascension of Our Lord

ACKNOWLEDGEMENTS

This is a true story. Incidents and conversations have been reconstructed from memory, my personal notes, and written documents, taking into account individual's personalities and other factors. Their only purpose here is to convey to the reader the story of *our journey in faith*. Names and places are real, with the exception of a few obvious ones which have been changed to protect the privacy of individuals.

I offer what I have written in a spirit of love and reconciliation for those of us within Catholicism and uniquely in the Diocese of Tulsa, for my brothers and sisters in the Episcopal Church, and for the reunion of all Christians with the See of Peter. It is my hope that sharing our story will serve to strengthen and encourage others in the fulfillment of God's plan for their lives and for his Holy Church.

There are no words to adequately express my gratitude to my husband and children, without whose love and support I could not have begun and completed this work. I am deeply grateful to Bishop Eusebius Beltran for his openness and encouragement, and to my friend Rita Bisdorf for the invaluable assistance of her insightful wisdom and editorial expertise.

Biblical quotations are taken from *The New American Bible*, St. Joseph Edition, Revised 1986.

MARY VINCENT DALLY

1

"Father Peter, did you read in the paper that the pope says married Episcopal ministers can become Catholic priests?" Tish asked.

"No. I didn't see that," my husband answered.

"Well, it was in this morning's *Post Intelligencer.*"

"Really?" Peter asked.

As I listened my stomach twisted into a knot and my hand tightened on the sailboat's wooden tiller.

No. Not the Roman Catholic Church, I thought as I looked away toward the shoreline with its friendly row of shingled roofs and picket fences. Its modest private docks. The tide was low, and I took a deep breath and savored it.

Above me a seagull swooped and screeched. It can't be true, my thoughts answered his cry. I won't let it be true. The gull screeched again, and flew off into the afternoon sun. Running away. Leaving me alone.

As I watched Peter sitting only a few feet away in the cockpit, I almost felt that he too had left me. My thoughts of him seemed trapped inside me and separated me from the group, though the laughter and voices swelled around me. I felt oddly wrapped in a loneliness that I couldn't explain even to myself, as thoughts rushed and swept me backward in time.

For as long as I had known him, Peter had been the only clergyman in our Episcopal diocese, first Oregon, then Washington, to celebrate the daily Eucharist. During all those years he went every Saturday night to hear confessions, though rarely did anyone come. I remember how soon after his ordination his bishop said, "The daily Mass? It'll just kill you!" The other priest at the table, an Anglican monk, smiled and replied, "Aahh . . . Bishop, but what a way to go!"

Names I'd heard when friends talked together in the privacy of our homes: Pusey, Keble, . . . Newman. All tractarians of the Oxford Movement. This had happened before to Anglicans. The remnant of the faith. Pusey and Keble held on. Now it's our turn to fight for what is Catholic in the Anglican Communion of the Church.

Still, the recurring Roman fever. Man's—Peter's link with God in the sacraments. His priesthood. "No longer there, Mary." "Where then?" The words and phrases bounced and echoed in my head like the screeching call of the seagull in the afternoon stillness.

My husband. He *is* a priest, I thought.

But as I turned away from the place where he sat, a chill swept through my body. In its wake I felt the gentle sun touch my skin. I tried again to listen to the carefree talk around me on the sailboat, but it was only noise.

There must be some mistake, I said to myself again. He wouldn't do that anyway! Or would he? I wanted to run from my fears, to enjoy this rare afternoon on the water, with my hand on the tiller of the sailboat, to pretend that our lives would always be the way they were that day.

As my eyes swept the island hills, thoughts and visions of years gone by accosted me again and again.

We had come to Vashon Island with our family in 1964. Peter served as the Episcopal Church's vicar, and I was his wife. Our lives were rich in warm experiences and friendships. Like today.

Our four children had grown up not knowing a time when summer afternoons of discovery on Puget Sound beaches were not a part of the rhythm of their lives. I smiled as I thought of the warm tidal mud that squished between their little toes, as they ran to lift rocks in search of baby crabs and starfish to carry home. Forgotten treasures until our noses reminded us of them stored in closets or under beds.

It was an idyllic place to raise a family. Isolated, yet only a short ferry ride to the city of Seattle.

The years passed quickly. We saw our sons and daughters leave the protection of the island cloister for bagpiping and ballet lessons, summer camp in the mountains, and later on college. I yearned for them not to forget these years, but to take with them the advantage of having one foot planted firmly in the best of each world.

My role as the vicar's wife was important to me too. Walking beside this man whom God had set aside in a special way, I felt equally called. No one could tell me that God did not give me his special grace to be the person who could make a difference in my husband's ministry. I found satisfaction and fulfillment in my role as strengthener and enabler. I was more than wife and mother. To our congregation I was a sacramental, the one person with the unique identity of priest's wife.

Life touched me with its full range of sensibilities. Vashon Island had become our family home, and when I took stock, I found our roots deeply anchored there, secure in the midst of the change and competition of life. So it was, that day in 1980 when Peter and I stepped aboard our friends' sailing yacht.

My thoughts returned to the task of steering as Don, our skipper, cut the engine. The sails caught the gentle northerly winds and swung us into the waters of outer Quartermaster Harbor, beyond which lay the southern reaches of Puget Sound.

"Oh, man! What a beautiful day. Couldn't be nicer," Marilyn shouted as the sails took a big gust of wind.

It was hard to believe that the mists and rains were only weeks away. I noticed that the surrounding hills were already dotted with the bright promise of fall colors. But for now, the sea water lapped soothingly against the hull of the boat, calling us to the rich enjoyment of good friends, a bottle of wine, and homemade delicacies. What friends we have, I thought.

Later, in the evening's stillness, the day seemed to have begun weeks before as I moved about the kitchen and became gradually aware of Peter reading the article in the Seattle morning paper.

"Archbishop Quinn. National Conference of Catholic Bishops. I know these other names. They're Episcopalian clergy. Do you know what this means?"

Stunned, I turned to see him bursting with excitement.

"I'll write them; find out what we have to do. There must be some conditions. Then I'll get in touch with Archbishop Hunthausen to talk about a date for my resignation here." He was elated as he took my shoulders gently in each hand. "Think what this can mean for us, Mary."

"The Roman Catholic Church have married priests? You can't be serious." I sneered at him and pulled away. "That's what it says here."

"Don't chase rainbows. They've made promises before. Crumbs tossed under the table to Henryites. Why they hardly know we exist and couldn't care less. The whole thing's crazy. Some hot-shot reporter got hold of it and made a big thing out of nothing. It can't possibly be true." I turned back toward the sink and said, almost to myself, "For the love of God, Peter, forget it. It'll never happen."

I loved my life. Peter's ministry. We had hopes and dreams of security for our future. Now they clattered together in a kaleidoscope of feelings. A childhood of insults and anger, long buried, assaulted me. My head reeled. I couldn't handle it.

"Mary. The opportunity. Have you any idea?" Peter seemed to yell at me.

"Why? Why do you have to do this? Why can't we just stay here? You're a Catholic. The *Roman* Catholic Church has never . . . " I turned and glared at him, my Irish temper flared.

"I want more. I want to *be* a Catholic. Don't you see, I don't want to settle for less and less all the time. A second-class citizen in a church that no longer believes it is Catholic? Sometimes I wonder if our bishops ever intended for the church to remain Catholic. A few years ago I thought Anglicans would reunite with Roman Catholics, but the Episcopal Church is farther away from reunion now than it has ever been." His voice softened as he said, "This is an opportunity.

An invitation. A homecoming. The state of the Episcopal Church. The implosion."

"But this is where we belong!" I cried.

"I don't care what you say. I can't turn my back on this. You know how I feel. Have always felt. My days are numbered in the Episcopal Church. The bishops won't tolerate men like me much longer. They want contemporary Protestantism, not Anglican Catholic theology and practice."

"But you've always said you are a Catholic. You've said it over and over, that we can be Catholic and not be Roman Catholic. Now, you're . . ." I said, weakly.

"Do I have to tell *you* how I love the Episcopal Church?" he asked. "I've always been alone in my stand on the Eucharist and confession. And now I'm even more alone. Not only faced with these issues, but questions about human sexuality, the sanctity of human life, of marriage, and that's just the tip of the iceberg!"

"How many Roman Catholic priests have you ever met who've even given you the time of day?" I asked. "They're not interested in us. We're just another Protestant group to them. I can't imagine that they'll ever accept us, under any circumstances."

"Mary, this is an opportunity. I have to do it. I believe I am a priest of God, but I want to be a Catholic even more. I've got to try for priesthood in the Roman Catholic Church." He stopped, seeming to dare me to continue. My husband's voice became soft as he said, "I've been called to priesthood and I must try. It is more important to try, and maybe even fail, than not to try at all."

For that moment, there in our kitchen, just the two of us, time stopped. I looked into his face. I saw there the years of shared vocations. The years of love. Of worrying about children, and how we'd pay the household bills. Why, I wondered. Why now?

"Come on, Peter. Can't you see what we are in this community? What our lives are here on this island?"

There never lived a man more like his namesake than Peter. Impetuous. Lovable. Earnestly sincere. And so terribly human.

Mistake? It's got to be a mistake. I know it. Still I couldn't deny there was, even now, an element of excitement welling up inside me, urging me beyond the gnawing fear that gripped me like a steel band around my chest.

Peter turned suddenly to me and said, "Of course it's true. The article is off the AP newswire. The Roman Catholic Church is too careful to let this out prematurely. I'll bet they're ready to take applications now."

"Sure they are," I mimicked.

"I wonder who else will go. I can think of at least six men from our diocese who will jump at this chance." His voice trailed off as he closed the stairway door and hurried up to his study.

"The others are too smart," I said sarcastically. "You're a rotten idealist about the Catholic Church!" I yelled after him.

No answer.

I slammed the door shut as hard as I could.

Still nothing.

I stared at the silent, closed door for a long moment. I felt helpless and numb. It was as if I didn't exist.

"He didn't hear a word I said," I muttered aloud to myself. The afternoon magic gone. Forgotten. How I wanted it back with the sunshine and the wind in my hair. Our friends. The water.

Mechanically, I put away the leftover food and supplies. Above me, the typewriter seemed louder than its normal clickety-click as it punctuated the stillness of the house with the reality of the day's events.

While I washed the plastic picnic containers, my thoughts turned to a future I could only guess and wonder about. There was no way I could know now all the questions that would haunt me in the months ahead. But, I wondered, what will happen to us? To Peter's ministry? He thought I would be happy about this? He's crazy. Would he ever hear me, how I feel about the Catholic Church? Mine was not the heart of a rebel. Would that gift ever be mine?

I wanted to scream. To be heard.

But there was only Peter.

Suddenly I understood that what I really valued was the respectability and acceptance of a proper Episcopal clergyman's wife. I knew who I was and what others expected of me. I liked my role, and within it I found independence and the freedom to be my own person. It was a privilege to share my life in warm and loving relationships with the people in our congregation, and I felt loved in return as the pastor's wife.

What of this new role in the Roman Catholic Church? Is there to be such a person as priest's wife? And what about the vow of celibacy? The article didn't say anything about continuing to live in the married state. Would we have to live separately? Others have done that. Will I be thought of as the housekeeper, or his woman? How will Catholic laypeople feel about a priest who has a wife? What of other priests. What kind of resentment will I have to face and live with?

Our children. What about our children?

Peter's voice haunted me across the years. I had heard it hundreds of times, "A sacrament is an outward and visible sign of an inward and spiritual grace . . . " For each of us, our relationship with God is bound up in our response to his sacraments. He calls us to a variety of gifts. From the beginning I sensed that this was it for Peter. His whole relationship with God and other persons was wrapped up in his ministry. That was it. All of it.

"Mary, if I marry you, my ministry and the Church will always come first. It's not that I don't love you more than life itself, it's . . ."

In my heart I knew then that he had to try, but I'd fight it. I had to. He's only a man. And I think I understand him. Yet I do not understand at all. Give all this up? Married Catholic priest? No.

How do I know when my feelings are real and when I am just plain scared? I had thought he was out of his mind when he wanted to teach blind kids to sail, but in the end I had encouraged him and helped with the weekends and summer camps, and the blind did sail! I knew now I'd do the same thing again.

One thing for sure, I thought, as I forced another large bowl into an already full cupboard. I definitely do not want to think about how I grew up in a family where my Catholic father married my divorced mother outside the church. The pans and bowls clattered and scraped together as I forced the cupboard door shut with a loud bang. I like being high church Episcopalian where I can be an Anglo-Catholic and not have to face painful childhood memories of hurts both spoken and silently endured.

Damn. Why did this ever have to happen?

Damn Tish.

Damn the Seattle *Post Intelligencer.*

And damn— No. There was something inside me that would not let me feel the way I really wanted to about the Roman Catholic Church.

2

I heard a car come into the driveway and looked up to see John, the oldest of our four children. He had stopped to pick up his clean laundry before returning to graduate school at the University of Washington. I listened as he came up the basement stairs and pushed the door open with a heavy thud.

"Mom? Where are you? Did Dad see the *Seattle P.I.*?"

"In the dining room. Would you like some lemonade?" I asked.

"Did Dad see the *P.I.*?" John demanded. "Mr. Pottinger showed it to me. Wow! Dad can be a Roman Catholic priest. Did he see it?" His face glistened in the evening light.

"Yes, we both saw the article. Dad's upstairs now. I think he might be writing a letter to find out about it."

"Wow! My Dad, a Roman Catholic priest," he said as he poured himself a big glass of lemonade. "Mmmm. This is good, Mom."

What can I say, I thought. "Well, we don't know what it means. But Dad will find out. Then we'll decide if it's what we should do."

"Oh, he should do it. It'd be so exciting. He'd be a lot happier there."

"We'll just have to see," I said. "We don't know exactly what it means, and we can't get our hopes up. It might not mean anything at all. You know how newspapers are. They blow everything out of proportion, and—"

"Oh, it'll be good. I can feel it. Where's Dad? I wanna talk to him," John said as he finished off the lemonade. "That's his typewriter. Wouldn't you know it? He's writing that letter right now."

I thought of the Episcopal Church, and how Peter had felt about it since the 1976 General Convention. He and his friends talked a lot about leaving, but to leave would mean to leave the ministry, and these were men who felt called to serve God, practicing and teaching the Catholic faith as they knew it. To become Roman Catholic would mean they would become laymen because they were all married. There were no other options for priesthood available to them within one of the traditional Catholic bodies of Christianity. They were high churchmen who looked upon themselves as part of the historic Catholic Church. Not Roman Catholic, but separated brethren. With the convention, the Episcopal Church had officially begun to change, to move farther away from Catholic practice and teachings and more directly into the stream of mainline Protestantism. There no longer existed a bastion of Catholic theology in the Episcopal Church within which clergy who were high church could take refuge. They felt deserted and alone, adrift in a body which no longer wanted them or needed to tolerate them.

Peter and most of the others decided to stay in the Episcopal Church and remain loyal to their theological convictions. However, by the late seventies congregations were shrinking in numbers, and there were many more clergy than the Church needed to fill vacancies. They agreed it would be just a matter of time until they were forced out. A few left with small groups of dissident laity, forming still other bodies, only to confuse more than ever the historic continuum of the Catholic faith as we experienced it. But that didn't fit for us. Peter was not a dissident. He simply believed that the Anglican branch of the ancient Church should recognize its unique identity within Catholicism. And more than anything, he prayed and hoped for reunion with Roman Catholics and Orthodox Christians.

I realized that Peter thought he would soon leave the Episcopal Church to become a Catholic layman, but for me it was just talk. I never dreamed that the time would come when he would actually do what he said. And I knew now that I had never faced the fact that he might be forced to leave. He worked too hard and was too beloved by his parish family for that to happen. I knew they would defend him against any bishop.

The muffled voices of father and son coming from the upstairs study interrupted my thoughts. They're quite a pair. John so much like his father, and still so different, his impetuosity, and then a moment later, his deep sensitivity. I knew that John would think about this move and within the week call me, fearing that his Dad might really decide to leave the ministry, to try for priesthood in the Catholic Church.

"Gotta run and get a ferry." John hugged me and left a kiss on my cheek. "I'll call you, Mom. Okay?" He yelled from the porch. Drive carefully, John, I said to myself.

Heavily, I got up and went to the kitchen. I put my hands into the warm dishwater and thought of this kitchen we'd remodeled with the money from my father's small estate. I loved the old Island house. It was modestly big and roomy with five bedrooms, (we added two in the basement when we moved in), a separate TV-study area for the kids, and a quiet attic study for Peter. The leaded glass windows and Eastern hardwood floors added a unique quality to the otherwise ordinary house built in the twenties by the Island's first banker.

The one bathroom with its beautiful antique fixtures soon came to be known as the "family room," having dared us to live here in any sort of harmony with four children about to become primping teenagers. I must admit it did demand time studies and engineering feats, and perhaps, most difficult for teens, consideration for the other person.

I thought of the evenings together as Peter and I painted and prepared the house to move into. We closed the sale in early December, 1971. Naturally, he wanted the family to spend Christmas there. And typically, I was against the quick move. The house wasn't ready, and with the demands of my full-time job, I couldn't work on the new house in the evenings. Nor could I take care of the family while packing our things to move from the other house in time for the holiday. Well, Peter had his own method of persuasion. One day I came home from work to find that he had moved all the beds from the old house to the new one. I yelled at him and cried for hours, and in his usual way he wondered what all the fuss was about. In the end I didn't make him take the beds back, and we got everything moved in time for a wonderful family Christmas.

It was a special house. It meant a lot to all of us to be a part of its history. A symbol of the early days, the old islanders loved it too. They often told us how it pleased them that our family lived there. The gesture made me feel warm and loved, as though somehow our lives were a symbol of the Island as it had become.

In Peter's long ministry on Vashon Island we knew people in an especially intimate way. We saw and listened to their struggle with "the rock," as we called the island. Some came expecting protection from the rest of the world. But it was only a dream for most of them, and when they didn't find the safe harbor they expected, they left. Others stayed, charmed by the daily ferry commute to their jobs in the city, the cup of coffee in the morning and the nap on the way home in the evening. The community also attracted artisans and skilled craftspeople, creating a kind of tiny "Carmel" of the northern Pacific coast. Their alternative lifestyles blended and mixed with the lawyers and Boeing Company executives to lend color and warmth to the island's character.

There were simple joys in living, as folks shared early summer news of ripened strawberries that you could pick for yourself. But of course it wasn't news at all, because the air was filled with the warm strawberry fragrance as you drove down the main road with your car windows open.

The summer people, more likely called "DSP's" (damned summer people), were barely tolerated by the locals. Most arrived on Memorial Day weekend with high-powered ski boats, barking dogs, and kids with ghetto blasters to take over our quiet neighborhood beaches until, finally, Labor Day signaled their return to the city.

I thought about our life on the island, the intimacy and strength we found among our friends there. But deep inside I knew that if the news article was right, Peter would do this thing, whatever it turned out to be. I remembered once he had asked a young seminarian why he thought he should become a minister. The young man replied with a question: Why do the geese fly south?

If we are truly called to this new ministry, if there is such a thing, I thought once again—instinctively knowing that both Peter and I had to feel that call together—God will enable me to rise above my anger and my fear of the loss of material security. Like for that other Mary in Nazareth, he will make it so clear that there can be no room for doubt. But I have to feel it's his plan, not ours.

The basement door closed. The sound drew my attention to the driveway where Peter looked up from his old bicycle, a wide grin on his face. He waved the white envelope in his hand. "Going to the post office," he shouted.

I smiled back. Tears filled my eyes as I slowly shook my head. He doesn't even have enough sense to wait until morning, I thought. All my talking, my emotional outbursts. Nothing I say ever changes his mind. I don't know why I waste the effort. Still, I envy his idealism. I guess when it comes right down to it I'll do anything he asks. I love him, and there will never be another like him. I dabbed my eyes and watched at the window until he was out of sight, the day's events sinking into my consciousness.

Peter had gone to mail the letter that would change our lives forever. Without regard for the way I felt, it seemed.

This time it isn't teaching blind kids to sail or moving the family beds into a new house. What has begun today will have an impact not only on the two of us, but on our children, and maybe even our grandchildren. Now, in the shadows of the kitchen I cannot begin to envision all that will happen to us. Perhaps that's best. This morning we thought we'd spend the rest of our lives on this island. Now I know all that has changed.

3

Peter's childhood was marked by parental instability and abuse. His father's alcoholism painfully fractured each member of the family with the inherent tragedy of that disease. His mother was the daughter of a Midwest banking family, his mother's loss of wealth and status left her unable to face even the challenges of daily living, much less the healing of an alcoholic husband. Lacking basic family stability, Peter and his younger sister, Elizabeth, fell back upon the spiritual strengths they found in the Church.

Determined not to live like his parents, Peter developed an insatiable drive to succeed, to pull himself out of the confusion and neglect which surrounded him throughout his childhood.

With God's grace he was able to persevere as he endeavored to enter the Episcopal ministry from a background of both material and emotional deprivation. It was not an easy thing to do, for he rarely had anyone to turn to for support and encouragement. On his own before he left high school, he often had to support the other members of the family. However, because he was willing to work hard, Peter was always able to get a job, frequently working nights while attending school during the day. Once when he desperately needed work, he agreed to clean up a suicide for a janitorial company, which got him a regular job with them. The summer he graduated from the University of Washington, before he went to the seminary, he lived in a storeroom at the bank where he worked, because he had nowhere else to go.

No one will ever know the triumph Peter felt as he began his first year in seminary, even though he had to work nights in a school for the handicapped to pay his tuition. However, with this grueling schedule he was physically and emotionally exhausted by the end of the first year. More important, he felt that he was facing the greatest spiritual crisis of his life. He needed funds to return to seminary in the fall, but above all else that summer he knew he must renew himself spiritually.

Peter learned of the Sisters of the Transfiguration, a small group of Episcopal nuns who ran a summer camp in the hills north of San Francisco. He was hired for a small sum to work as boys' counselor for the entire summer. There he met Sister Marjorie Hope and Father John Baldwin, a monk of the Order of the Holy Cross. It was in their spiritual depth, simple devotion to God, and the historical traditions of the Church that he received renewed energy and peace, the strength to continue toward his goal of ministry.

Near the close of Peter's third and final year in seminary, Bishop Dagwell of Oregon asked for unmarried clergy to go to the isolated, sparsely populated southern Oregon coast. He volunteered and was assigned to work with Father Robert Greenfield, a learned liturgist and theologian. Father Greenfield's scholarship was an inspiration, and his devotion of offering daily Mass was a practice Peter continued throughout his ministry. In fact, that one year with Father Greenfield shaped Peter's ministry and his view of the Episcopal Church in a way that nothing else would ever affect him again. He devoured the works of Pusey, Keble, and other Catholic reformers, seeking and finding in them a belief and validity for the practice of the historic Catholic faith within contemporary Anglicanism. These men, C.S. Lewis, and other moderns like Father Greenfield, brought to the Episcopal Church of the 1950s a depth and balance that extended far beyond pretty liturgical ceremonies and well-cultivated social graces.

Perhaps if then Peter's longings and questions had fallen on the ears of a sympathetic Roman Catholic priest . . . But those were pre-Vatican II years, and Catholic priests found little time or interest for the questions of Protestant ministers. So Peter stayed, loving the richness he had discovered in those first months of his ministry, but also wrestling with the inevitable bouts of Roman fever. Like other high churchmen, he saw his role as one of strengthening and teaching the Catholic faith in the Episcopal Church, praying that renewed understanding and love would lead to reunion with the Holy See.

As with Peter, his sister Elizabeth's life was a struggle for survival and a desire for firm roots which eventually led her to a religious vocation. She began her life as an Episcopal nun when she was eighteen years old. But she had little education beyond high school, and the community she entered lacked the stability and the depth of faith that Peter found in his association with Father Greenfield. While there were individuals who inspired her, Elizabeth longed for something more than what she had found there. She and two or three others left their religious community in 1970 to become Roman Catholic laywomen. Elizabeth joined an informal community of persons who like herself were searching for their vocations. More and more she felt drawn to St. Teresa of Avila and the cloistered prayer life of the Carmelite Sisters. Within a short time she found her way west where she established a friendship with the Seattle Carmel. Through them she learned of the Carmel of the Our Father, a French- speaking community located on the Mount of Olives in Jerusalem. She petitioned that community for postulancy in 1973.

When she entered the Carmel she announced to us, with the zeal of a true convert, that the entire community would now pray for our conversion too, and that Peter would one day be a Catholic priest. I was shocked and furious at her audacity, and I felt alienated and offended by her meddling in our personal affairs. Priest, I thought, she's crazy. Any sane person would know that a married man could not be a Catholic priest.

I remember thinking as I mentally planted my feet firmly on mother England's soil: Not me. Those sisters aren't going to pray me into popery.

And now look what's happening. At the dinner table I looked from one family member to another. God has not only heard her prayers; he seems to be answering them. I felt startled by the reality which my thoughts brought to light. Lord, I hope you know what you're doing.

We had finished our evening meal and I sat there

listening as Peter read the letter he'd just written to Sister Elsbeth. It was September, 1980, and one month had passed since our reading of the papal announcement in the *Seattle Post Intelligencer.*

> I get a few facts occasionally, but things are still vague, and of course I would like to see them move much faster. Still, it is God's will and his time. I am totally convinced this is the right road to take, and I ask your prayers and those of your community as I complete the last four months of my ministry in the Episcopal Church.

Unable to believe what I'd heard, I shrieked, "Last four months of your ministry? You can't be serious! Peter, you haven't heard a word from Archbishop Hunthausen yet. We don't even know for sure there *is* such a program."

"I'll hear any day now. And as soon as I do, we'll leave. You don't think I can stay in the Episcopal Church and be a Roman Catholic at the same time, do you?" Peter finished his dessert and looked at me across the table. His face expressed the same benign determination that I heard in his voice.

"Well, no. I don't expect that. But four months?"

"I know it seems quick. But life here is so short compared to all eternity."

How many times have I heard *that* in a crisis, I thought.

He continued, "I've wasted enough time. If I'm going to be a Roman Catholic, then I've got to get on with it."

I felt the eyes of our two younger children, Kurt and Tess, move from Peter to me and back again. They were uncommonly quiet, listening to this conversation about a decision that, whatever the outcome, would have great impact on all of our lives.

"What about the kids' educations? We've got to get our finances in order. We can't turn our backs on our responsibilities, and we can't live on what I make."

"We'll make it okay, Mary. The Lord will see us

through this transition. It's the right thing to do, and I know everything will work out."

He seems so sure, I thought, but . . ., "It's not good sense. Nobody ever said we didn't have to pay our bills. What will people think? We've got to take care of our financial obligations before we can do anything. What do you want to do, claim bankruptcy? That would be wonderful. Ha. Come on, Peter."

"No. The Lord has a plan. Our job is to pray that we will know what we are supposed to do."

"Are you sure it's not *your* plan?" I asked. I felt upset and confused. Why does it have to be this way, I thought. Why do we have to do this?

Peter reached for his clerical collar, stretched his neck to attach the button to the front of his shirt and with his right hand felt the ends of the collar snap over the second button at the back.

He came to my chair and kissed me goodbye.

"You're still the best thing that ever happened to me, Love. I'll be home around nine," he said as his hand brushed my shoulder in a gesture of assurance.

The collar ritual, usually preceded by the family's frantic search, was a familiar scene. As he closed the door, I wondered what it must be like for the children of this man. He was a child at heart, an exciting and energetic parent who took his sons and daughters sailing and backpacking in the summer, and carved time from parish responsibilities to see them in school events in the winter. The father who taught them to paint rocks at the beach, who tumbled about with them on the floor of the family room. Who, when they were small, created the Saturday night habit of root beer floats and Jackie Gleason on TV, and who read all of C.S. Lewis' *Narnia* books to them more than once. I wondered how they felt about his wanting to be a Roman Catholic priest. Did they have any idea how it would change their view of the world? And the world's view of them?

The kids cleared the table and loaded the dishwasher, and as I finished tidying up the kitchen, my thoughts returned to the present. The idea that Peter considered giving up his ministry, his lifelong profession, and without any income whatsoever expected to wait for the Roman Catholic Church to receive him as a married priest stunned me into denial and disbelief. Yet I knew that was exactly what he planned to do.

With a wave of my hand, I absentmindedly sent the kids to their studies. I was baffled, too, by Peter's blindness to the fact that more than a month had passed without a reply or even an acknowledgment from Archbishop Hunthausen. There was no word, either, from Father Clark, the Island priest. Truthfully, I wondered if he would ever hear from them.

Always in the past, when Peter had written to Archbishop Jean Jadot, the Apostolic Delegate in the United States, a reply had come by return mail, and always, I noted, accompanied with the official correspondence number in the upper right-hand corner. But those letters were only inquiries by Peter, hoping that some notice might be taken of him and other Episcopal clergy who wished to be reunited with the Holy See.

So far the bits of information we had received came from a group of Episcopal clergy who called themselves the Pro-Diocese of St. Augustine. They planned to hold a meeting in November in San Antonio, to which all those ministers interested in the program were invited.

Saturday morning came and the mail revealed another newsletter from the Pro-Diocese and still nothing from the Catholic Church. We sat at the dining room table enjoying a leisurely cup of coffee together.

"I know these guys are a bunch of spikes." Peter used the slang for extremely ritualistic high church people in reference to the Pro-Diocese clergy. "I'm not sure what they're after, but I've heard that some of them have already left the Episcopal Church with their congregations. I know at least one parish that is trying to keep their buildings, though they've had a law suit brought against them by the Diocese of Los Angeles."

"Does this mean they won't be a part of the mainstream Catholic Church?" I asked, knowing that there are some connected groups of Christians under the pope here in the United States.

"I can't see any other route but the usual Roman

Catholic priesthood for me. I don't want to belong to just another little schismatic group. Besides, while I know some Episcopalians would leave with me, I'd only be kidding myself if I thought the whole congregation would want to become Roman Catholics."

"Oh my, it would cause a terrible split in our congregation," I said, appalled that Peter's convictions rooted in a desire for reunion with Rome might cause still more pain to either church body.

I poured another cup of coffee and set the pot on an antique trivet in the center of the old dining room table. The oak table had first belonged to Peter's grandparents in Illinois a hundred or more years ago. The wood was beautifully scarred and stressed the natural way from generations of use. The chairs had worn out long ago, but I had been lucky enough to find six matching antique oak chairs at an Island yard sale. It was wonderful at Thanksgiving time when the kids' college friends came home with them. We'd put all the extra leaves in the table, extending it beyond the dining room into the living area. It was then I thought of the hundred or more Thanksgiving feasts before ours, and I enjoyed the warm feeling of knowing that we were firmly rooted in our intimate history through so traditional and simple a gesture as the family meal.

"I could go that way," Peter said, speaking of leaving with the whole congregation, "though I do feel uneasy about it for some reason. I'd only do it if Archbishop Hunthausen says it's what he wants."

"Well, I can't imagine it. The Episcopal Church on this island is so small and struggling. And then to take some of their strength away! Anyway," I said hotly, "I don't believe Anglicans want the Roman Church. They're actually anti-Catholic. Why else be Episcopalian?"

"Oh, I don't know. I've been their pastor since 1964. If I feel called to leave now to fulfill and uphold the faith, why wouldn't they want to go with me?" Peter's tone seemed to change.

"I'm an Episcopalian because I can have the Catholic faith and still not be Roman Catholic. Look at the Church of England. They sure don't want Rome." I looked down at my hands and twisted the wedding band I'd worn for twenty-three years. "I don't want to be a part of a split. And how would Catholics feel about it? Causing trouble in another Island congregation? No thanks. Not me." I felt the anger surface within me and I looked away, out the window to watch the Saturday morning ferry traffic scurry by.

"The Catholics? They'll be delighted. Of course they'll want us. They want *everybody*. Why these guys in the Pro-Diocese are using Catholic churches for their congregations to meet in. And they haven't even been officially received yet."

"I don't know if I believe that."

"Don't be silly. The Catholic bishops have welcomed them with open arms," Peter said. "I've got things to do. I can't sit here all day." Abruptly he went upstairs to his study.

Peter believed everything the Pro-Diocese clergy told him. Well, maybe it is true, I thought, but the whole picture of malcontent Episcopalians, no word from Archbishop Hunthausen, splits in congregations, it all filled me with anxiety and fear. And I felt angry. Angry that Peter would put us through this ordeal. For what? Who knows if he will ever be received or ordained, or if the program even exists. I followed him upstairs to his study. He sat with his back to the doorway where I stood.

"It sounds to me like they're starting a new church. You talk about reunion with Rome. If it's another church they're starting, why do you want anything to do with it?"

"Mary, I don't know what this offer means yet, exactly. But I do feel that any invitation from Rome is almost an edict from God," he said without turning to face me. "All Christians should be working toward reunion. That's what it's all about. Jesus said that we should be one, that the world might believe (John 17:20-21). How can non-Christians believe there is anything to Christ's love when we're all fighting and squabbling among ourselves? Don't you see that if Rome is making an offer, each of us has a responsibility before God to respond? You may as well realize right now that if it means that the congregation or part of it will go with me and it's what the archbishop wants, then I'll do that too."

"But you haven't even heard from him," I cried.

"I know, but I will." He still did not turn to face me, and I saw his right knee bouncing up and down impatiently under the table.

"Peter, I can't bear the thought of a struggling group that can't pay its bills, with all the infighting that breeds. And you know as well as I do, they wouldn't be accepted by either the Episcopalians or the Roman Catholics." I did not believe the future held anything good for us, but I felt helpless to stop my husband. How to do it when I felt so defeated and lost. As I turned to go I said, "Count me out. I'll not be a part of it. I think you've lost your mind."

Peter came over to where I stood and put his hand on my arm to stop me. "Trust me, Mary. And trust the Pro-Diocese people, too. We don't know yet what miracle God is working in all this, but we can trust him, and a part of that is your trusting me."

"I'm afraid this will fizzle just like all the other rumors of reunion with Rome we've heard in the last twenty years." I pulled away and faced him. "Haven't you noticed, when Rome goes to the bargaining table they're just like the Russians. They don't bargain. They hold all the cards. The rest of us poor suckers just hope and pray they'll throw us a few crumbs. And we wait breathlessly for them!" I was starting to cry. I wanted to get away from him. I turned again to go.

"Mary, come here, my little red hen. I know you're scared. I am too. I don't know how we're going to live and keep the kids in college." Peter put his arms around me and held me close. "You've just got to have faith that it will work out. By Christmas it'll all be settled. We'll be Catholics. Don't you know what that means? We'll never have to face the uncertain ambiguities of the faith again. We'll be at home in the Catholic Church where the faith is protected by sound . . ."

"You're really crazy, aren't you!" I drew away from him. "My father was a Catholic. I've always been an outsider looking in. They treated my mother like a tramp. I can remember them saying to me when I was no more than eight years old: "Your parents weren't married in the Church. You know what that makes you, don't you?" Do you know what that did to me? Please, Peter. Don't talk to me about the uncertain ambiguities of the faith. I know too well what there will be for us. If I'd wanted to be a Roman Catholic, I would have been one," I sobbed.

"Mary." Shaken by my sudden outburst, Peter put his arms around me again. As intimately as he knew me, Peter would never understand the whirlpool of conflicting emotions within me.

"Don't you see, my father allowed them to degrade my mother. Yet he respected the Church. He was wrong to let them hurt her because she was divorced and couldn't marry him in the Church." My feelings poured out in an emotional confrontation I'd avoided all my life. "They blamed *her*. Why not him? *He* was the Catholic. *He* married outside."

"I know." Peter held me tightly in his arms.

"He never went to Mass, but he never completely rejected the Catholic Church either. He used to talk to me about the Church. That's why I asked the priest to come before he died. I knew the family wouldn't like it, but I did it anyway. And that's why I insisted he be buried from the Church. Some of them will always hold that against me."

"You did the right thing."

"I'll never forget the hurt in his face when I told him I was going to marry you. He said, "I thought you'd be the one who would be a Catholic." I think that somehow in me he saw the means for his own peace and reconciliation. He was such a proud, stubborn Irishman."

The story that I'd never before told Peter poured out, cleansing and healing me in a way I could not have imagined. I was freed by the sharing of this awful burden of my childhood.

Peter held me close. Peter, whose faith is bound in Scripture, history and tradition, who knows that what he wants most is the Catholic faith wherever it is found. There is no way he can know how I feel about the Roman Catholic Church. How much I feel drawn, and yet how overwhelmingly painful it is for me.

"Dear love, all that was yesterday." He stroked my hair as he held me. "That was your childhood. Put it behind you now. This is a new day with opportunities none of us have ever dreamed of. I want you with me. I can't do this without you beside me." His voice was soft and in that moment I almost felt he understood.

4

The weeks passed slowly by. Though Peter met with Father Clark, the Catholic priest on Vashon Island, several times during this period, we heard nothing from Archbishop Hunthausen. Father Clark himself discouraged Peter from making the move, saying that we would not be welcomed by most priests and sisters in the archdiocese. However, for Peter, nothing daunted his optimism and enthusiasm for whatever lay ahead.

Because I couldn't face "swimming the Tiber," I spent the days thinking of the economic impossibilities facing us. They overwhelmed me and became the more immediate impediment, rather than my revulsion and fear of Roman Catholicism.

With two children in college and two others to enter in the next two years, there would be three children at once in college for several years to come. It took every penny Peter and I earned together just to keep the family going financially. How would we manage if he were unemployed? Was it morally right to jeopardize the kids' educational needs, or would this challenge be good for them? We owed the orthodontist, and there were car payments to make. Without employment we could not afford the medical and dental insurance we now had. It was insane to think we could manage on one-third of the income we now enjoyed.

In that fall of 1980 our savings account had only a few dollars in it. Still it was not in 'a living' that our interests lay. Over and over again God had shown his great love for us by providing everything we needed. However, I was a firm believer that we had to do our part, too. Now, it seemed, only a miracle would allow us to meet our financial demands if we were to leave the Episcopal ministry in the next months.

No matter how I tried to muster faith, I felt convinced that everything was against us. The sacrifices, both personal and professional, were not worth martyrdom to me. It seemed clear that my husband's idealism was way out of hand, and I felt determined not to find myself caught in the same trap. After all, I rationalized, God gave us brains. He expects us to figure a few things out for ourselves.

I convinced myself that I was the only hope for our future. I decided to fight Peter every way I knew how, and I put God in an unimportant corner where he belonged. I got nowhere. Peter was as stubborn as a mule; he'd put on his blinders and made up his mind. He again wrote to his sister in Jerusalem:

> Mary is beside me, but not always behind me. She feels I can witness for the Catholic faith within the Episcopal Church. I am convinced I cannot. Still, I could not do what I am doing without the support and companionship of my wife and children.

At times I resented Peter's letters to his sister. It seemed in their religious zeal that sooner or later I'd get caught in the snare they had set to convert me to Roman Catholicism. Then one day I found the way to get Peter to see the terrible mistake he was about to make. I asked him to write down on a sheet of paper two lists. One list would be the reasons to stay in the Episcopal Church. The other, the reasons to become a Catholic. I thought that the rationale to stay would become so clear that he would have to give in to me. I knew I would win.

To my surprise, it did not take Peter long to produce a long list on both sides of the page. We sat in his study and looked at his notes together. I was startled when I read the first two statements: Catholic—I feel called by God. Episcopal—I have a strong feeling I must leave.

I took the lists and walked out of his study. I needed a

little time to think. Peter seemed to sense the impact they had upon me.

Of course, I thought, it's so obvious, so simple. It was the second statement, I have a strong feeling I must leave, that hurled itself at me from the page. Like Sarah and Abraham, *called out*. Faith is leaving, I thought. The opposite of faith is fear. I understood then that I was filled with fears and anxieties of ghosts real and imagined. Oh God, help me, I prayed.

I began to read again: Catholic: I feel called by God. Episcopal: I have a strong feeling I must leave.

I continued. Under Catholic he listed all that he had taught and practiced throughout his ministry in the Episcopal Church: (1) I believe in the lifestyle, the sacraments, the meaning of the Eucharist; (2) I must be loyal to the teachings of Jesus in the Gospels, the universal Scripture of the Church; (3) the historic continuum is important to me; (4) Scripture alone leads me to the papacy, the successor of Peter, as the source of unity and authority within Christianity.

On the other side I read reminders of the faith as I knew it was generally believed and practiced in the Episcopal Church today: (1) the perfunctory weekly celebration of the Eucharist as emphasized by an overall lack of commitment to the other sacraments; (2) authority of Jesus in the Holy Scriptures dwindled, bringing in its wake a rationalization of Christian morality, reflective of modern sociological pressures and schemes; (3) the congregational aspect of the minister's personal popularity.

I sat in the old captain's chair beside the window in our upstairs bedroom for a long time. The window was open and I leaned forward, my arm resting on the peeling paint of the windowsill. I looked down onto the tree-shaded patio where we had spent so many carefree afternoons with our family and friends. I thought of the gallons of homemade ice cream we'd eaten there. First we had bought a freezer with a hand crank and I, being the purist, was surprised to find that turning the hand crank on an ice cream freezer was not the kids' idea of fun. So I put it away in a corner of the attic and bought an electric ice cream freezer. The next step for me was to learn the simple recipe for Philadelphia ice cream. We began to use it instead of the complicated custard base, which had to be stirred over a hot stove the day before. Should I mind? The ice cream tasted just the same. Maybe even better. And we made it a lot more often with a lot more enthusiasm, especially from me. A faint smile touched my lips.

"Are you all right, Mary?" Peter's voice startled me.

"I guess it's like making ice cream," I said, still seeing the scene on the patio.

"Ice cream?"

"It's in the eating." I turned to look into Peter's questioning eyes.

I had thought I knew it all. I had been the devil's advocate, and I had lost. In the simple integrity of his faith, without understanding the impact of his words, my husband had converted me.

5

I was stunned by Peter's answers. But I could see that if he continued to live the integrity and honesty I admired so much, Peter's reception into Catholicism was the inevitable answer. And I would go with him down whatever road we found open to us, knowing that this step could mean the loss of lifelong aspirations and dreams, the loss of our way of life, both professional and personal.

Loss of status and position in the community.

Loss of a comfortable income.

Loss of our home.

And more than anything, it meant my acceptance of the role of a priest's wife, a complete unknown, in the Catholic Church.

"Why did you do this to me?" I said, tears filling my eyes. Unconsciously, I rubbed the arm of the old chair. I looked away from Peter, once again to the patio below, still alive with thoughts of homemade ice cream and the laughter of friends.

"Do what?" Peter asked.

"You're right, of course. We must leave the Episcopal Church. The way you see the situation, it doesn't hinge on whether you can become a priest or not."

"You mean you agree?" he asked softly.

"I'm sad, but if you really feel this way." In resignation, I gently motioned, my hand filled with the lists of reasons.

"I think it's the right way, dear."

"Once you leave the ministry, we can't come back if they don't let you become a priest in the Catholic Church.

When we walk out the door, it's over," I said half to myself. "We have to face the fact that former ministers are a dime a dozen. There probably won't be decent employment for you." I felt a lump fill my throat. "We may find ourselves having to give up everything we've ever hoped and worked for, the rugs we've been saving for, that vacation without the kids." I could see it all coming to an end at that moment, and in a sudden movement I got up from the chair and walked quickly across the room. "And I'm scared. We don't know what's waiting out there."

"I know. It's an unfair thing to ask of you," he said.

"We need time to get our bills paid and prepare the kids for this change. They'll all need to get part-time jobs and student loans. We need to have a good talk with them. It will mean so many adjustments for all of us. I don't know how we'll manage on so much less money. We barely make it now."

"It's not the best time to do this to the kids, I know. But I guess there'd never be a good time," Peter said. "Those rugs. You have almost enough to buy them, don't you?"

"Yes," I said as I started to cry all over again. Our eyes met in the instant communication of our marriage. We both thought of the sorry bargain basement rugs we'd used for nearly ten years in the living and dining rooms of our home. Though money was tight, we'd decided to set aside a few dollars each month to replace them with wool oriental design rugs from Sears Roebuck. I was just a few dollars short of the needed $1,200, and I saw them slipping away from me now. "We've never bought any decent furniture," I said through my tears. "Oh, well."

"The rugs. Yes, Mary, you must get them. You've saved for them, and we need them. We all need them."

"But the money. We're going to need that money for other things. Our bills, the kids' education."

"That money is for the rugs. I want you to order them tomorrow." Peter's words were final and it pleased me. I went to him and we held each other for a long time.

But I wondered about our future. What would unfold for us and for the children? Will this invitation really materialise, and will Peter ever be a priest in the Catholic Church? I could not understand why Father Clark was so reluctant to become involved, and why Peter had heard nothing from Archbishop Hunthausen. I felt a new heaviness in my chest. This step was not my choice, but perhaps mine were the wrong reasons. I, the woman, the protector of the nest, still the rib of Adam, created to walk beside my husband. I would accept the decision and the reasons Peter had for making it. I felt I could do anything, accept anything. I knew I could, and I would do it for him with a little help from God.

As I left him and walked down the stairs, my thoughts turned to the other Mary in Nazareth. She must have felt frightened and alone. In her humility and innocence, yet unafraid, she had said yes to God. So I must try to find that same yes within me.

The next day Peter again wrote to Sister Elsbeth:

> Without even a request, Mary signed the statement from the Pro-Diocese that she will accept full Roman Catholic doctrine and the care of souls by the Holy Father and the Bishop he is going to give us. I think she is beginning to feel as I do . . . that God is calling us.

I was busy cleaning the upstairs family area when Peter came out of his study. "Now that you've accepted Roman Catholic doctrine I want you to read theology with me. We can talk it over, and this will prepare us to be received into the Church."

"There you go again deciding what I'm going to do." I slammed the bookend down on the shelf and kept right on dusting. "Mary, do this. Mary, do that."

"Okay, okay. You make the decision," he said impatiently. "But you need to prepare, and this seems a good way to begin."

"Prepare for what? You can't even get Father Clark to listen to you. Well, you can forget it. Roman Catholic this and Roman Catholic that. It's all you talk about. I'm sick of hearing it. I've made the decision to support you, but it will take a long time to convert me." I turned away to hide the tears of anger that wouldn't go away. It seemed that just when

I felt a softening toward him, Peter wanted more from me. Somehow, what I felt willing to give freely was never quite enough for him.

"Aren't you feeling God's call?" Peter asked.

"Well, yes. A little," I said reluctantly.

"I know the intellectual rationale is there. We agreed to that yesterday. But the step toward priesthood really isn't valid for me if you don't feel called. You're so much a part of this." Peter followed me around the room as I cleaned. I felt trapped by him and all that was happening to us.

"Called to what? *Your* priesthood in the Catholic Church? What about me?"

"The early Church had both celibate and married priests. You know we've talked about the Apostle Peter, the first head of the Church. He was married."

"I like my life now. What if I'm not accepted?" I demanded.

"How could anyone not accept you, Mary," he said as he tilted his head to emphasize that the remark was a statement, not a question.

"I know I'm selfish, but I do feel it. You're gaining everything and I'm losing everything. It's hard for me. Don't you see?" My voice grew shrill as my eyes filled with moisture. "And what if they turn you down? It will all be for nothing. Nothing."

"Mary. My life has never been more directed toward God than it is now. I don't feel that I'm forcing my way. Doors will open for us. That feeling is as real as the fact that I'm standing here with you."

"You're always deciding my life for me. Why don't you let me be myself?" I turned to him. "And stop following me around."

Peter sat on the edge of the study table and looked down at the floor, "It's so clear to me now, Mary. That Peter is the spokesman, the source of unity and authority within Christianity." He looked up at me, and with gentle determination said, "In God's grace I will serve him as a Catholic and a priest, and I want to share all of it with you, Love." He used the old pet name, his eyes pleading with me. But I would not give in, even though I felt moved by his love for me.

"Save your sermons for somebody else. I'm sick of your idealism about the Roman Catholic Church. You're so blind. You have no idea how foolish you sound," I finished dusting the bookcases. "Why is it suddenly so clear to you now? Ask yourself that."

"I am called only if we both are." Peter ignored my question.

"Okay. I feel called. I think it's what we should do. Are you happy now? I'm going downstairs to fix dinner."

Still he followed me. It seemed that Peter would never stop talking.

"It's simply a matter of loving our Lord and being with him now, knowing that wherever we must go and whatever we must do, he will protect us."

"If there's anything I can't stand, it's your syrupy piety." I took the leftovers from the refrigerator and set the dishes down hard on the ceramic tile counter top. I wished he would stop bothering me . . . I was tired of coping, and I didn't want to hear any more, but he continued.

"It's not that other ways—Episcopal, Baptist, Methodist—are wrong. It's just that the Catholic faith is right and whole. Complete. Don't you see how I feel?"

"I read all your reasons for wanting to leave, and I know it's what we have to do, but it's painful for me. The decision itself is enough right now, Peter. I can't go any further, so don't push me." I turned to him and hoped that somehow he could understand and continue to love me. I needed time to work my way through the maze of anger and brokenness I felt. My love for Peter depended on it. For without my wholehearted acceptance, I sensed even then, the Catholic Church would not give him priesthood. I had to do it not only for him, but for God.

"I know it's hard for you not knowing what's ahead and . . ." Peter said as he leaned back against the kitchen cupboards.

"I can't imagine you anything but a minister," I interrupted. "I guess that's why the uncertainty is so difficult for me. I think about it all the time. Who knows if you'll be allowed to function as a priest, even if they do ordain you. Ordination is no guarantee that you'll be used. I keep thinking that at least here in the Episcopal Church you have a real ministry."

I had to admit, Peter's words today had touched me in a new and different way, even though his syrupy gloss had turned me off. He was filled with beauty and the hope of fulfillment in spite of his slim chance of success. I felt grateful too that he was able to go beyond my anger, accepting my feelings, but not giving up on me. Still, there was something inside me that kept me from giving myself completely.

"The Catholic Church is as corrupt as any institution you can name. There will be the same deficiencies and short-comings we knew in the Episcopal Church, and I wonder what real difference our switch will make when all is said and done. I will become a Catholic. After all, it's just another church. But I don't expect it to shower any new graces on us. I simply feel that you made the decision for the right reasons, and I want to go with you and support you." Anger swept over me once more as thoughts of Peter's constant demands and assumptions assaulted me, and I turned from the sink to face him. "So please don't ask me to read theology. I don't have time and I'm not interested. I consider that your job."

That night when we had gone to bed, I said to him, "Peter, I do feel that somehow God is calling us . . . even though we are confused and fearful. And . . . the excitement of pioneering a new ministry challenges me, but there's so much against us."

"Don't worry, Mary. We'll take it one day at a time."

"But you don't take it one day at a time," I said as I snuggled down in the covers. "You grab the brass ring on the merry-go-round, and you think you've got it all. You rush on ahead leaving chaos everywhere you've been. The kids and I are the ones who suffer."

"We can't talk about it now. You'll get me all steamed up and I won't sleep." Peter cut me off and turned away. Soon I heard his heavy breathing. He slept soundly.

I listened to the gentle pelting of soft October rain on the wood-shingled roof. The sound had comforted me before, as I lay sleepless. I loved the old house, our bedroom under the eaves, and the security of the old pine tree's whispered movements in answer to the night winds that swept the top of the island. I reached with my foot and touched my husband's leg. His skin was warm and I felt secure at that moment.

I hoped that some things would never change.

6

Peter was like a race horse in the starting gate. I felt like a jockey about to begin the most important race of my life, impatient for the starting gate to open, terrified that when my waiting ended, I would be thrown to the ground and trampled. Still, I felt compelled to keep my poise while inside me the doubts, fears, and anger raged without relief.

Peter couldn't wait. He wanted to become a Catholic and a priest, and it seemed he could think of nothing else, waking or sleeping. He had made the decision and he wanted to get on with it.

Once again, I felt swept along by decisions and circumstances over which I had no control. Exhaustion overtook me as I urged him to be patient, to allow events to take their natural course. I felt barely able to accept daily events, much less find meaning in them for my life.

Though busier than ever with our Episcopal congregation, Peter seemed compelled to keep his request moving with the Roman Catholic Church. Typically, he felt that the end result depended entirely upon his action. It seemed to me that his impetuosity took control. I often felt that God had given me the more difficult job in this partnership, as I begged him to be patient, to wait on Father Clark and Archbishop Hunthausen.

More and more it seemed my life was over, that I had nothing good to look forward to. I tried to face up to the fact that the anxiety and anger I felt had begun to dominate my life, especially my relationship with my husband. I began to realize that the challenge of a new pioneering experience, and our decision to accept that call did not fill me with enthusiasm and excitement as it should. Instead, I felt hopelessly condemned. Every day I slipped deeper into depression, and there was no one to whom I could turn. I felt alone and adrift.

Every day I went to my job as secretary to the Superintendent of Schools, grateful for the opportunity to lay aside the fears and sadness that colored my life. Each evening I returned home to focus my growing resentment and anger on Peter, not simply because he wanted to be a Catholic priest but because once more I found myself rejected and shut out by the Roman Catholic Church. Each day the mail delivery reminded me that months had passed without so much as an acknowledgment from the archbishop. Somehow I blamed Peter for this lack of courtesy.

Then finally, after three months' wait, Peter received a reply from Archbishop Hunthausen. He asked us to be patient. He said that he would be in touch with Peter as soon as he found a source for the instructions and norms required by the Church for the reception of the former Episcopalians.

"Well, there goes your theory that they're all set up and ready to accept applications. I knew it," I said as I thrust the needle through the thick layers of cloth in Kurt's school jacket. Peter ignored my sarcasm. I glared at him across the dining room table as he continued to open his stack of mail without looking up.

"You're a hopeless idealist, Peter. The Catholic Church is an ugly bureaucratic machine. I can remember when people waited years just to get an annulment. And you're asking for priesthood with a wife and four kids in the pew? Don't make me laugh."

"Do you think he's saying that he doesn't know anything about this program?"

"Yes, dear. I think that's what he's saying." I mimicked. "I wouldn't resign yet, if I were you." I forced my chair back with a loud thud against the window sill. "I knew you'd be treated this way. Bunch of heirarchic slugs." In my anger my tongue stumbled over the words, but I meant what I said, and Peter knew it.

He picked up the letter again.

"He says he'll be in touch with me. That sounds good." Peter looked past me, out the window.

"Peter, all he's saying is that he received your letter. In August. It's nearly the end of November now! He doesn't want to be bothered with you. He wants you to give up! Do you need a picture?"

"Well, he can forget that. We both know that persistence is one of my best gifts."

"Ha," I said and laid the jacket over the back of the chair. "The letter says nothing."

Perhaps the archbishop won't allow anything to come of this, I thought. I was surprised to feel a tiny twinge of disappointment emerge from somewhere in my soul. I wanted to share Peter's enthusiasm for the possibilities this new life held, yet I could not shake the sadness and depression which so dominated me.

Lord, I want to grow, to know and freely welcome your plan and purpose for me. Help me. I cannot help myself.

Peter wrote to his sister in Jerusalem:

We have learned of a meeting in San Antonio for the Episcopal clergy who wish to be received into the Roman Church. We really can't afford for me to go, but yesterday Mary told me that she used her own small personal savings to purchase a plane ticket. I protested the use of her money, but she said with her own brand of Irish defiance, "No. We don't do things half-way . . . let's not start now. This may be the most important meeting you'll ever go to."

A few days later Peter boarded a plane for San Antonio for the three-day meeting. In spite of my pessimism I was curious to hear about the meeting, and I found myself waiting impatiently for his return. At least now, I told myself, we would know if there was any credibility in Rome's offer, and learn about the Pro-Diocese of St. Augustine.

But I found myself on a see-saw much of the time, as I clung to the idea that there was still a small chance that I could talk Peter out of making what I could not help but think was a terrible mistake in judgment.

I went alone to the airport to meet Peter. Standing in the crowd of greeters, I watched the passengers pour into the waiting area. Feeling like a school girl again, I spotted him quickly, and it reminded me that I never tired of seeing him for the first time. He seemed taller than his six-feet-one, his nearly black hair alive with movement. I felt stirred by his handsome rugged features, his distinctive Swiss ancestral nose. Or was it Chippewa? I smiled to myself as I thought of his mother who would not admit to her native American ancestry. His face still hinted of severe scarring. Eyelids that were cut open when the car he was driving between Oregon coastal missions was hit by a drunk driver on that Sunday morning, the Fourth of July weekend in 1955. We nearly lost him that time, I remembered.

Peter smiled "hello" over the heads of the other passengers. He was dressed in his black clerical uniform. What will it be like to see him stripped of the identity I have always known to be basic to Peter the person, the husband, the friend? I would have to face that, too.

He greeted me with a kiss, and we headed for the baggage claim area. Finally, as we drove toward the Vashon Island ferry, Peter began to tell me about the meeting.

"To my surprise, when I changed planes in Denver I was met by Father Clark Tea from Las Vegas. Somehow he found out my flight schedule and arranged to be on the same plane from Denver to San Antonio. Nice guy. He and his congregation have already left the Episcopal Church." He chuckled to himself as we turned onto I-5. "Actually, there were only a few of us there still serving congregations in the Episcopal Church."

"What?" I said. "That's hard to believe."

"Yup. They all left right after the 1976 General Convention, mainly because they wanted to retain the 1928 Book of Common Prayer and were opposed to the ordination of women."

Peter waited for my reaction. The sound of the windshield wipers dominated the atmosphere inside the car. "So this is it, so this is it, so this is it," they seemed to say again and again.

"Were all of the clergy there like that?" I asked finally.

"Yes. Well, most anyway."

Now the windshield wipers seemed to warn more loudly, "not for us, not for us."

There were long periods of silence between us as Peter waited for my comments and questions, but they did not come.

"We were told we have to go Anglican Rite."

"Anglican Rite?"

"That would mean the use of the 1928 Book of Common Prayer, with some adaptations appropriate to the Roman Church, of course. They say that the only way a married Episcopalian can be a Roman Catholic priest is to stay with the Pro-Diocese of St. Augustine, of which these clergy are all a part. They call themselves Anglican Rite or Anglican Use. It's the same thing."

Once again Peter waited for me to react. He knew how I felt about these dissident groups in the Church.

"I don't feel at ease about them. There's just something—well, I guess I simply want to be a Catholic priest in the traditional way," he said when I didn't answer.

"What if that's not possible?" I asked finally. More crumbs under the table, I thought. Why did we ever get sucked into this mess?

"Tokenism," I muttered.

"What did you say?"

"Don't you think it smacks of tokenism?" I laid my arm on the back of the seat and looked over my shoulder. "And what will you do if you can't be a Catholic priest in the traditional way?" I asked a second time. I noted Tess's school notebook, and a soccer ball as it rolled casually back and forth in the back of our family station wagon. What are we dragging these kids into, I wondered. "The Roman Catholics will never trust us. We'll be shuffled off into this strange small Anglican-whatever group without moral support or perhaps even any real credibility or recognition."

"Newman said Roman Catholics never trusted him. And they didn't. They frustrated him in every possible way, and he was a saint. I don't know, Mary. I don't know what I'll do."

"You know the history a lot better than I do, but I

don't think anyone, Roman Catholic or Anglican, would say Cardinal Newman was a right-wing radical."

I didn't want to be identified with the right wing of the Episcopal Church for the rest of my life. All I wanted was the Church, pure, simple, unadulterated. Humanly corrupt? That's to be expected. But shattered, trying to exist outside the norm? No. That's not for me.

"No Roman Catholic representative met with us. That made me uneasy. Why weren't they there?" Peter said.

"Now that bothers me," I said. "Did you hear anything that helped you understand how all this got started?" The August 20th newspaper announcement had seemed to us to come out of nowhere, yet reasonably we knew there had to be a complicated series of events leading up to it.

"Well, yes," Peter said as he stopped the car to wait in line for the ferry. "Do you remember hearing about the late Canon DuBois? He was the head of the American Church Union which led the high church movement in the Episcopal Church and, of course, lost out. Among his supporters were the clergy who now call themselves the Pro-Diocese of St. Augustine."

"I remember the American Church Union . . ." I mused.

"They were the group that submitted the first request to the Holy Father. That was Paul VI. Then he died and they resubmitted it to John Paul II."

"Okay . . ."

"The Pro-Diocese, it seems to me, is pushing their own agenda. They think they can go to Cardinal Ratzinger in Rome and dictate to him what conditions and terms they will accept." Peter shook his head, "I don't know where they think they get their bargaining power. Our numbers are so small compared to the vastness of the Roman Church. If we swim the Tiber, we are in their waters, and we come on their terms."

"Do you really want to be a part of this Pro-Diocese thing?" I asked. "I wasn't there but it almost seems that it's a splinter group."

"I felt alone there too, Mary." The cars moved onto the dock and the ferry to Vashon Island. "And many of them were older men, I mean much older, retired or semiretired. Their tiny congregations have left the Episcopal Church, and they're not a part of anything. To be truthful, I was very uncomfortable about the whole thing. Do you realize there were only a couple of us there still in the Episcopal Church ministering to Episcopalians? I didn't fit in. I was too normal for the group." He chuckled. Peter's Catholic theology was not considered normal by most Episcopalians.

"Well, what are you going to do?" I asked as I folded my arms across my chest. I'm really tired of the whole mess, I thought.

"I'll stay with them. It's all I can do. Then I'll hope that something more healthy develops out of it."

"Okay. I guess I can handle that for now," I said, relieved to hear the resolution in his voice.

The ferry engines started and the boat began its fifteen-minute trip to Vashon Island. I heard the water swishing and stirring as we got underway.

Peter placed both hands on the steering wheel and without looking at me said, "They want me to leave the Episcopal Church now and bring the congregation with me. They say I can't be received as a priest in the Roman Catholic Church unless I leave now."

"Leave now?" I looked ahead of us across the Sound. My heart sank as I watched the other drivers and passengers leave their cars. It was windy, and above the drone of the engines I heard the flat-bottomed steel ferryboat hit the swells as it moved across the water. Slap. Bang. Slap, slap. After a long time I asked, "What did you tell them?"

"That I have asked Archbishop Hunthausen for his counsel, and I'll do whatever he tells me," Peter said quietly.

"I don't understand. You can't be a Catholic if you don't bring your congregation with you?" I asked, still not believing.

"A priest. A Catholic priest. They say that if I don't leave the Episcopal Church now, and bring the congregation with me into their group, I cannot be received into the Roman Catholic priesthood when the time comes."

"I don't understand. You have to work with the archbishop."

"Well, of course," he looked across the Sound to the Island. "In one sense I want to bring my flock back to the Catholic Church. Reunion with the mother church is what it's all about. But on the other hand, I want good feelings between the Episcopalians and the Roman Catholics."

"Oh, I think it would cause a terrible row. This island is too small."

"You know sheep stealing has never been my way of getting ahead. I want peace and wholeness, not more division. The idea of three Roman Catholic parishes on this island seems ridiculous anyway."

"I imagine there will be a few Episcopalians. . . . Peter, we can't leave now anyway. Take the congregation?"

"Well, one of the things I need to do is write to Jim Parker. He's an Episcopal priest working with Bishop Bernard Law in the Diocese of Springfield-Cape Girardeau in Missouri. It appears that Bishop Law will be appointed by the Holy Father to oversee this program. I have to go through him or I cannot be considered. So that's the first thing I have to do, write to Father Parker and make my request."

"Was he at the conference?" I asked.

"No. I don't understand that either. If he's going to be involved, why wasn't he there?"

"Maybe contact with Father Parker will answer a lot of questions. It can't make the situation any less clear, that's for sure. Maybe Archbishop Hunthausen could get the norms and requirements he's looking for from Jim Parker or Bishop Law. Why don't you suggest he write them?"

"Yes. I thought I'd do that," Peter said. The ferry horn sounded to signal its arrival at Vashon Island, and passengers poured onto the deck to return to their cars.

"Another thing that came up at the meeting was the question of conditional ordination or re-ordination in the Roman Catholic Church. I don't mean to put myself above these issues, but it seems so immaterial to me. I simply want to be a Catholic, and I feel called to priesthood. How I get there makes no difference to me. I know that my ministry the past twenty-seven years has been valid. I don't need to have that proven to me with conditional ordination by the Catholics. It's like the old prayer book with the Elizabethan English. Who cares? If we're not careful we'll lose the essentials while we're sitting around nit-picking. The most important thing is to do this for healing, to be reunited with the Holy See."

"It sounds like you got a lot from the meeting," I said, suddenly overcome by the familiar deep sense of sadness and fear. "Even if you don't agree with them, at least you know better where they're coming from. I'm wondering about this Jim Parker. Do you think there is something the Pro-Diocese isn't telling you about because they want your support? It just seems so strange that Father Parker wasn't there. And no Roman Catholic representatives either."

"It did make me uneasy. I need time now to think and pray about all of this," Peter said.

I heard the heavy chains fall to the steel deck as the workmen released the barrier which allowed the foot passengers to walk up the ramp and leave the boat ahead of the cars. The familiar sound triggered memories of years of living our lives according to the ferry schedules. Lives intersected again and again by other lives simply because there is no other way to reach this island but to ride the ferry boats. Strange that we should have been called to this place. And that we have stayed so long. Now it seems we are being called away. I suppose if I could lay aside some of my fears and bad feelings toward the Roman Catholic Church, I might find happiness there. After all, people are people wherever they are. Within minutes Peter will drive our station wagon off the ferry and up the long winding hill, a part of the parade of returning islanders. Home again, I thought. Then what?

7

The following day Peter sent a letter to Jim Parker, and he wrote again to Archbishop Hunthausen. He told the archbishop about his experience at the San Antonio meeting. He also asked permission to announce to our congregation that we would leave the Episcopal Church at Christmas and be received into the Catholic Church on January 1, 1981. He again asked whether or not he should establish an Anglican Use Church with our congregation.

I was in our bedroom changing my clothes after work the day Peter shared this with me.

"Christmas?" I screeched. "That's only four weeks away. What if he says yes? Our bills . . ."

"Now Mary, just calm yourself."

"You really know how to spoil Christmas, don't you? Have you mailed the letters?"

"Mary, stop. Haven't I told you we'll make it okay? These things take care of themselves. Haven't we always been given everything we need?"

"Take care of themselves?" I glared. "Sure, God provides everything we need, but he expects us to do our part."

"We will, Mary."

"Dull household bills? You'll be too busy writing letters and setting dates. What you really mean is *I'll* do our part."

"Well, I can't sit here forever doing nothing."

"And where do you think this constant barrage of letters will get you, Peter?"

"Sometimes your faith is small," he said. I felt shut out by the aggravation in Peter's voice as he emphasized the word "small."

"Don't you realize that your demands on the Roman Catholics, and even on God himself, might in the end destroy your goals?"

Peter seemed not to hear me as he gathered up his notes and walked out of the room.

Another week passed without word from Archbishop Hunthausen. We both experienced a new state of anxiety. Peter, because he wanted to resign. I, because I feared that the archbishop might let him.

One evening as we drove to a friend's house for dinner, I said, "You're putting too much pressure on Archbishop Hunthausen, Peter. You're forcing him to make a move; it may not get the results you want."

"He knows that I've tried to resign since last August. He's had plenty of time to figure out what he's going to do about it." He paused. "No point in waiting."

"I don't know how this is any different from the way the Pro-Diocese is acting with Cardinal Ratzinger. It's insane. A tiny group of Episcopalians telling Rome what to do?"

"Mary, to have faith in God is to have faith in his Church. Archbishop Hunthausen is the Church. I am the Church. Have a little faith in both of us."

"I'm the Church, too. And you don't care about my feelings or what I think is best in all this. I'm tired of being swept aside for all this craziness about being a Catholic priest. That's the thanks I get . . ."

I despised myself. I've never been like this before. What's happening to me? To us?

Then I tried to concentrate on the true meaning of Christmas, to lay aside, at least for the evening, the anger and fears which had consumed me since this all began.

I thought of the other Mary's words:

Behold, I am the handmaid of the Lord. May it be done to me according to your word.

Luke 1:38

What power there is in her words, Lord. Help me to experience the power of the Word made flesh.

As we passed Hollymere Farm, I looked through the mists in the winter dusk. Fleeting forms and shadows stepped out and danced before my eyes in the dim rows of holly trees. Fear. Loneliness. Once again, I thought, fear is the absence of faith.

I thought of the holly we'd soon be gathering from the abandoned orchard across from our home. The trees were not trimmed and nicely shaped like these, and the grass around them was high from lack of care. Not even the birds had been able to thin the heavy clusters of red berries before heading south to escape the cold, wet Puget Sound winter that was now upon us. I could only wonder where Peter's excessive energy would take us as we progressed through this holy season.

As the children arrived home from college, there hovered over our days the shadow that next Christmas would find us displaced and located who knew where. Peter had set into motion his target date of December 25th for the announcement of his resignation.

But we had not received a reply from Archbishop Hunthausen.

Finally, when he could wait no longer, Peter called the Island pastor, Father Clark. The following day he gave us a message from the archbishop not to leave the Episcopal Church now. Peter was completely frustrated and bewildered. Thank God, I thought, to leave now would be impossible. But I felt angry, too. Why couldn't the archbishop at least answer Peter's letter? Or telephone, himself. It seemed obvious to me that he didn't take us seriously, and I feared for the future more than ever.

As I look back to December, 1980 and see the hand of God at work in our lives in those years, I wonder at our courage, and I know that the Lord never gives us too great a burden to carry. Back then it didn't seem like courage. It was enough just to hold on to each day and to cope with the decisions Peter had eagerly made. In my weakness I could do no more than force myself to accept them without any desire to determine their greater meaning. Now I know that our path then was truly of God's hand, that in our frailty we did all that our faithfulness enabled to follow. I prayed every day for the grace to follow him, to truly put ourselves into his service. In my anxiety and depression, faced with Peter's eagerness to push the Roman Catholics into action, this season of hope and expectation became a time of fear that our holiday experiences were happening for the last time. Instead of the new beginnings of Advent, I found myself wrapped in a cloak of silent finality from which I was unable to escape.

In a lifetime some things happen to make a few holiday gatherings stand apart from the others. Our family Christmas that year was one of those memorable ones. Though there was little money for gifts, being together was a special gift in itself, perhaps more so because of the uncertainties. We found our pleasures in the simple family traditions we'd gathered around ourselves over the years, like decorating the tree when the children arrived home from college, popping corn, Tess's favorite Nacho recipe, and the Christmas Eve Mass that we all feared would be Peter's last. Our traditional family Christmas dinner of roast beef and Yorkshire pudding, with the grand finale of plum pudding and brandy sauce, seemed the best yet.

It was during this Christmas holiday that John confided to me. "Dad is a fool. He will never be ordained in the Roman Catholic Church." It was like a knife in my heart as I listened to our son, whose excitement had filled our home that first day when we read the announcement in the *Seattle P.I.*, who on that day had made me feel that my faith was small.

I felt sad when the children returned to school, preoccupied with fears that their father would soon be out of the Episcopal Church with nowhere to turn. Yet I felt thankful that they did not have to face the daily uncertainties that confronted us.

In the archbishop's message I received a reprieve, but for how long? I knew that Peter would soon set another date. God only knew what else he might do. I wanted to forget the threats which his impending resignation placed upon me. I could not. My survival instinct demanded that I maintain as much control as possible, a laughable illusion, for Peter and I both knew that he was in control.

Peter received frequent phone calls and letters from the clergy in the Pro-Diocese of St. Augustine, and particularly from Father John Barker. He constantly pressured Peter to leave the Episcopal Church with the congregation now, not to wait for Archbishop Hunthausen's approval. Peter felt strongly that he should not take that step without the approval of the archbishop because Jim Parker had said he must have a Catholic bishop to sponsor him in the program. To go out on his own in opposition to the archbishop's counsel was against his ethics and the personal discipline he felt was so important to his relationship with any bishop he served. Jim Parker seemed supportive of the Pro-Diocese, but he agreed with Peter. He should not go against the archbishop. Jim, for example, was not a part of the Pro-Diocese, and he had left the Episcopal Church without taking his congregation. In fact, he had become a Catholic with the blessing and support of his Episcopal bishop.

So there was another way. Peter did not have to be a part of the Pro-Diocese and did not have to establish an Anglican Use congregation. I was glad to hear that. Jim tried to establish communication between Bishop Law and Archbishop Hunthausen; but from all that we could gather, he was not completely successful. It was from Jim that we learned that the August 20th announcement had been leaked to the press prematurely through the Pro-Diocese of St. Augustine, that the bishops had hoped to establish guidelines before they made any public announcement. It was unclear whether the guidelines had even yet been established. Indeed, confusion seemed the only certain element in the program.

Then one day Father Barker called to say that a Cardinal from the Vatican was in Vancouver, British Columbia. Could we drive up there the next day to meet him, the purpose being that he had never met a married priest.

"I think I'll call Father Parker and see what he thinks about this," Peter said to me, after he explained Father Barker's telephone call. I waited for what seemed a long time while Jim and Peter talked. I could hear the kitchen floor squeaking as he paced back and forth.

"That seems like good advice, Jim. I'm glad I got hold of you. Yes. Please give my love to Mary Alma. Yes, I will, and thanks again, Jim." Peter hung up the phone and came quickly into the living room. He continued to pace back and forth from one end of the room to the other.

"Well?" I asked. He did not answer. "What did Jim say?" I demanded finally.

"I learn a little more each time I talk with him. If I understand it right, Barker and the Pro-Diocese want to go over the heads of the American bishops and deal directly with the papal authorities. Jim is a bit uneasy about the whole thing. It's all political. I think I'm being used in this situation. Jim's advice is to play it cool. That's good enough for me."

"What are you going to do?" I asked.

"I'm going to call Barker and tell him I can't come."

As Peter left the room to make the call, I remembered years ago how we had gone to St. Mark's Cathedral in Seattle to meet the Archbishop of Canterbury, Dr. Michael Ramsey. It was Dr. Ramsey's Catholic leadership which had nearly reunited the Anglican and the Roman Catholic Churches in the early 1970s. This would have been an incredible victory for the Catholic cause of Episcopalian high churchmen. Ramsey was not only a leader, but a scholar whose spiritual depth and maturity were held in high regard among Christians throughout the world.

I remembered that Peter had taken a favorite book of the archbishop's for him to sign. As the white-haired prelate began to write his name, he paused. His soft grey eyes looked out from beneath huge bushy eyebrows and he said, "And who might you be?" His bright eyes sparkled, then softened, as Peter told him of our small island mission in the middle of Puget Sound. For that moment we were alone in the crowded room with the Archbishop of Canterbury as he listened with undivided attention to our words.

How often I have thought of his question, "And who might you be?" Who *am* I, Lord? Mary, a child of God. But a shadow of that other Mary. Her courage. Her integrity. Her love. I thought of the journey that she made to visit her cousin Elizabeth. The dangers she faced. Her promise to be God's vessel for all of us. I must hold to her and the example of her faith. But, I wondered, why is it I am drawn to her now, when I never used to think of her at all?

Peter wanted to begin preparing our congregation for his resignation, so his January, 1981 vicar's report to the congregation included the following comments:

> "It is my intention to assist you in making application for parish status. However, my long and joyous ministry here must come to a close. It will be a time of new leadership for you, and a time for me to seek new pastoral responsibilities."

As I attempted to accept and deal with my feelings about Peter's announcement, I tried to label some of the vague, yet overwhelming fears which haunted me. There was the constant worry that unsympathetic members of our congregation would discover our plans and inform the hierarchy. The fear that Peter would face unemployment and our children would be forced to drop out of college. And of course the overshadowing possibility that Peter would never be accepted for the priesthood in the Roman Catholic Church. It seemed that I was overwhelmed by fears, fears that took shape in images and shadows that I did not know existed. Looking back to those moments, I realize that I lacked any real faith in God, and my relationship with him was so thin as to be practically nonexistent.

Weeks went by and Peter did not hear from Archbishop Hunthausen. He was impatient and anxious to make the change. Once again I was struck by panic as Peter, pressured by the Pro-Diocese of St. Augustine, talked with several people in our congregation whom he thought were sympathetic to him. He asked them to meet on a regular basis to explore the idea of forming a new congregation under the Pro-Diocese of St. Augustine if the archbishop granted his permission. I thought, if only the archbishop would meet with Peter, at least the question of an Anglican Use congregation could be settled.

Peter contacted Father William Treacy, a sympathetic Irish priest in Seattle who had been involved in ecumenical relations for many years. With half a dozen laymen he began to attend Father Treacy's noon Mass once a week in downtown Seattle, after which the group met for a brief discussion. Father Treacy encouraged them. He told them it was important to be a Catholic. That conversion to the Catholic Church did make a difference, that it was worth any personal sacrifice.

Peter's brazen disregard for secrecy alarmed me. I felt sure that now the word would get around the parish, and perhaps even back to our bishop. We still had not heard a word from Archbishop Hunthausen. I felt deep down in my heart it would only be a matter of time until we were thrown out of the Episcopal Church for Peter's disloyalty, without the door to the Catholic Church opened to us even a crack. And I thought if that happened, what chance would there be for him? Looked upon as a troublemaker, I felt sure he would not be given so much as a hearing by the Catholics.

Father Patrick Clark, the Catholic priest on Vashon Island, had been a good friend of ours since he'd first arrived. But he was less than enthusiastic about our plan. Peter had confided in him from the beginning, only to be discouraged by Father Clark, who now often stopped at the vicarage on Saturday mornings for a cup of coffee.

"You don't *really* want to leave the Episcopal Church, do you? You have so much here, a fantastic ministry to the people of this island." Father Clark repeated this each time the two men got together.

"Oh, I love the Island and my people, but this is our chance for a real gesture of unity between the Episcopalians and the Roman Catholic Church. We have an obligation to respond to the invitation," Peter said.

"We don't believe any more that you have to be

Catholic to serve God or to have a valid ministry," Father Clark said.

I sat at the table with the two men and listened to the same script each time they were together. I'd think: Wait a minute. All my life I've been told that the only true church is the Roman Catholic Church. I can hear my dad saying now, "but you're not the Church." I thought Catholics wanted everyone to be Catholic.

But I never got into the conversation much, afraid that if I spoke too strongly, Father Clark might not come back. I was never sure how he felt about women, and I wanted him there. I wanted Peter to hear the Catholic Church speaking to him in this informal setting. Even at this late hour I hoped that through his questions and doubts Father would bring some sense to Peter.

It was in this context that I first became aware of the depth of the problem my presence might be. As I listened to the conversations, my head filled with questions I was afraid to ask, not because I feared the answers but because I kept getting the message that though present, I wasn't there at all. I didn't feel that Father Clark disliked me. He simply didn't know how to react to me any more than I knew how to react in the situation we were in.

In the privacy of our family I felt filled with contempt and anger for Peter and the meetings he had with Father Treacy and the several members of our congregation who met with them weekly. I had no one to turn to, so I buried the anger I felt inside me, in what had come to seem like a permanent condition. Nor could I speak of how my depression affected every one of my days and nights. I began to think a lot about taking my own life. I told myself I wouldn't give in, and I willed the evil thoughts out of my mind. Even so, they crept back, and I found I had to fight them almost constantly. I wished that I could set aside the constraints of God's laws, and my own lack of courage, to carry out a plan. In this dark night of the soul I thought little of the mother of Our Lord. Indeed, I thought little about anything except myself.

It was during these weeks that Peter was called in to

see Bishop Cochrane. We both felt uneasy about this meeting, the purpose of which we had not the slightest hint from the bishop's secretary. My eyes hardly left the clock all day, as I counted the hours and minutes until his return.

"Mary. Mary, are you home?" Peter shouted as he ran up the basement stairs.

"Yes, I'm right here," I called back as I hurried to meet him. "What happened?"

"You'll never guess. Why, this is the best thing possible," Peter said as he fussed with the lists and notes beside the kitchen telephone. "Where's Larry Johnson's number?"

"Do they know you're going to become a Catholic?" I thought his call to Larry Johnson, an attorney in our congregation, could only mean one thing, that Bishop Cochrane had heard we were leaving the Episcopal Church and had terminated Peter.

"No! It's the clinic. You know, I went there and questioned them about the contraceptive and abortion counseling they're giving.

"What? . . . I don't . . ."

I listened as Peter told me about his meeting with the bishop that morning.

"Take a look at this, Dally." Bishop Cochrane's gruff voice almost shouted as he threw a sheet of paper in Peter's lap. "Do you realize you're causing a legal suit against the diocese?"

I smiled to myself as I imagined the anxiety our bishop would have over the loss of prestige and social approval that a legal contest over feminist health issues might bring to him and the Episcopal Church in western Washington.

Peter explained that Bishop Cochrane wanted him to sign a statement that he would stop his attack on the health clinic.

"Attack? I haven't attacked them at all, Bishop. I met with them confidentially, as a professional person in the community concerned about *lives*, Bishop. You should be on my side!"

"You sign this statement, Dally."

"Bishop, when children as young as seventh grade go to the clinic for their athletic physicals, the staff is telling them how to have what they call 'no risk' sex. The nurse practitioner spends only minutes talking with each one—hardly adequate to the seriousness of the physical disease and emotional problems related to sexual promiscuity. Parents came to me, and our own kids were confronted with this too. I see nothing wrong with talking to the doctor and nurse practitioner about my concerns, either as a clergyman in the community or as a private citizen."

"I don't want the Church involved here at all, and I want you to sign this now," Bishop Cochrane demanded.

"No, Bishop. I'm not going to."

"So what do you think you're going to do?"

"I'm going to take this letter to a lawyer in my parish and see what he says. They don't want publicity about this. It would ruin them. Bishop, you know what islands are like!"

"I'm warning you, Dally, I want this dropped immediately. Don't use church stationery. Don't mention the Church in any way. Now I'm serious, and I'm through discussing it with you."

"Bishop, will you give me your blessing before I leave?"

"Yes, yes, you have my blessing," Bishop said.

"No, Bishop. I mean *your blessing*. You know . . ." Peter raised his hand, as though to give the Church's blessing.

"Oh, yes. Well, of course."

Peter knelt before the bishop to receive the Church's blessing. With incredible timing, the volunteer fire department plectron which Peter wore sounded its screeching alert. Peter tried to turn it off, only to accidentally increase the volume. The dispatcher's loud voice shouted the location of the Vashon Island fire throughout Diocesan House. Bishop Cochrane waited, while Peter, still on his knees, frantically pushed buttons and turned knobs to quiet the blast. He got to his feet and shook the thing. Nothing helped.

"Okay, Dally. That's it for today," the Bishop shouted.

A moment later Peter located the right button and switched off the volume. As he hurried past the dignified offices, every head turned to see him go. He couldn't wait to get home. "Damn it," he muttered to himself as he closed the car door. "The bishop should be on my side."

As Peter told me of the morning's events, I thought of the warm relationship that should ideally exist between Episcopalian bishops and their clergy families, of other bishops under whom we had served.

Our previous Bishop, Ivol Curtis, was a lovely man, but he wasn't sympathetic to Catholic teachings in the Episcopal Church, and he and Peter had had their differences. Together they had worked them out, and Bishop Curtis supported and backed Peter's ministry. I had felt sad when he retired, because I knew I would miss the warm friendship I shared with Lillian, his wife. And I loved the way he hugged me and said, "You're my best clergy wife!" He said it to all the priest's wives, but no matter. It was a great line.

Before him was Bishop William Fisher Lewis.

"You and I are the newest men in the diocese," he had said to Peter that first day, acknowledging that we and the Lewises had arrived in Washington state at about the same time.

Such warmth was characteristic of Bishop Lewis. For when he made parish visitations, he stayed in the home of each clergy family whenever possible.

Since he was a diabetic, and I was almost always pregnant during those years, I enjoyed the privilege of having him all to myself over Sunday morning breakfast while Peter went ahead to get things ready for the morning services.

But most of all, I shall never forget Bishop Lewis' face, so filled with peace and joy in those last cancer-ridden weeks of his life, as he turned to me that morning in his office and said, "My dear, there is no competition in the Lord's work."

That was 1964, and Bishop Lewis had called us in to talk about a move to Vashon Island. We realized later that he knew he would live only a few more weeks, and he wanted to see us settled in a new parish before his death. It was the only time I was ever invited to the bishop's office.

As Peter talked with Larry Johnson on the telephone, I thought of that office. It was spacious with large windows overlooking the Lake Union yacht basin, Queen Anne Hill, and the downtown Seattle skyline. Behind the bishop's beautiful old mahogany desk hung an arrangement of original paintings. Everything about that room characterized the affluence and conservative good taste of the Episcopal Church.

"Great! I'll be right over." I heard Peter say as he hung up the phone.

"Mary, this is fantastic! Larry is having dinner with two lawyers who specialize in this field right now?"

"Where are you going? I'm cooking dinner for you and you're—"

"Mary, just cool it. I'll eat when I get back. This is wonderful," he said as he looked in the refrigerator. "The bishop doesn't have the foggiest idea where I'm coming from. And that health center! I'd be delighted to expose what they're doing. The people of this community would be so angry if they knew what was really going on up there."

"Peter, remember you're trying to be a Roman Catholic. My God, now you're taking on the whole United States healthcare system! If you get involved in a civil suit . . ." I couldn't believe what he was doing.

"Do you know that those people don't talk to the kids at all about venereal or pelvic disease? Or about the emotional consequences of promiscuity? And when I asked about the counseling given to a woman wanting an abortion, the doctor just smiled."

Peter grabbed his coat. "See you later," he called over his shoulder.

I could only look after him and shake my head as the door slammed shut behind him.

Now eager to take on feminist health issues, Peter had gone to see Larry Johnson. Lord, I hope he can talk some sense into him, I prayed. Well, Bishop Cochrane doesn't know we're going to become Catholics anyway, I assured myself.

As I prepared our evening meal, I thought of this man I had married. Peter sees himself as one whose role is primarily spiritual, but he lives in the world. I thought of John the Baptist in Luke 7:24, "What did you go out to the desert to see, a reed swayed by the wind?" Well, Peter could never be accused of that!

I wondered, was my husband simply tilting windmills? No. Now I understood that he was not really an Episcopalian. And I knew more than ever that ours was a Catholic morality; that no matter what, this new path would be better than the one we now walked.

8

Things had no sooner quieted down than Peter wrote another letter to Archbishop Hunthausen, again with a direct request for an appointment with him. This time the archbishop invited us both to meet with him on February 24th, 1981. It had been six months since Peter first requested a meeting.

Peter wrote to Sister Elsbeth at the Carmel du Pater in Jerusalem:

> I have nothing but good feelings about this. I'm convinced by my life's past experiences that God is opening doors and giving us grace to go through them. I don't feel I am forcing my way anywhere. Indeed, I feel a deep sense of humility that God should even consider to call me, poor sinner that I am, to be so blessed in every way as his servant. I deeply appreciate your prayers. You are moving far greater mountains than you are aware of.

In spite of my personal pain, I felt deeply warmed by Peter's words. He seemed never more in tune with God's will for his life than in his letters to Elsbeth. It was good for me to read them, for they were filled with peace, and confidence, and hope. Truly the prayers of the sisters were moving mountains, but I suspected we would encounter many more mountains before our journey ended, and the hour would be late.

Typically, February 24th was a rainy day. Peter drove the car to Seattle, though it was a luxury we had denied ourselves in recent months. I remember we parked on the hillside next to St. James Cathedral and walked around the corner to the Chancery. That day I was the one filled with hope and expectation. The blood rushed through my veins, making pink roses of my cheeks in the excitement I felt. Perhaps it was my unusual optimism that lent an air of fantasy to the day, as though it was happening to someone else. For I had not really expected Peter would ever get so far as this first appointment with Archbishop Hunthausen. And the invitation to me to come along? I assumed that the archbishop would want to meet me. I suppose I didn't view it as anything unusual. Little did I suspect how how unusual it was.

As we walked up the steep hill, I looked up into the dripping maple trees overhead. It seemed that from among the bare branches, I saw us. This is not the first nervous couple seen huddled together on a rainy afternoon, walking toward the Chancery, I thought. But none of them came for the same reason. I smiled to myself and my pulse quickened.

I remember Peter opened the door and we stepped into a room that seemed to glow with candlelight, though there were no candles. I felt nervously conscious of my damp clothing and hair.

Soon a priest came into the waiting room and walked directly to us.

"I'm Archbishop Hunthausen." He offered his hand first to Peter, then to me. He wore a black suit and a plain black clerical shirt. There was an aura of humility and meekness about him. I almost expected to find the knees of his trousers baggy and shiny from wear. I liked him immediately.

"I've just come in from the anti-abortion rally in Olympia. I'm sorry I'm late for our appointment," he said. To myself I thought, these are my people.

I had not expected this shy, self-effacing man with his simple clothing. In my more than twenty years experience in the Episcopal Church, he seemed to me out of the context of his office without the purple clerical shirt, the pectoral cross, and the large bishop's ring that were so familiar to me.

"Please have a seat over there." He gestured to the semicircle of armchairs off to one side of the room. The plainly furnished office held only the archbishop's large working desk, a conference table, and chairs. Through the window behind the table we could see the construction of an apartment complex not more than a few hundred yards away.

"That new construction will be low-cost housing for the poor. The inner city is ideal for it because the poor are already here and will not have to be relocated in the unfamiliar suburbs," Archbishop Hunthausen explained with a smile. I noted that the finished building would completely close off the view of downtown Seattle and Puget Sound in the distance. Then, I thought, the poor will have the view.

I watched as the archbishop seated himself near us. Above his head hung a large crucifix. Somehow it dominated everything and everyone in the room.

"Tell me about yourselves," he said.

Archbishop Hunthausen was warm and easy to talk to. Peter described his ministry and relationship in the Episcopal Church, how he'd worked for reunion with Rome for most of those years, and how he felt that the August 20th announcement was an opportunity that no Episcopalian should let pass without prayerful consideration. He told him about our family and our work on Vashon Island, and about the recent incident with our bishop.

"I've asked you to come here to meet you, and to give you the opportunity to meet me. But more important, I want you to know that I am concerned for your family and what you are all going through with this decision," the archbishop said. "Mary, how are you doing?"

"I'm fine, Archbishop."

"I do not think it a wise idea for you to leave the Episcopal Church until your situation can be more completely worked out with the archdiocese. I don't know how long that will take."

"I understand," Peter said, disappointment in his voice.

"I still do not have the norms and guidelines. There is always confusion with a new program. The Vatican is very slow. However, I do want to assure you of my desire to cooperate and of my daily prayers on your behalf."

"Has Bishop Law's office contacted you? Or Father James Parker, the Episcopal priest who is working with him?" Peter asked.

"These things always go much more slowly than one would expect," the archbishop said. Did he avoid answering the question or did I imagine it?

"Shall I continue to meet with Father Treacy?" Peter asked.

"Yes. However, I want us to keep all of this confidential until the details are worked out. I don't want to jeopardize our good ecumenical relationship with your bishop."

"I understand, Archbishop," Peter said.

"For now, I assure you of my prayers. If there is anything at all that I can do for you or your family, please call me."

We left the Chancery offices and stepped out into the late afternoon darkness. The gentle drizzle of raindrops seemed to hang in the air as we walked quickly down the steep slope.

"I've never met a bishop like him." Peter said, once inside our car. "So humble and simple. And did you notice he looked like any priest?"

"Yes. I liked him. He seems to understand what we are going through."

"But I still don't understand why it is so difficult to get the norms and guidelines for this program," Peter said.

Clearly, we liked Archbishop Hunthausen, but as we analyzed our meeting with him, we both began to feel less enthusiasm for what had occurred there.

"I wonder if they're trying to get them, or if they just want us to wait. You know he really didn't say anything new. His comments repeated the letter we got from him months ago," I said. I felt disappointed by the meeting. Shouldn't we expect something more definite after six months? "He almost acts like the whole program is our idea, not something the Holy Father has offered to Episcopalians. It's as though we're here out of a clear blue sky and we're trying to twist their arm. Don't they realize we're trying to work within their system?"

"Well, it wasn't a bad meeting. At least maybe now that he knows us things will begin to happen," Peter said.

We drove in silence toward the Vashon Island Ferry. There was an air of resolution between us. At the archbishop's mercy, there was nothing we could do. We would continue to wait.

The weeks and months that stretched ahead of us came and were gone again. A sudden quietness enveloped Peter. I wondered if he felt as discouraged as I suspected he did. We talked less about the day we would finally leave the Episcopal Church, and about what we would do when the time came. It seemed to both of us to be in the far distant future, an act that we no longer had control over. Peter was not anxious or manipulating, as I had seen him so often in the past when confronted with crises. Oh, he was still impatient, but it was different this time, I couldn't deny it. I thought of how I must be hurting him with my anger, and the hate I thrust upon him at every opportunity. I felt a certain comfort that he was so consumed with his call to the Catholic Church that he hardly noticed me most of the time.

There were times when I felt I was losing touch with myself. The person I had become little resembled the person of my past. It seemed that we were trapped between what we felt we must do and the passive repression of Archbishop Hunthausen's refusal to get things moving. I was angry with both of them. This was just what I thought I could expect from the Roman Catholic Church. I gained weight. My old energy was gone. I couldn't say even when it left me. I didn't sleep well, though I wanted to sleep all the time. I was dominated by an overpowering urge to go to bed and stay there, to pull the blankets tightly over my head. The thoughts of self destruction came, attacking me again and again. It became increasingly difficult to brush them aside, and I had to keep telling myself I would not do it.

Then, on one of those wet gray days in Lent, I went to the mailbox to find a copy of *The Progress*, the Seattle Catholic newspaper. I was deeply touched by something I saw there. In a large photograph of a human hand there was gently cradled a sprouting seed. I thought of God's springtime promise of new life and the Resurrection of Jesus. The caption under the picture read:

People look ahead to the future with hope and

expectation. They plan for the future and hope to shape it. But like the seed that grows, the future is surprising, always a bit different, sometimes a lot better than we expect.

I read and reread the message, as it unleashed a torrent of tears I'd held back too long. I taped the page to the front of our refrigerator. I needed its gentle reminder of God's plan, especially his plan for me in the days ahead. It was everything I felt, all my fears for the future. The future that I had not given myself the faith and luxury to hope for. In its simplicity, this became my infantile act of abandonment to God's will. In it I sensed that God wanted something good, something very special for us. The words and the symbol of the seedling became a constant prayer and reminder for me every time I passed by the refrigerator.

Had I known the paper would become stained and yellow with age, I could not have accepted even this small sign of God's revelation and hope.

9

Peter asked to be received into the Catholic Church again at Easter. Once more Father Clark brought the message from Archbishop Hunthausen: wait.

Peter was humiliated. He felt hypocritical and disloyal toward his flock, and yet it appeared that he was suspect and unwanted by the Roman Catholic hierarchy for the same integrity. Peter and the six or so men from our congregation continued to meet with Father Treacy, but they seemed only to be going through the motions. The waiting, the lack of communication from the archdiocese left them floundering; and while Father Treacy firmly supported them, it seemed unreasonable that we should be expected to wait indefinitely.

April and May that year were filled with wonderful warm spring sunshine and the flurry of showers and rainstorms that characterize the Puget Sound region. Peter worked in our vegetable garden every opportunity he got. "I know we'll need the vegetables, and at least when I am working in the garden I see things growing and changing," he said one day.

Or he would say to me, "This is just a game they're playing, a cruel tease. Why can't I give it up?"

It was not too late to turn back, but his desire to be a Catholic and a priest was greater than the pain and derision he felt at being put off by the archbishop. We could only continue to wait and wonder what the future would bring. I agonized for him. Without a definite date for Peter's resignation, we seemed frozen in this world of uncertainty.

Then June arrived with unusually cold, chilling winds and low overcast skies which dumped rain and more rain. Peter could contain himself no longer. He wrote to the chancellor of the archdiocese:

As you know I have twice previously tried to be received into the Catholic Church. Both times I was asked to wait. I don't need to tell you that it is not necessarily easy.

And then later in the same letter:

The arrangement I made with Father Treacy is that in the event of imminent death, Last Rites will be given to me by a Catholic priest, and that requiem and burial can be within the Church. Again let me thank you for your continued kindness and prayers. It is reassuring to know that you, the archbishop, and others are supporting us with your good will and intercessions.

As I read his letter, I felt pain and anger intermingled. Why are they doing this to him, I wondered. What can possibly be gained by this delay, this putdown? Peter's letters to the archdiocese angered me. They were not him at all. They seemed to helplessly beg.

Yet I knew that a more real problem we faced was that if we expressed our anger and frustration over this unreasonable treatment, they would say we were malcontents, archconservatives, and troublemakers. And they would drop us. We had to wait for their time. We had to hold on and hold back.

Peter wrote to his sister in Jerusalem:

The waiting is the most difficult. I've heard no word from anyone for months. I have tried to be received twice, and now I am told just to wait. I feel as though I am sitting on a time bomb. I don't know how long I can continue here with the harassments of the present Episcopal bishop. He must know that I am trying to become a Catholic, but he has not actually confronted me with the issue. He seems bent on discrediting me, though I don't understand what he hopes to gain. It isn't as though I'm the first priest to leave the Episcopal for the Catholic Church.

Sister Elsbeth wrote back:

. . . you have all my sympathy and especially our prayers for you. It is hard to wait, I know, and to live with the continual indecision. When I became a Catholic and when I started to seek out a Carmel, I never dreamed that I would end up in Jerusalem. He has given me much more than I could ever have imagined. I would never want to be anywhere else. Those years of waiting, the anxiety of not knowing what was coming next were worth it. Our Lord has something special in mind for you. It might be a surprise, but you know it will be greater and more wonderful than anything you can possibly imagine. Just flow with the Spirit and he will lead you.

Those years of waiting, I thought. Can we expect years? Yet when it all began last August, I instinctively knew it would take years, if it were to happen at all. And now it seems so unpromising and dreary, caught as we are between the hierarchy of the two religious bodies.

Peter hung up the telephone and turned to me. "Bishop Cochrane wants to see me again. I wonder what it's about this time."

"I'm so tired of the whole thing. I don't even care," I said and turned away so he wouldn't see my tears. "Peter, don't you see, there are bound to be harassments. No matter what he says or doesn't say, he's got to be hearing rumors that we're leaving the Church, and maybe even that you're causing a split in the congregation."

"I suppose you're right," he said.

"Besides, this is nothing new. He's always been on top of you for every little thing. I wouldn't worry about it." I put my arms around him and looked up, waiting for the kiss I hoped I'd get.

"Yeah. I guess that's it." Peter turned away. He seemed not to be aware of my arms around him and I let him go uneasily.

On the following Wednesday Peter left early for Seattle. He had hospital calls to make on his way to see Bishop Cochrane. When he was shown into the bishop's office, Hayman and the other archdeacon, Langpaap, were there as well. Hmm, must be important, Peter thought to himself. He couldn't help but notice that while the two priests greeted him, the bishop did not.

"Sit down, Dally," the bishop said.

"Well, how are things on the Island?" Bishop Cochrane asked, as he thumbed through the thick file in his hands. Then without waiting for an answer, he said, "Few things we want to talk to you about."

"Your assessment payments are late, Peter," Archdeacon Hayman said. "We need that money for operating expenses."

"I think you're mistaken, Bob. The payments were late a few times in the past, but my treasurer tells me that hasn't happened for some time."

"He's right, Holy Spirit is paid up. But you've got another payment due in just two weeks. I want to see that on time too," Bishop Cochrane said.

"There won't be any problem with that," Peter said.

"Another thing, I don't like that recorder on your telephone," Bishop Cochrane growled.

"I'm out a lot, and I don't have a secretary. As you know, Mary works, so there's no one around to take my calls. I don't see how—"

"It's that message you have on there. Do you have to say "and God bless you?""

Peter laughed. He thought the bishop was joking.

"Don't laugh, Dally. I've had complaints about the recorder and your message. People don't like it; they're offended."

"I don't know what to say, Bishop. I am a minister. What's wrong with saying God bless you?"

"Peter, it's just offensive to some of the older, more reserved people over there," Archdeacon Langpaap explained.

"I'm glad they don't have anything big to worry about." Peter paused. "I can hardly take that seriously."

"It seems small," Archdeacon Hayman said, "but you know, the sophisticated retirees from the East Coast. You know the type. You need to make more of an effort to accommodate their needs, and not spend your time in the community."

"This is ridiculous." He turned to Hayman, "Okay, what else is there?" Peter asked impatiently.

"I think that's all, Peter," Hayman said. "Just a few little pointers to help things go more smoothly."

"Oh, sure." Peter looked down at the design in the oriental rug. "Well, if that's it, I'll just excuse myself and get on back to the Island." Peter could not get out of Diocesan House fast enough. He was furious. As he came around the corner past Dr. Hodges office, he nearly ran over the elderly gentleman.

"Peter, what's the hurry? We don't see enough of you around here. Where are you keeping yourself these days?"

"Oh, hello, Dr. Hodges. I'm fine. Busy. How is Mrs. Hodges? Yes. Well, be sure to say hello for me."

As Peter hurried on, Dr. Hodges turned and stared after him. "I wonder what's gotten into him," he said to no one in particular.

Peter returned home angry and frustrated. There was little appetite for a legal battle, as there had been with the health center issue. We agreed, it seemed that our lives in the Episcopal Church could end abruptly at any moment.

"And God bless you," he muttered sarcastically, as he followed me around the kitchen, pounding his fists on the cupboard doors. "If he thinks I'm going to change that message, he can wait til hell freezes over. I happen to like the message, and I like the guy who says it. Besides, what have we got to lose anyway?"

"They probably know every move you're making with the Roman Catholics. They'd so love to see you stumble. Just keep the assessment paid. Two can play their little game." The hot oil in the electric frying pan sputtered and sang with each fresh oyster I laid in it, and I had to pull my hand away quickly to keep from getting burned.

"You know, I think you're right. Of course. That's why he had both archdeacons there. They want to make me appear incompetent . . . that's of more use to them than firing me. Ha!" he shouted. "That's it." He threw his head back. It forced the cabinet door shut with a bang.

Kurt appeared in the doorway, a surprised look on his face. "Everything okay in here?" he asked.

"You bet!" Peter said.

Our teenaged son shook his head slowly as he rolled his eyes.

"We'll come through this okay." For the first time in months I felt as though we had a purpose. Peter was David against Goliath. We realized now that Bishop Cochrane would do anything to make Peter look bad, to keep the Catholic Church from accepting us. We knew we had a fight on our hands. We weren't looking for trouble, but we'd be ready when it came.

Our lives reentered the now familiar holding pattern, but with a renewed peace of mind and purpose it became a period of purification for me. With fresh knowledge and confidence, I was able to let go of my fears and anxiety, if only a little at a time. There were more frequent moments now when I realized that the Lord was leading us. Yet at times I still felt tossed about, angry, frustrated, and out of control. In spite of these feelings I took comfort in the direction he began to reveal, the revelation of the vocation, a special purpose for my life too that began to unfold slowly but steadily before me.

Driving home from work, I thought of the Harmony Baptist Sunday School I walked to when I was a small child on the farm. Years had passed since it had crossed my mind. I remembered the musty once-a-week smell of the little pioneer church building. The hot fire that Ernest arrived early to build so Neppie Lou and the other ladies could take the cold. This last, he never failed to explain as he rubbed his hands together just when the fire began to roar. Then his eyes would follow the rickety stovepipe up to where it entered the wall, and we'd both watch the red sparks pop out into the air to become gray cinders as they fell to the old plank floor around us. "The Lord shore takes go-od care o' us," he'd say. During those years of nurturing by that group of simple Godloving people, I developed a strong sense that God had a plan and purpose for my life.

More naturally now, I embraced my thoughts of the other Mary, the mother of our Lord. I felt a strength and confidence from her that was difficult to share, even with Peter. She became my mother, my sister, my self. Even as I grew closer to her, however, I felt tempted to push aside my thoughts of her and the path we seemed to walk together. Episcopalians do not have as deep a reverence for Mary as Catholics do, and I began to question my motives and thoughts. To compare myself to the mother of God surely must be a sacrilege, but there seemed no one to whom I might turn for guidance.

Our daughter Theresa completed her first year of college that spring. She spent a good deal of time when she was at home with us questioning and rebelling against her father's decision to leave the Episcopal Church. This letter to Peter signaled understanding and perhaps a certain resignation:

Dad,

I went for a walk on the beach the other night. It was dark, the sky was overcast, and the air was thick with fog and the smell of Puget Sound. There was no moon or stars and the phosphorescence sparkled and glittered like stars falling at my feet. I was silenced by a feeling to want to share such beauty with those I love.

I remember some of my first encounters and explorations on the beach. You were always there, Dad, with paints and with each new shiny rock and squirmy hermit crab, your strong and caring hands would take the time to share love and appreciation for his most wondrous creation. These and other times of growing are the wisdom you've given me to fall back on and guide me.

Well, we all are growing and changing. God has a hand in all of this. Sometimes we find interest in new shells, or a shinier rock, so we move on farther down the beach and find contentment on other sandy shores. But the most amazing thing, and important to remember, is it's all the same body of water from which they flourish.

> Take care, Dad.
> God bless you,
> Love — *Tess*

As I read my daughter's letter, I thought of a day years before when the sun was warm and radiant and the Puget Sound tide was low. Those were the best times, I thought— when the tide was low. I could see John, the oldest, pulling an aluminum rowboat across the soft tidal mud, scraping it over the rough patches of barnacle-covered rocks on the beach. He was ten years old, and the boat was new. Monica, the little mother, tried to help him, as Tess wandered into the path of the rowboat.

"Wait. Dad will help," I yelled from the hillside.

But they couldn't wait, and by the time Peter got there, they had nearly reached the water, no thanks to Tess. I leaned back in my chair and smiled to myself, remembering.

10

Bishop Law's official appointment of Father James Parker as full-time coordinator of the Pastoral Provision was an important milestone. Jim and his wife Mary Alma moved to Springfield, Missouri where he worked out of Bishop Law's office. Mary Alma soon set up a lending library for the theological books that were required study for the academic examinations. Peter telephoned Jim there frequently.

"I'm surprised, Mary. No Episcopal pastors who are former Roman Catholic priests will be allowed to apply." Peter filled me in as we walked together one afternoon.

"Why is that?"

"Most of them have married, of course. That's why they left the Catholic priesthood, to get married. The difference is that these men had made a promise of celibacy. With their marriages, it has been broken," Peter explained.

"Naturally," I said, "the Episcopal Church doesn't require celibacy. That's the technicality for receiving married Episcopal clergy; they haven't made that promise." It seemed so logical to me now.

"The Catholic Church has always received and trained former Episcopalians who are celibate. It's the marriage condition that makes this program so special," Peter said.

We turned the corner onto the point, and we could see the blue water of Puget Sound ahead of us. I was surprised to see fog in the distance, and I had forgotten that this Saturday was the day of the Seattle Yacht Club's annual race around Vashon Island. There were literally hundreds of sailboats of every size and shape. We watched them emerge from the fog. Ribbons of white mist curled around their sails as they moved silently ahead. I recalled that running with the wind in a sailboat one does not feel the wind because you become a part of it. I recalled Peter telling the blind teens we taught to sail that a good sailor must cooperate completely with God for the winds are his. It is for us to set the sails. We watched the boats move past the point, disappearing mystically into the fog to the south.

"I've always loved the race around the island," Peter said absently. I realized we had stopped walking and talking, overcome with the beauty. This place was truly home to us. If we had to leave, we would miss it sorely.

"Jim says there is to be great stress on a healthy family life. You will have to write a statement for the Holy See on how you feel about this, Mary," Peter said, looking at me as we walked more slowly, moving on around Dilworth Point.

"Okay," I said with a sigh.

"Also, I've been praying about it, and I think I should separate from the Pro-Diocese of St. Augustine," he continued.

"Oh? Why the sudden change of heart?"

"I've been talking to Jim about it. I don't want to serve in a separate jurisdiction. I'd rather be a mainline Catholic priest. Besides, I know there's no future for an Anglican Use congregation on this island . . . three Catholic churches? That would be ridiculous."

"What about Archbishop Hunthausen? Have you talked to anyone from the chancery about this?" I wanted to know.

"No, but I'm sure they're not going to be disappointed. This concept may be one of the things holding them up. Archbishop Hunthausen is overly concerned about the Episcopalians. He'll probably be relieved."

"It has always seemed to me terribly unfair to place Episcopalians who have been torn and ruptured in the Episcopal Church, and are leaving for that reason, in a tiny group where they are once again separated from the main body of Rome." I hesitated. "Well, I know they wouldn't be separated in the sense that Anglicans are, but they would still be a small struggling group, misunderstood by both sides."

And our tradition is Western. I want to relate to the

strictly Latin tradition of the Church. I think there is a real danger that the Anglican Use congregations will be seen as Latinized Episcopalians. I don't want to take those Episcopalians who leave with me away from the larger body of the Church," Peter said.

"What about Father Treacy?" I asked. "What does he think?"

"He's such a fantastic person. I think he would like to see all the Episcopalians on Vashon Island become Roman Catholic." Peter laughed. "Well, I would too. His attitude is different from the archbishop's, but he supports me. I'm not really sure how he feels about the Anglican Use concept."

"Well, I'm relieved. I don't know if I could have handled the Anglican Use thing at all. I only hope that the different factions among those clergy already in contact with Bishop Law will now unite . . ."

"And get on with our work of love in the Lord." Peter finished my thought for me.

11

Peter built an oratory in a corner of our basement and had an altar made for it. He painted a crucifix and icons, including one of St. Frances Cabrini.

"Once I leave the Episcopal Church, I'll have a place to pray and say Mass. That is, if I'm permitted," he said to me one day.

Not say Mass? The thought struck me as bizarre. For all the years I had known him, since the spring of my sixteenth birthday, Peter had celebrated the daily Eucharist. I could not imagine it otherwise, and yet I wondered what right will he have to say Mass once he has resigned from the ministry and has not yet been ordained a Roman Catholic priest? He can't be an Episcopal priest after he has become a Roman Catholic, surely?

"Peter, a chapel to pray in? Yes. But, to say Mass? You can't have it both ways, Love." I turned my back to fold the laundry. Tears filled my eyes. How will he handle this, I wondered. Not to celebrate the sacraments?

"Oh, that won't change," Peter brushed aside my concern. "If Father Clark had a daily Mass, that would be one thing, but he doesn't, and I'm used to the daily sacraments." He saw my tears and put his hands on my shoulders, "Now don't go worrying about that too, Mary."

Clearly, Peter thought nothing would change, that no one nor any circumstances could take away the authority of his ordination.

We had adopted a thrifty lifestyle since the August

20th announcement nearly a year before. Our Dodge station wagon was paid for, and we had no other outstanding debts. It seemed almost a miracle that we had managed this first step toward our goal. We needed only to finish with the orthodontist and the student loans and work-study funds for Monica and Tess who were still in college. John, our oldest, would finish his Master's degree at the University of Washington in the fall quarter. Kurt was a senior in high school. I hoped that now we could save part of our income to meet the expenses of the transition and any unforeseen emergencies.

In addition to his parish responsibilities, Peter was busy putting together his dossier which would go to the Congregation for the Doctrine of the Faith in Rome through Bishop Law's office. A detailed history, it included both of our baptismal and confirmation records, our marriage records as proof that neither of us had received baptism or any other sacrament in the Catholic Church. Health records and grade transcripts were required, as well as verification of the line of Episcopal and Old Catholic bishops down to the bishop who ordained him in the Episcopal Church. It required references from our physician and other professionals as to the health of our marriage, and a detailed statement from him outlining the reasons for his request. It took weeks and countless letters to gather the information. To be complete it required two additional papers: a letter of sponsorship from Archbishop Hunthausen and the results of the psychological examination which had yet to be ordered by him. Peter mailed the copies in triplicate to Jim Parker's office only to have them returned. Bishop Law could not accept them until Archbishop Hunthausen agreed to sponsor Peter.

We faced disappointment and frustration once again. We had foolishly hoped that at least the documented portion of his application could be accepted by the Curia in Rome on the condition that a bishop sponsor Peter. This latest development meant that every move was blocked without Archbishop Hunthausen.

More waiting. It was obvious to me that the interim period between leaving the Episcopal Church and ordination in the Catholic Church would now be extended by months, perhaps even years. Once again for me, the weeks of relative security and peace became the disillusionment I expected from the Catholic Church. It turned to anger and frustration, directed at the only available person, Peter. We were told that the request could not go to the Holy See until we left the Episcopal Church. We would learn later on that this was not true. Archbishop Hunthausen did not understand the ruling, or he simply wanted us to wait. At any rate, nothing could proceed until he committed himself. It was midsummer, 1981. Soon it would be a year since the announcement, and we had made little progress. Yet our lives and the lives of our children had been disrupted from the beginning. It was difficult for me not to feel rejection.

However, in spite of all this my feelings were mixed. On the one hand I felt angry and frustrated that Peter continued to be put off by the archbishop, but on the other hand I was relieved. I wanted to delay our move as long as possible. We needed to save some money. We needed to educate our children. These were not options for us, and I felt concerned for their outcome.

Also, leaving all that we had and stood for still seemed unreal and a bit unstable to me. I could not see where we were headed, and I continually fought back my old fears and depression regarding the future.

Although I considered myself a practical sort of person, I could not accept the fact of our change and get on with the business of living. I knew that time and God's love would heal my hurts and anger, but I began to feel that the faith I tried to live in the Episcopal Church was nothing more than a facade. I felt like a hypocrite.

Peter talked constantly about interim employment, which he thought would be provided for him by Archbishop Hunthausen.

"I might teach in a Catholic high school or work in a Catholic hospital as a lay chaplain," Peter said to me one day as we talked while I prepared dinner.

"No Catholic school in this state will hire an unlicensed person to teach. They'd lose their state accreditation if they did," I explained. I pulled the large griddle from under the other pans in the stove drawer, allowing them to fall together with a loud bang that told more of my impatience than did my words.

"Oh, they can do anything they want."

"Not today, dear. It's not like it was in the fifties. Besides, what would you teach? About the only thing you're qualified for is Old and New Testament. I doubt they'd expose those sweet little Catholic children to what you know of Roman Catholic theology," I said contemptuously.

"Thanks a lot, Mary."

"The archbishop will have no obligation to you. Not even to help you find employment. They don't think in terms of a priest supporting a family," I said and banged the griddle onto the stove.

"Frankly, I don't know what they think in terms of. And you don't either," he said, as he left me alone in the kitchen.

Without a resolution to our situation, the days and weeks hung over us like a black cloud. We thought this summer might be our last on Vashon Island, but we seemed so affected by anxiety that we did not make the effort to enjoy the beaches as in past years. It was not a healthy time; it was filled with sadness, fears in many shapes, and a deep longing for peace in Peter's decision. During this period we received two or three phone calls from the chancellor of the archdiocese, inquiring how we were holding up and offering us the assurance of their prayers. However, in my state of mind even this seemed to be indifferent to our situation. It was one thing to deal with my own depression; it was another to see Peter discouraged.

I thought, all we need now is more harassment from the bishop. Then, sure enough, we got it.

Archdeacon Hayman called to say that he and Bishop Cochrane would like to see Peter about something "very serious" the following week. The somber tone of his voice gave Peter a sense of foreboding about the meeting.

"Sure, Bob. Would you like me to bring a delegation from the Bishop's Committee?"

"No. Absolutely not. Err, ah . . . you may bring one other person, but that's all. Do you understand?"

Peter asked Tom Felker, a young attorney and close friend to go with him.

"I called Hayman, Father," Tom said in a telephone call that same evening. "He says they've been told that you're leaving the Episcopal Church to become a Catholic. He asked me if it's true."

"What did you say?"

"I hedged."

"Thanks Tom. I appreciate that."

The following week as Tom and Peter drove to Seattle together, Peter asked, "What should I do if they ask me if I'm becoming a Catholic? Archbishop Hunthausen has told me to keep the matter completely confidential."

"Has he counseled you on what to do if they ask?"

"No, he has only said to wait."

"Well, my advice is to roll with it. Don't offer any information. I didn't tell them anything, so let's just see what happens."

When Peter and Tom entered Bishop Cochrane's office, there was an unusual air of solemnity. The greetings were formal. Peter was terrified. He felt sure they knew he was going to become a Catholic. In a state of inner panic, he wondered what he should do, even though Tom had urged him not to volunteer anything.

As the meeting began, Bishop Cochrane patted a thick file folder on his desk. "Your file is thicker than any other priest in this diocese."

"Well, I've been here a long time, Bishop. Since 1959."

"I mean, there are all sorts of complaints here about your ministry." The bishop frowned.

"You know, Peter, we talked to you about the telephone recorder," Hayman began, drifting off into other vague complaints. Comments about Peter's years of service on the Children's Centre Board, involvement as a volunteer E.M.T. and firefighter, time taken with the Washington State Guard, and finally the health center incident. Peter was not surprised, because he knew these involvements had been an embarrassment to some socially sensitive Episcopalians.

As the session droned on and on in a series of petty incidents from the past, Peter realized that they were not going to mention the Catholic Church.

"Bishop, I'm happy to cooperate with you in any way to help the Island church succeed, but I don't understand what you're getting at? Could you be more specific?

Bishop Cochrane again patted the file on his desk, looking at Hayman.

Peter continued. "Holy Spirit is one of the few parishes in the Seattle area that has experienced continual growth without community population increase. We've paid our assessment, as well as making other major outlays and improvements. We're approaching parish status, having been financially solvent for five years now, and that's because many of our families tithe. Our program is alive spiritually. We have good lay involvement, and there is community outreach. What is it you're trying to say to me?"

"Well, uhh, we've had complaints that your magic acts verge on the occult," replied the bishop.

"You mean my summer family Eucharist? Where in place of the Sunday sermon I do a simple magic act with the kids to teach some moral or doctrine?" Peter threw his head back and laughed. He couldn't believe they were serious.

"Don't laugh, Dally." The bishop glared.

"They seem okay to me, Bishop. My kids love them," Tom volunteered. "In fact, all the children try to sit in the front rows so they can figure out how Father does them."

Peter sat in relieved silence as the bishop and the two

archdeacons droned on about his magic acts and the other complaints they'd mentioned.

Then the bishop said abruptly, "I want you to apologize to the three men who came to see me, Dally."

"I'd be happy to go talk to them. I only wish they had talked this over with me! You know, Bishop, I live in a small island community. Believe me, if I were doing anything scandalous, you'd surely hear about it soon."

All this time Archdeacon Langpaap sat in silence, almost with liturgical solemnity. Now in round, piously intoned syllables he sighed. "Peter, I do hope that in your future employment you will not be permitted to work with people."

"I thought sure they were going to tell me they know I'm leaving," Peter said when he and Tom were outside.

"I thought so too, Father. The whole thing's strange."

"I'm sure they know. Why don't they just say it? Langpaap and his syrupy little talk. Yuk."

"Well, lay low now. Don't do anything. Let's hope Hunthausen gets things moving soon."

"I wouldn't worry, Peter. You're not that good," I said, laughing as he told me about the magic acts.

"They know I'm leaving, and obviously they want a scandal."

"But why? Why not just let you go? It isn't as though you're the first Anglican to become a Catholic. Or as someone said, why shouldn't they take our married priests? We've been taking theirs for years!" I laughed.

"I'm going to see these guys right away. I want to heal this relationship between us. They're my people, my flock, and I love them. You know, for years I've prayed for each person in the parish by name."

Peter went to see the first two men who both declined

to discuss the matter with him, one refusing even to pray with him.

When he called the third man, Peter was surprised when Richard suggested that I come along for dinner with him and his wife Margaret.

"First of all, I want to apologize to you, Father. I went to see Bishop Cochrane because the others asked me to go with them. When we got there, I was surprised and embarrassed by the kind of meeting I found myself involved in. Margaret and I appreciate your ministry. I had no intention of making trouble for you."

"Oh, that's okay. It really doesn't upset me." Peter smiled.

"I'm from the Church of England in Canada, as you know," Richard said. "I prefer a much more sedate, formal liturgy. It was very upsetting to me that you would give those magic act sermons." His concern was sincere.

Peter's eyes twinkled. I braced myself, fearing what might come next.

"All I can say is that tomorrow morning there are three men on this island who are going to turn into frogs . . ." For just a fraction of a second I thought I saw terror in Richard's eyes. Then we all burst into laughter and proceeded to enjoy one of Margaret's delicious gourmet dinners.

To this day I don't know why the Episcopalian hierarchy did not confront us. It would have been so simple for them to say, "We hear you're leaving the Episcopal Church. What's happening with you, Peter?"

Did they not want the publicity? Or perhaps they thought if there was a scandal, the whole issue of married Episcopal clergy becoming Catholic priests would be unattractive to the local Catholic hierarchy. If they had terminated him for no good reason, others who knew him and his style of ministry would have been sympathetic to his cause. Then too, Peter's martyrdom by the diocese could have triggered a further exodus of lay persons. The bishop would have been sensitive to this most of all, because Episcopal congregations

had been dwindling in western Washington since the mid-
seventies. A number of dissenting Anglican groups had already appeared in our area.

Still and all, this was their way of doing things. They
had never been direct with Peter. It was not their way to call a
spade a spade.

Lutherans, Orthodox, Catholics, and some Protes-
tants can define theology in objective terms, and they live
their lives accordingly. Wasn't it a former bishop of Olympia,
Stephen F. Bayne, who said, "There is no such thing as
heresy in the Episcopal Church," a church that would tolerate
a Bishop Pike who made fun of the dogma of the Holy
Trinity? Or the East Coast bishop who doesn't believe in the
physical resurrection of Jesus? No. They could hardly confront Peter on doctrinal matters. This is why the Episcopal
Church is not honestly close to the Catholic. Lutherans and
Eastern Orthodox are, because they reflect objective theological doctrines and morality. I remembered the phrase, "the
blessed ambiguity of Anglicanism."

That thick personnel file was the same one Bishop
Cochrane later showed Archbishop Hunthausen and the chancellor of the archdiocese. To this day I have no real answer as
to why Bishop Cochrane handled our situation the way he did.

12

The archbishop's words to Peter still ring in my ears:

The answer is yes, I am willing to consider your
eventual incardination into this diocese as a priest.
In saying that, however, I need to make it clear that
I am not in a position to consider your incardination
a foregone conclusion, one for which we merely
need to wait until we receive some official adjudica-
tion of the matter from the Congregation of the
Doctrine of the Faith. It will be theirs to pass
judgment on the question of the validity of your
orders, but it falls to me to make the decision about
incardinating you as one of our priests. For that
decision I shall rely on our Priesthood Discernment
Board which functions under the direction of Father
David Jaeger. I intend to ask Father Jaeger to contact you in order to discuss with you the procedure
that is normally followed whenever the question
arises as to the acceptance of a priest or seminarian
for service here. A series of interviews along with a
battery of psychological tests are the principal com-
ponents of the process, but Father Jaeger will be in
a better position than I to explain that to you. Once
that process has been completed, I will look to
Father Jaeger and his board for a recommendation
regarding your eventual incardination, and we will
be in a position to forward your case to the Sacred
Congregation in Rome.

Peter read the letter aloud to me. I felt numbed by the

import of its message as my eyes fixed on the flowers in the center of the table. They were orange-red geraniums, and they reminded me of fall evenings with a cozy fire in the fireplace, of family dinner together around this table, of simple food and candles lit, and the fun of shared experiences that made a difference to all of us.

> You are free to make your profession of faith and to receive the sacrament of Confirmation at any time you and your pastor see fit. Your decision to take this step will, I realize, make it necessary for you to resign your present position as vicar of the Church of the Holy Spirit. I wish there were some concrete suggestion I could make to you regarding employment, even temporary employment, but I am afraid I have nothing specific in mind at this time. May the Lord who has begun this good work bring it to a fruitful conclusion.

"Is this the way the other Catholic bishops are handling these cases?" I asked. We had waited one full year for a response to Peter's request, and he was jubilant. As for me, I felt only bitterness. More waiting, I thought, and for what, so a committee can turn us down?

"No, I've not heard of any committees from anyone else," Peter seemed thoughtful. "I wonder what it means."

"Committees take forever. I bet it'll be another year before we know whether Hunthausen is going to sponsor you or not."

"It doesn't seem fair, but I want to cooperate with Archbishop Hunthausen in every way I can. So I guess if this is how he wants to handle my case, then I'm for it. It may go a lot faster than you think."

"It can't go to Rome until he okays it, and who knows how long Rome will take," I said.

"Oh, Rome's a simple rubber stamp."

"Sure. After the petition has laid on some cardinal's desk for six months." I crossed my arms in front of me in a gesture of self-protection against him and all that he was doing to us. "And there'll be no help getting a job either." I knew it, I thought. "What will you do?"

"First, I'll talk with Father Clark and decide on a date to be received into the Catholic Church." Impatient with my cynicism, Peter went to the kitchen telephone. I sat quietly, looking up into the branches of the old pine tree outside the dining room window. The small statue of St. Francis stood where Peter had placed it in the crotch of the tree the day we moved into the house. Each year the pine needles buried him waist deep, and so he was again. His patience was a vigil of warmth and acceptance, a reminder of God's profound love for all his creatures. I thought of the prayer of St. Francis, "Lord, make me an instrument of your peace." Your peace, Lord, I thought again.

I heard Peter talking to Father Clark. I felt deserted and thrust aside as they made plans for Peter to announce his resignation September 1st, effective September 30th. We would then be received into the parish of St. John Vianney on the Feast of St. Francis of Assisi, October 4th.

Our children, scattered throughout the Western Hemisphere for the summer, created a joyful diversion by their homecoming during the last two weeks of August. Kurt from Minnesota, where he'd spent the summer working in the Student Conservation Association. Monica from her job as a counselor at Camp Huston, the diocesan summer camp in the Cascade Mountains. Tess from Ponce, Puerto Rico and a summer with Episcopal sisters doing a demographic study and volunteer work in the slums. John, who had remained in the Seattle area for the summer, came home for the day as each one arrived. These were good days, filled with experiences to share and excitement for the future of the whole family. Still, far in the distance for the moment, the cloud of doubt and foreboding hovered, never out of sight for any of us. I wanted to make good the days that we had, for now more than ever our future seemed hopelessly uncertain and out of control.

Monica, John, and Kurt agreed they wanted to be received with the family, but Tess wasn't sure. She was ill when she arrived home, having spent her last days in the Caribbean with an amoebic disease. Her summer with the sisters had left her with a certain bitterness toward religion. She saw few examples of understanding and love between Roman Catholic and Episcopalian sisters, and instead of empathy for the poor of Puerto Rico, she seemed repulsed by what she had seen.

I think every member of the family, including Tess, wanted us to be together on October 4th, but we were all apprehensive. It was confusing, to say the least, that Peter now felt compelled to leave the church we had sacrificially served as a family all of their lives. We had given them the faith in infancy. They had grown up with it, accepted, and lived it. Now they were being asked to relinquish it. It was difficult for them to say, for what? We emphasized that our move was the fulfillment of that faith, not conversion. We weren't losing anything, only complementing and completing the faith we'd always had.

Wherever we had lived, we'd been greeted and nurtured by a ready-made parish family who took a personal interest in each of our children, all special to them. We all felt as though we were divorcing people we loved.

The children also asked if their Dad would ever be allowed to exercise his ministry in the Catholic Church. They knew how hard it was for me, and they worried how I would be treated.

John, the oldest of the four children, talked to Tess. He felt it was important to remain within the support of our family faith experience. It was painful for all of us to think of this kind of separation.

Peter and I both felt that the decision was a personal one of conscience which each of our children must answer for him or herself. Yet I hoped and prayed that the family could stay together in one church. This, after all, was not so much a conversion as a fulfillment of the faith we'd always lived.

To Sister Elsbeth, Peter wrote:

John has little faith that I'll ever be a Catholic priest. He thinks it is too big and there are too many prejudices against a married man for me to be accepted. We'll see. Anyway, it is the way God is calling me, and sometimes it is more important to do the right thing and fail than not to try at all. I hope the kids will be received with us. I do not look for quick decisions nor am I impatient about the process. Like John, I feel most of those responsible will not treat my petition in any hurried or concerned way. I plan to get a secular job and then see what will come of it. I can only do my part. Others must do theirs.

There were moments in those weeks when I too felt called to be a Roman Catholic regardless of whether Peter would ever be a priest. But it was quite another thing to resign myself to the fact that he probably would not be ordained. That would mean a loss of his identity as a person and in turn a loss of my identity that was so completely intertwined with his. It seemed that we were forcing ourselves to turn our backs on all that we had believed for most of our lives. It was a turning away from the validity of that existence. Or was it a turning toward a greater reality? As Episcopalians we had often justified ourselves in the face of Catholic criticism. So it was not easy now to convert from what we had lived and believed for nearly thirty years. We talked of fulfillment in the Roman Catholic Church, not conversion. We had struggled to defend and justify the Anglican Communion as we knew it through men like Pusey and Keble, only to discover that their standards, like our own, were simply theirs and not the theology of the contemporary Episcopal Church.

I thought of friends forced to face the death of a husband or wife, or worse, the tragedy and rupture of divorce. I understood how it was for them. This too was divorce, a death experience.

In those final weeks in the Episcopal Church each act brought Peter face to face with the life he would leave, and he began to realize how much he would miss his pastoral relationships, if there were to be none in the Catholic Church. Not being able to speak of these feelings to our parishioners, there sprang in us a renewed ability to savor and enjoy each remaining moment.

For me, those last Sundays before Peter's announcement were a hazy dream world of collage and confusion, of details and challenges to be faced. Added to this, I was preoccupied with the needs of Monica and Tess as they prepared to leave for college.

On one of our walks Peter said to me, "I can't help but feel concern for some of the works I have begun. Can I just walk away from the work with the blind, for example? This is the thirteenth summer we've had sailing with the blind, but probably more important is the audio cassette and large print study and worship materials the guild provides for the infirm."

"Better put a lid on your conscience. You can't have it both ways," I said.

I noted that it was already August again, and the trees were painted with bright fall colors. I thought of the sailboat ride on that afternoon of the papal announcement. A year now. It seemed so long ago, and yet only yesterday. Perhaps I'm too hard on him, I thought. These days are difficult enough for me, but they must be especially hard for Peter.

"The new pipe organ will arrive any day. But Jim Brumbaugh is the inspiration and energy behind that. They don't need me," Peter said. His voice seemed to suddenly drop.

"Yes. That's a headache I don't mind missing." I laughed, thinking of the thousands of pieces of antique pipe organ spread on the parish hall floor for months as volunteers tried to rebuild the instrument. Of well meaning fuss-budgets bustling about, sputtering and generally making life miserable for everyone, as they feared damage and loss of the precious parts. The scene amused me, and I laughed again to myself.

Peter seemed unaware of my laughter as he continued his serious reverie of concerns and sentimentalities.

"I can't help wondering whom they will send to replace me. I'm sure it will be someone to contradict what I've taught, and save the congregation," he said. "Probably a divorced priest, maybe a woman." He smiled, but I sensed a sadness in Peter's voice in spite of his attempt at lightness.

We talked of many things during those days. Of the time that Peter had awakened in the early morning hours with an abnormal feeling of freezing cold. The telephone rang. It was the husband of a parishioner. Catherine was critically ill. He feared she was dying.

"Can you come, Father?"

Peter dressed and drove to their home at the north end of the island, down a narrow road along a remote beach. Catherine was still conscious when he arrived. He learned that she was bleeding internally.

"I'm so cold, Father. So cold." Peter gave her last rites and she died within a few minutes.

There was a sensitive communication between Peter and the people he served in the island community. It was not unusual for him to awaken in the night minutes before the phone rang, to be summoned to a bedside or the scene of an accident.

These were gifts of the Holy Spirit out of the great depth with which Peter loved his people. Once again I wondered, what will happen to this man if he is not allowed to express priesthood in the Catholic Church?

I could not imagine him anything other than a priest.

In the end we would turn our backs on the people we had served for more than eighteen years, realizing that God the Holy Spirit was in charge of this too, not we. We had to do what we had to do, and like Lot's wife we could not look back with longing for what might have been. We could continue to love them and care greatly, but when we left the Episcopal Church, we would walk out the door and leave them behind. It would have to be a clean break. We could not worry either about the rupture in relationships our announcement would create. One day I hoped they would come to realize that the decision was not one against the Episcopal Church, but made for the whole Church out of the same love and integrity that Peter had given them, and which they had accepted and freely returned.

I found comfort in the words of Isaiah 49:15 as I faced the most difficult and painful period of my life:

Can a mother forget her infant, be without tender-

ness for the child of her womb? Even should she
forget, I will never forget you.

I went to work every day knowing that my employment made a vital contribution to my husband's hope of
priesthood in the Roman Catholic Church. While the overwhelming sense of hopelessness remained with me, I was able
to get through each day because I knew I was doing everything I could to help our family deal with the uncertainties
ahead. Peter's resignation was no longer something in the
vague future; the time had arrived, and I discovered myself
far more capable of dealing with it now than in the past. I
awaited each new development, and except for momentary
glimpses I refused myself the luxury of looking back. I was
determined to look forward. I told myself I must lay aside the
past. I would need all my energy to face the challenge of the
future.

I made a private inventory of the children. I thought it
would be hardest for Kurt. A senior in high school that September, he would know the uncertainties firsthand, as well as
each decision we must make or that would be made for us. I
felt most concerned for him. The others would be away at
college. John finishing his last quarter on his Master's degree
at the University of Washington, Theresa at Evergreen State
College in Olympia, Monica had decided to return to school
in Spokane this year after a semester off. How grateful I felt
that they would be spared the stress and pressures that would
be a large part of our lives from this point on.

Peter kept his appointment with Bishop Robert
Cochrane on August 24, 1981. It was one year since we had
read the announcement in the *Seattle PI*. That same morning I
left on a three-hundred-mile drive to take Monica to college in
Spokane with little thought of Peter. I remember his surprise
when he learned I planned to drive Monica on that same day.
Somehow it didn't enter my mind that he needed me. Or
perhaps it was my way of avoiding the whole issue.

To save money Peter took the transit into the city and
walked from the downtown area up Capital Hill to Diocesan
House for his meeting with Bishop Cochrane.

When he entered the executive office, the bishop did not look up as Peter handed him the letter of resignation.

"I have here something for you to read, Bishop," he said. "I doubt this comes as a surprise."

Peter leaned back and looked around the room for a crucifix or cross on which to concentrate. It was not a light moment for him, giving up twenty-eight years of ministry in the Episcopal Church. But he could see nothing in the room to draw him to our Lord. Then his gaze stopped on an amethyst crystal paperweight on the bishop's desk. It was purple, the bishop's color. It seemed to reflect in its many surfaces the purple of the bishop's shirt and the garnet gems set in his large pectoral cross. Bishop Cochrane impatiently tapped his large ring on the desk as he read the letter.

"As a matter of fact, I am surprised," he said as he tossed it on his desk and looked out the window beyond the cathedral gardens. "Since you intend to enter the Roman Catholic Church, you will need to submit a letter renouncing your ministry."

"I would like your permission to remain at the Church of the Holy Spirit until the end of September, Bishop."

"Yes. That'll be fine." Bishop Cochrane moved some papers on his desk, then looked past Peter out the window again. "Your stipend and medical insurance will terminate on that day, as will credit toward the Church Pension Fund. This will also deny benefits to Mary and the children in the event of your death. You, personally, will be able to draw a small pension should you file when you are sixty-five."

"My Bishop's Committee has offered to continue my salary until the end of the year and medical benefits for the family for six months in appreciation for my years of service."

The bishop examined the letter of resignation again. "No. They can't afford to do that."

Here was a man who'd served the Diocese of Olympia since 1959, without personal ambition, wherever his bishop needed him. Yet the bishop seemed unable to show any warmth at all toward him.

"I'll need to get that letter from you right away, Dally."

The bishop appeared preoccupied and turned his attention to a stack of papers on his desk.

The meeting was over. It was hard to believe.

A smile touched Peter's lips as he instinctively adjusted his collar in a gesture of personal identity. He took one last look around the room where he'd met with four different bishops over the years. Again his eye fell on the amethyst paperweight which seemed unique to Bishop Cochrane. He turned and for the last time walked slowly through the walnut paneled rooms of the Victorian mansion. Through the doorway of the diocesan council room he saw the oil portraits of the bishops who had served the diocese. Drawn into the room, he stood before the likenesses of Bishop Bayne, Bishop Lewis, and Bishop Curtis. His thoughts turned to the familiar loved Anglican liturgies. The memories of Evensong with the soft rain falling on the roof of old St. Mark's Church. Weathered faces of the fishermen and ranchers in the coastal missions of Oregon. The revered beauty of the Collects in the Book of Common Prayer, and the many hundreds of other experiences where God's presence was made real throughout his ministry. All such a terrible majesty, uniquely valid for historic Christianity. Still it was the Catholic Church he wanted. Peter had made his move. He felt a peaceful mixture of sadness and joy. Without looking back, he reverently closed the door behind him.

He pushed open the heavy glass doors and stepped out into the fresh air. He hesitated for a moment on the steps where he had stood when he came to meet Bishop Bayne in 1948. He thought of the Lord's words in Mathew 10:14

> Whoever will not receive you or listen to your words—go outside that house or town, and shake the dust from your feet.

His lips parted in a smile as he kicked his shoes against the old stone steps. It felt good. There was no looking back.

13

"Well Dad, how do you feel?" John asked, as the two settled themselves in the restaurant booth.

"I'm glad it's over."

"You're still wearing your collar." John smiled. He knew his dad well. The two, father and eldest child, communicated in a special way.

"Yeah. I wasn't going to see Bishop Cochrane without my collar." The man across from him had been a child only yesterday. Somehow today Peter sensed their roles were reversed, that John was here to take care of him.

"Did he accept your resignation?"

"Oh, sure." Peter's relaxed smile told John that everything was okay with his dad. "I wish Mom hadn't gone to Spokane this weekend, but I guess she had to."

"Monica could have gone alone, but you know how Mom is. She thinks none of us can do anything without her help."

"Anyway, I'll be glad when she's back safely."

"Do you want me to come over Sunday when you make the announcement? I mean so you won't be alone."

"No. I don't think so."

"Kurt'll be there, but he's not really into all this. It goes right over him," John said of his adopted younger brother.

"No. I'll be okay. A lot of the congregation know already. I feel good about it. Mainly relieved, I think. I'll be glad when the whole thing is settled with the Catholic Church. I told Bishop Cochrane that the Bishop's Committee wants to continue my salary until the end of the year and our medical insurance for six months." A faint smile touched the corners of his mouth. "He said they couldn't do it."

"You're kidding? That old . . ."

"I don't know what we'll do; no job with Archbishop Hunthausen and Cochrane says the congregation can't give us anything."

The silence grew between them as Peter's gaze moved across the restaurant to the far wall and fixed on a yellowed Coca-Cola poster.

"There are a lot of people who think you're crazy. I hope you and Mom are ready to face that." John seemed suddenly self-conscious as he fingered the condensation on the water glass and looked up shyly into his dad's face.

"I know they do." Peter laughed. "I guess the truth is we are. I just don't want your mother hurt anymore. She's been through enough."

"She's going to be hurt, Dad. You can't be there for her unless you're honest with yourself about that."

Peter stared at his son, amazed and bewildered at the wisdom coming from the mouth of this young man he'd cradled in his arms not so long ago.

The waiter brought the wine, and John filled the two glasses. He raised his in a toast, "To you and Mom."

"Yes, to Mary and me. And all of us." Peter lifted his glass, "and to St. Frances Cabrini."

"St. Frances Cabrini?" John laughed.

"Yes." Peter looked around the little restaurant. "She was an Italian, you know. This is a good place to begin."

"Oh Dad, you and your friendships with dead people."

"Haven't I taught you anything? She's not dead. She's in all her glory in heaven, and she's praying for us right now."

"Dad." John looked furtively around the room to see if they were overheard. "No wonder people think you're crazy, especially when they don't know you."

"I walked to Cabrini Hospital after I left Diocesan

House. I got there just in time for Mass. The chapel's in the original part of the hospital."

"Dad, do you know how far that is? Why did you walk?"

"I loved it. Besides, I needed the chance to cool off a bit."

"I can't believe the things you do," John moaned.

"Do you know that St. Frances Cabrini had a fear of water that was nearly pathological? Nevertheless, she sailed across the Atlantic Ocean more than sixty times to raise money for her charitable works in the new world." The waiter served the pasta and Peter continued, enthusiastically swept up in the life of the saint he loved. "The story is that she wanted a hospital in Seattle. Bishop O'Dea wouldn't let her have one. So she asked permission to buy a building on the corner of Terry and Madison to use as a hotel, I suppose for the homeless. He said yes, and within a year her hotel became a hospital."

"Sounds like you, Dad."

"There are so many stories about her work in Seattle. Did you know she became an American citizen here?"

"No. I wonder why I never heard that before," John's friendly mimicry pleased Peter. "It's no wonder you like that old chapel. You and that saint are two of a kind." John laughed again and looked warmly across the table at his dad.

"It's because of people like her that we know and love our Lord today, John. And she and all the others, the host of heaven, are praying for us right now. The example of her life gives me courage to do what I am doing."

"Yeah, I know, Dad. You'd better eat though. The pasta's good, and you've never been one to let food go to waste."

It was early evening when Peter boarded the ferry for Vashon Island. Keenly aware that he had resigned his ministry in the Episcopal Church only hours earlier, he felt strangely self-conscious as he talked with other islanders during the crossing.

When the boat reached the island, he walked alone up the dock to the parking lot where he'd left his car. His coat was too thin for the damp, chilly night air. He felt rejected and isolated. Tomorrow he would mail his letter of resignation to the parish, and those who were not in the congregation on Sunday would receive it in the mail Monday afternoon.

In the phone booth three hundred miles away, I let the phone ring a long time in the vicarage on Vashon Island.

"Hi, dear. It's me. I've been thinking of you all day and wondering how things went with the bishop," I said, relieved to find him home at last.

"I'm so glad you called, Mary. I was hoping you would."

"Did it go okay?" I asked again.

"Oh sure. He accepted it."

"Didn't try to talk you out of it, huh?"

"Nope. He didn't waste much time with me.

"Did you expect him to?"

"No. I guess it would have been a bit out of character. Bishop did say the congregation cannot give me the three months salary and six months medical benefits that they offered. I guess I should have expected that too."

"Well, it really says more about him than it does about us." To myself, I thought, without a job or the gift from the congregation how on earth will we manage? But I said to Peter, "Don't worry, Love. We'll get along without it."

"I'll be glad when you get home on Sunday. Give Monica a hug for me. Drive carefully. I love you."

"I love you too, Peter."

Saturday was a quiet day for Peter. He contacted the two head laymen in the congregation to confirm that he had seen Bishop Cochrane on Friday. He mailed the letters to the congregation, then prepared for the Sunday service as usual.

On Sunday morning Peter walked down the aisle to stand between the front pews as he always did to speak to the people. He preferred the warmth which his physical nearness to the worshipers created. Rarely did he speak to the congregation from the pulpit.

". . . I have decided to leave the Episcopal Church. I'm sure this comes as no surprise to most of you. Mary and I love you all more than we can say. However, the time has come when I can no longer justify separation from the vicar of Christ, (Pope John Paul II), and the Catholic Church. In conscience I must be loyal to the ancient church's tradition, the Scriptures, and the magisterium. I believe that I can do that only as a Roman Catholic. The implosion we have experienced in the Episcopal Church has been an agonizing tragedy, causing sorrow and bewilderment for many of us. Some of you will note that I've been saying for years that I cannot remain in the Episcopal Church." Peter looked out the window to the majestic evergreens beyond and smiled, recalling the many occasions on which he had said that it would be just a matter of time until he would leave.

"Mary and I reached that conclusion privately about two years ago. The Holy Spirit does mysterious things when we make these kinds of choices . . . I no more than set my heart on leaving when Bishop Cochrane asked me to transfer to a larger mission in our diocese. I turned him down because I knew I would soon resign my ministry. Then a short time later I was contacted by a parish in an ideal location for my family. Again I declined. I felt I could not go to a new congregation and continue to teach a faith outside the present norm in the Episcopal Church, a faith which would be denied by succeeding pastors. I realized that I was just another person trying to make the Episcopal Church what I wanted it to be. I had to face the fact of what it has become. There is no longer room for Catholic theology and teachings in the Protestant denomination that the Episcopal Church is today."

Peter looked into the faces of the people whose lives he had shared intimately for eighteen years. He knew better than any other person in that room their tragedies, joys, human foibles. Their disappointments. They loved and accepted him with all of his faults and weaknesses. It was not easy to leave them, and he hoped they could understand.

"I planned to continue here for a limited time only when quite unexpectedly a year ago the pope announced that married Episcopal priests could become Catholic priests. That opportunity for reunion was all I needed. I am in conversations with Archbishop Hunthausen now, and I hope, God willing and by his grace, to eventually serve as a Catholic priest. My resignation will become effective on September 30th, and Mary, the children, and I will be received into the Roman Catholic Church on October 4th, the Feast of St. Francis of Assisi. Please pray for us. I continue to pray for each of you and the Church of the Holy Spirit. God bless you always."

When the liturgy was over, people crowded around Peter and gathered in little groups, reacting in various ways to his announcement. More than anything, no one was very surprised.

Edith Williams, the granddaughter of Teddy Roosevelt, took Peter's hand and said, "Father, I'm shocked, but I'm not surprised. And I wish you the very best. You deserve it." While another long-time parishioner to whom Peter had ministered through several family crises over the years muttered some anti-Catholic comments under her breath and refused to shake his hand when he offered it.

Most, however, were warm and supportive, with concern for our future. And of course they thought we'd lost our minds. He was puzzled by the members of a small charismatic prayer group who stood on the edge of the activity, watching without comment.

Interstate 90 from Spokane to Seattle was long and straight, and that Sunday afternoon it seemed longer than ever. True, I had left to take Monica to school without any thought of Peter and what he faced with Bishop Cochrane. Now I wanted to get back to him in a hurry. While on this drive I was caught in the mystery and wonder of what was happening to us.

My hands tightened on the steering wheel of our old station wagon, and I turned the radio a little louder to drown out the loneliness of the empty car. My feelings of fear and anxiety renewed again on this long drive across the state, as I thought about everything that lay ahead of us.

When I started up the east side of Snoqualmie Pass, I was struck by the variety of fall colors all around me. The air was invitingly crisp and clean, and I stopped at a view point near the summit to stretch my legs and enjoy the quiet panorama of the Cascade Mountains before I began the western descent to Puget Sound. As I drove on, the hills and valleys became a spectrum of emerald evergreens in the irridescent evening light. It was like a fairyland, and I half expected to see a leprechaun waiting to hitch a ride with some passerby.

I thought, how could I have been so insensitive as to leave Peter alone on this weekend, of all times. I felt an urgency to get home as fast as possible.

It was evening when I drove onto the ferry, and I decided to stay in the car. I wasn't ready to face the reactions of islanders who would by now have heard the news of Peter's resignation. I felt too tired to explain and face the eyes that I knew would say, "Those crazy Dallys. Now they've really gone bonkers."

Peter was waiting up for me. We talked until we could stay awake no longer and then fell into bed exhausted and sure that the worst was behind us, hardly aware that the next months would be crazier than we could possibly imagine.

On Thursday the story broke in the Island newspaper, *The Beachcomber*. "Dally Switches Church" it said. I wasn't prepared for the front page headlines, even in our little community. Nor was I prepared for the television cameras and photographers from the Seattle papers. I felt a certain excitement that at last our adventure was really underway, but it was more difficult now than ever to face people, knowing that hardly anyone would believe that a married man could be a priest in the Catholic Church.

During that first week after the publicity began, Father Ryan from the archdiocese kept in close touch with Peter. I felt comfortable in knowing that now they considered us part of them and that we were working together toward a common goal.

Then we began to receive mail. It came from all over the country. One of the most memorable was a poignant letter from a young woman in Maryland who was confirmed in the Episcopal Church at the age of twenty. Because her own parish church was kept locked, she frequently stopped at a neighboring Catholic church to pray. There she felt drawn more and more into Catholicism, and in spite of her somewhat frantic efforts to remain loyal to the Anglican Communion, she came to feel that her true home was in the Roman Church. She said that no priest, Anglican or Roman Catholic, would take her seriously. They thought she was flighty and immature. She said that the Catholic Church, in contrast to the Episcopal, was strange, vulgar, full of cheap gaudy art, needlessly authoritarian and narrow, and they simply did not know good liturgical music, nor could they sing.

Fears assailed her on every side, and she became filled with dark visions of such magnitude that she backed away from being received. Drawn forward again, apparently in an act of blind obedience, she told us how she was finally received into the Catholic Church nine months after she had become an Episcopalian. In her words: "It was like crawling through a narrow dark passageway and suddenly coming out into dazzling light. Ten years later now, still a deep peace, a sense of being at home."

Her letter ended, ". . . I hope, I pray that they will let you be a priest (and that they will show you the respect of making the ordination conditional). But if not, or until then, I hope you will be at peace living the sacramental life of the Church, that you will enjoy being in full absolute, total, unreserved communion with the Church Christ founded on the rock of St. Peter."

I found power in her words, power to face the next day, the next week. Here was a person who saw both sides and loved each, who has lived on both sides, and who understands who we are and where we are going. A person who knows the validity that is Rome and still recognizes the validity she experienced in the Anglican Communion. A person who had the courage to change and now, ten years later, continues to be at peace with her decision. I found in her words confidence and hope for our future as well.

There were sad letters too, from clergy friends and acquantances, some filled with envy at our courage, others with bitter accusations of desertion. After the initial spilling of guts, nearly all expressed good wishes and prayers for our future. To many of these people it was one thing to leave the Episcopal Church for the Protestantism of, say, the Methodists. It was quite another for an Episcopalian to convert to the papacy, pragmatically denying the catholicity and hence the validity of Anglicanism. Their sense of resentment, bitterness, and insult was familiar to me because of my own experience as a loyal Episcopalian. Reading their letters I felt hurt, but I understood and accepted their feelings.

That first Sunday after Peter's resignation I forced myself to go to church. Each time I faced the mixed reactions of our friends and parishioners I held my head high by sheer will, and I talked little, the ever-present tears caught in my throat. There was nothing to say anyway. How could I explain? It was just something we had to do.

While there were those who felt betrayed by our move, there were also many who supported it. It was almost easier, at that point, for me to understand those who felt betrayed than those who said they understood. I felt like a traitor to everything I'd stood for and believed all my life in the Episcopal Church. Feeling somehow caught between them and my husband, I could only hope and look forward to the day when, like our young friend in the letter, we too would find peace.

Many Episcopalians are extremely anti-Catholic. I believe that's why they're Episcopalians. They want the pretty religious things, reflecting beauty and culture, but they do not want to be identified with the doctrinal theology or the practice and lifestyle of the Roman Catholic Church.

In our congregation those who supported our move fell into two groups. Some wished us well and remained loyal to the Episcopal Church. They understood Peter's desire for reunion with the Catholic Church, and they simply wanted the best for us, while not necessarily always agreeing. Others would leave with us. Some to become Roman Catholic, while a few left because of personal dissatisfaction with the direction the lay leadership in the congregation was now taking. Many of these later began to attend other mainline Protestant churches in the community, or sadly, none at all. In the end about fifty persons went to the Catholic Church with us.

That first Sunday after the announcement I thought of the mother of Jesus. The contempt and derision which surely were directed at her by family friends and neighbors at Nazareth. And she was only a child. I was a child of nineteen when I married Peter, I thought. I was not only attracted to the man, but to the exciting life I knew I'd have with him. But on this day, I reflected, it's been a long and weary road for me. Now this struggle. This new challenge. I'm not ready for it. I wondered if I would ever be. I seemed unable to think beyond the last Sunday in September. I wanted only to get through the days and weeks, the memories, which now fell together in a turbulence of impressions and feelings. Every morning was covered by a cloud of dread. I prayed again and again that I could share some of the joy and beauty of the other Mary's earthly life, but my prayer lacked the joy of anticipation that was so completely hers. I felt swept along in the whirlwind over which I had no control. And I mourned the life I would leave behind.

Years later I would hear my husband, the Catholic priest, pray Mass, ". . . make us worthy to share eternal life with Mary, the virgin Mother of God . . ." and I knew then that only God in his gentle mercy and the wisdom of his time can make us worthy to share in the life, both earthly and eternal, of Mary the woman. His mother. Our mother.

Since those early days when I first felt drawn by Mary's example of faith, she has become a real person for me. In my moments of suffering and pain I am reminded of her suffering. Acknowledging my human weaknesses, we have smiled together too, sharing those strengths and shortcomings that a woman can only share with another woman. Somehow I knew from the beginning that our Blessed Mother knew me and the challenge that I faced, that she would help me find my way.

Even as I write this, I am surprised that my thoughts became directed to her, that in my hysteria I remained open to the grace she gave. In the Blessed Mother's love for me I understood that my entire life had been a preparation for what was happening to me now, that everything that had ever occurred in my life, every choice I'd ever made, was somehow in God's infinite plan directed toward this juncture in my life with Peter. Still I felt compelled to push the thoughts away, finding in them an egotism that was contrary to God's will for a life centered in Christ.

It was on a weekday morning that Peter returned from the celebration of the Eucharist puzzled and hurt.

"Mary, as I looked out the window by the altar, I noticed the little statue of St. Mary and the Christ Child weren't on the stand in the back garden. I was sure the wind must have tipped it over, so Gwen and I walked out after the Eucharist to put it back. Well, it was smashed into a million pieces on the sidewalk."

"Why would anyone do that?"

"I can't imagine. It's been there ever since I planted the Cedar of Lebanon, must be twelve years."

"It wasn't an accident, was it?" I asked.

"No. There is no way it could have been an accident. The statue was taken off the stand and carried to the cement sidewalk where it was broken."

"Why? Why would anyone do that?"

"I don't know. . . ."

Later that day I sat alone at the dining room table with scratch paper, a calculator, and our family account book open in front of me. Peter was in the vegetable garden preparing the soil for the winter. But I knew the more likely reason for his sudden burst of energy was to rid himself of the frustration and anger he felt about the destruction of the statue. Reluctantly, I went to answer the ringing telephone.

"Hello?"

"Mary?" It was Mike Pottinger, the Junior Warden at the church.

"Yes, Mike. Peter's in the garden. Would you like me to have him call you?"

"No, I can tell you. You know about giving Father three months salary and the medical insurance for the family? I wanted the two of you to know right away that we have polled the Bishop's Committee. We all agree that we will go against Bishop Cochrane's directive not to give them to you."

"Mike, are you sure? I mean, the bishop refused."

"It was unanimous. Father will get a letter confirming it. Your family needs it and, more important, Father deserves it."

I couldn't answer Mike. The tears ran down my cheeks as I began to sob, and I gently hung up the phone. I knew Mike understood. Words could not express how I felt anyway. Our prayers were answered. The money and insurance would make the difference for us economically.

The following Monday's mail brought more good news. In a letter from Bishop Law we learned that November 12th through 14th he would hold a conference at Holy Trinity Seminary in Dallas, Texas.

"This meeting will be official, Mary. Bishop Law will be there. It's his meeting." Peter was elated.

"That's wonderful. I hope it really is everything it seems." At last everything was coming together as it should.

"I will be able to start looking for a job when I get back. The timing is perfect," Peter said as he opened the mail on the kitchen counter. "I almost forgot, can we afford for me to go?" Our eyes met. We both just assumed he would do it.

"You have to go. You can take a night flight; that'll be cheaper. We'll make it okay," I said as I turned back to the sink to finish washing salad greens for the family dinner. Then my eyes returned to my husband, his head down, reading his mail. I love him, I thought. Nothing will ever change that.

14

"Mary, this letter is from Father Jaeger. It outlines the processes I'll be going through."

I stopped and dried my hands. "Let's see. You'll have interviews with five priests and one sister."

"He says the archbishop will poll the diocesan priests to see if they will agree to have a married priest. And he says he has to find a parish that will accept and pay a married priest. Oh. This is a good one! Archbishop Hunthausen says he must have a favorable written recommendation from Bishop Cochrane."

"Are you sure it says that?" I looked at the letter in disbelief. Yet there it was. "Well, Archbishop Hunthausen and his committee don't understand that no Episcopal clergyman is going to leave with the approval of his bishop," I said.

Peter waved the letter, "A man who would leave isn't an Episcopalian. In theology and morals he has left long ago."

"Naturally, Cochrane or any other bishop is going to be dissatisfied with any priest who rocks the boat. He's a threat to everything the bishop stands for."

"We're leaving an organization that is officially pro-choice on abortion. Doesn't that say anything about us? How they feel about clergy like me?"

"Hunthausen's got his head in the clouds all right. He certainly has no concept of a Protestant minister's relationship with his superior. Or maybe he's looking for a reason not to ordain you," I said cautiously and turned my attention to the kitchen sink once more. "Well, there's always something to bring us back to reality, isn't there?" I added with a nonchalance that I hoped didn't betray my real feelings.

While I felt disappointed in the archbishop and the process, I thought, we've come this far, we have to go on. It's almost as though we've been turned down already, though.

"What does a recommendation mean, anyway," Peter said. "Cochrane's got to have his day. Let him have it. Who cares what he has to say about me? And I thought he was such a good pastor when he was a parish priest. Oh well."

"Peter, I'm beginning to feel that there is no way we can stay in the Seattle area."

"Don't be silly."

"What would you say if I told you I didn't want to stay here?"

"I'd say you're being very childish. It's this business about a recommendation from Cochrane, isn't it?"

"That. But it's too big. We don't need the pressure of being in the same diocese as we have been in the Episcopal Church. I wouldn't mind living in another part of the country."

"We have to stay with Hunthausen. He's the bishop in our area. He's the one I must ask to sponsor me. If he turns us down, then . . . Well, we'll cross that bridge when we come to it. Right now I've got to set up these interviews and see Dr. Reilly, the psychologist. You may have to see him too. I'll ask Father Jaeger about that."

Oh Lord, I thought. I don't think I can go through an interview with a psychologist. I'm a nervous wreck as it is. I realized that if I were to have a psychological examination, Peter could be turned down because of me. I didn't want his priesthood to hinge on that, and yet there was nothing I could do. I had no choice. If they required it, I would have to see Dr. Reilly too.

The week following Peter's announcement of his resignation, we began attending Mass on Saturday nights at St. John Vianney, though we would not receive communion until after we became Catholics on October 4th.

The second Saturday evening, as we were leaving the

church, Father Clark asked to speak with us privately. We followed him back to the sacristy.

"I have some news about the question of your reception into the Church," he began, his eyes avoiding ours. "I've talked with the liturgist in the diocese. The custom now is that candidates receive instruction for a period of months as catechumens, after which they are received or confirmed before the congregation on a major feast day." He waited for the words to sink in. "You could be received next Easter."

The small room filled with tension. Father Clark leaned on the vestment case and studied the tile pattern at his feet. Someone came to the door and pushed it open far enough to look in. I heard it click shut again.

"Easter?" I said as I looked from Father Clark to Peter. "What's going on?"

"It would be pretty impressive for this congregation if your faith meant enough to you to wait seven months until Easter," Father Clark said.

"I think it's pretty impressive that this man is willing to give up a good job, with no promise of priesthood or anything else, to be a Catholic." I glared at him. "Wait? We've waited a year already," I said thinking of how we were ignored, then the numerous excuses and delays.

I knew too that some Episcopal ministers who had requested priesthood stayed in the Episcopal Church, waiting for permission from the Holy See to be ordained, before they made the commitment to become Catholic. This assured their families of economic security in either case, but it denied them the sense of integrity and risktaking, of being open to all the possibilities of grace and challenge. Peter felt he could not ethically choose the sure path. He could only be a Catholic first and a priest second. His loyalty had to be to one or the other. Ours was the more difficult path. Now I resented more than ever the burden placed upon our family's economic and emotional security. The least we could expect was support for our lay status within the Roman Catholic Church. I was furious. How could I ever be a devoted Catholic? I felt the old hate welling up inside me. I wanted to walk out the door, and I wanted more than anything to slam it shut behind me, to be done with the whole idea. But I forced myself to stay in the small sacristy with Father Clark and Peter, to hear out this man who would be our pastor in the Catholic Church.

"Mary." Peter said in an effort to quiet me. "What about the sacraments, Father? We're going to need sacramental grace more than ever to face the difficulties ahead."

"You would not receive any of the sacraments before you are confirmed. Except, of course, in the event of death."

"And then I suppose you'd bury us in the Protestant cemetery," I said. I remembered as a small child standing beside my uncle's grave. He had died of a brain tumor and a self-inflicted gunshot wound. I heard the adults say he could not be buried in the Catholic cemetery because he had taken his own life. We should have expected this, I thought.

"But I've made my confession to a Catholic priest for more than a year now. Would I have to stop doing that too?" Peter asked, baffled by the change in Father's attitude.

"Yes. You could not make your confession until after you're a Catholic," Father Clark said.

"It doesn't make any sense. I know none of the others have had this imposed on them. What does Archbishop Hunthausen say?" Peter asked. He looked in my direction. I fumbled to find a tissue for the tears in my eyes.

"The archbishop agrees."

"I don't understand this. Haven't we proven ourselves? I have never missed Church on Sundays unless I was having a baby. Now you are saying that we are barred from the sacraments. Father, we don't deserve this."

"You might not like the Catholic Church. If you wait until Easter, you'll know what you're getting into."

"It's not a matter of liking the Catholic Church. Believe me, we know what we're doing if that's what bothers you," Peter said angrily. "We want to be Catholics. Isn't that enough? Ours is a decision that comes from years of thought and prayer. It's not something we've done lightly. Father, you know that."

"You might find little difference here from the Episcopal Church once you get acquainted," Father Clark said.

"It's still the true Church isn't it?" I asked bitterly. "Or has that changed too?"

"Well, if this is it, I guess we'll do it, but I don't agree.

Don't you see, ours is an entirely different situation than the unchurched convert? You're wrong, but we've placed ourselves under the discipline of the Catholic Church, and we'll do what you ask."

"I don't think you'll be sorry. It will be quite a victory when you're received next Easter. You feel all right about it, don't you, Mary?"

"No. But, I'll do whatever Peter says. And, well, what choice do we have anyway?"

"You do have another choice." Father Clark hesitated for a moment, as though he was questioning his own judgment. "You can talk to the liturgist and see if he'll allow you to be received under special circumstances. "I'll give you his telephone number. You can call him for an appointment, Peter."

"Okay." Peter said half-heartedly. We waited for Father Clark to give us the information.

"Good luck." Father Clark patted me on the shoulder as we opened the door to leave. In my heart I knew that in spite of what he said, Father Clark could receive us on October 4th if he wanted to. The fact was he didn't want to.

"No one else has been treated this way," Peter said to me when we were alone in the car. "It's not just the two of us, but our kids. Especially now when they need warmth and acceptance from the Catholic Church."

I realized that Peter was hardly thinking of us, but the cruel impact all of this would have on our sons and daughters. I wondered how much more they could accept and still be faithful, not only to the Church, but to us and our ideals and goals.

"This is the Roman Catholic Church. You might as well get used to it," I said as I fastened my seat belt. "They have no intention of ever ordaining you. If receiving us as laymen is such a trauma, think of what ordination is to them. What a farce. Crumbs for dogs under the table. That's all it is. We're outsiders and we're not welcome."

"They have no idea where we're coming from, Mary. They're just playing games with us."

As we drove home through the rain, the silence between us hung like a pall. Only the swish of the windshield wipers penetrated the shock of the last few minutes. "Playing games, playing games," the wipers seemed to repeat again and again.

Back home, I said, "I'll have to call Marie and Aunt Sue. No point in their driving up here from Oregon if we're not going to be received." My dad's elderly sister and my sister were Catholics, and they had planned to be there when we were received. "Well, it will be no surprise to them," I said. "They don't think you're going to be ordained anyway."

But somehow I didn't have the heart to call them then. I'd wait until morning.

Peter woke me after a sleepless night. "I'm going to phone Jim Parker. I just can't believe this is happening to us. It can't be right."

After speaking to Jim, Peter came downstairs, grinning from ear to ear. "Jim's first comment was, "My Lord man, they're treatin' you like Buddhists." So you can guess how the rest of the conversation went. He won't see Bishop Law until tomorrow morning, but he will talk to him then, and he is sure something will be done to help us. Jim says I'm right. No one else has been treated like this by any Catholic bishop."

"I wouldn't count on it. No bishop is going to go against another one," I said.

The next morning Jim Parker called. He told Peter that Bishop Law had talked with Archbishop Hunthausen. It seems that the archbishop was unaware of the proper procedure for the reception of former Episcopal clergy and their families. Now he understands, and he will speak with Father Clark. We would be received on October 4th, as planned.

One more dragon down, I thought. There seemed to be a succession of them.

15

Peter's letter to Bishop Cochrane dated September 23, 1981 read:

> In keeping with Title IV, Canon 8, Section 1, of the 1979 Canons of the Episcopal Church, I do hereby renounce the ministry of the Episcopal Church and I desire to be removed therefrom. You and my former brothers in the Episcopal Church will always be assured of my prayers and love in Christ Jesus.

He received this release from Bishop Cochrane on October 1st:

> I do hereby accept the renunciation and resignation of the Ministry of this Church . . . by George Peter Dally, who is now and hereby released from the obligations of the ministerial office and deprived of the right to exercise gifts and spiritual authority as a Minister of God's Word and Sacraments conferred on him in his Ordination. This action is for reasons which do not affect his moral character. Done at Diocesan House . . .

In the midst of this painful disarray, Peter went to see Dr. Reilly for his psychological examination. He spent an entire day taking personality inventory tests, plus three more afternoons in interviews. Then it was my turn. The events of previous weeks and fear of the weeks to come found me in a state of quiet hysteria. I was terrified of the psychological examination. Up until now no one else knew of my depression. I hoped I could bluff my way through.

My first interview with Dr. Reilly was brief and friendly. At the end of it he handed me a packet containing a personality survey form and suggested that I take it home, do the test, and bring it back for a second interview the following week. I was relieved to do just that. I took the test as I had been instructed, in one sitting. Then on the morning of my second appointment I arrived in downtown Seattle early. As I waited in a nearby coffee shop, I took the survey out of its envelope and impulsively changed many of the answers. Thinking of what I had just done, I felt guilty, so I took the test out of the envelope again. I tried to spot the answers I had changed so I could change them back to my original responses.

I was overcome by my own insecurity and fear, and I wondered how this confusion would affect the interview I was about to have, and more importantly the recommendation which Dr. Reilly would soon give to Father Jaeger and the Priesthood Discernment Committee. I was embarrassed and ashamed that I had done such a silly thing. Still I could not tell anyone. Most of all I could not tell Dr. Reilly. So I went to the second appointment feeling even more terrified than before.

Dr. Reilly scored the test and asked, "What did you think of the survey, Mary?"

"It was interesting. I've never taken one before," I said, as I nervously examined my hands.

"The results are interesting too. Actually pretty typical of individuals who want to be sisters or priests. By that I mean a lot of what you express is: I'm okay. I know you think I'm crazy, but I know I'm not."

We both laughed.

"Did I say that?" I asked. I looked away again. "That's exactly the way I feel. I know that you Catholics must think we're crazy. It doesn't make sense to anyone but us, and sometimes I wonder if it does even to us." I fumbled in my purse for a tissue.

"It's all right, Mary. Your feelings are very normal."

Dr. Reilly's tenor voice comforted and strengthened me. "You're bound to have all kinds of doubts, and feelings of anger too. They're okay to have."

I quietly dabbed at my eyes. A sob escaped as I said, "I was so afraid I'd blow this thing. I know a lot of Peter's being accepted depends on me."

"The thing I am concerned about is that I detect a bit of depression in this instrument, and the test is only an instrument, a tool."

"That's not so bad, is it?" I asked.

"No, not now. But you mustn't let it fester and grow either. It's important for you to realize that the feelings and emotions you are having now are normal. You're facing a lot of change. It's tough and it's probably not going to get easier, but I think you can handle it."

"Yeah. I'll be okay. I've got to. I'd do anything for Peter, and I know he'll help me through it too. Thank you, Dr. Reilly."

"The stress you and Peter are under now is only the beginning. The next few months, after Peter receives permission from Archbishop Hunthausen, while you are waiting for the decision from the pope, are going to be especially stressful. You have no idea what this is going to do to your husband. Stay close to each other, and if there is anything I can do to help, please call me."

"Thank you. I appreciate that," I said quietly, the real import of his words not reaching my consciousness. I didn't expect it to be easy. Dr. Reilly's warmth and understanding had unleashed my pent-up emotions. As we talked tears streamed from my eyes in a flood of relief.

"I think it might be a good idea for me to meet with your children. What do you think? Would they mind coming in?"

"No. I don't think so. Monica is at school in Spokane. It wouldn't be convenient for her to come, but the others are at schools in this area."

"Okay. Let's set a date now. You can call me if it is not convenient to their schedules. You and Peter come too."

When I left Dr. Reilly's office I was a reddened, swollen mass, but I was so relieved I almost danced to the elevator, not caring in the least who saw my red eyes and swollen face. It's over. Thank God, I thought.

As I drove to church alone that last Sunday in September, it seemed that everything was mixed up and out of order. We had been saying goodbye in our hearts for more than a year now. These people were my friends and I loved them. I would miss them more than I could say. How I dreaded this day, and now this final farewell seemed an agonizing anticlimax. To once again hear the silence, as their eyes spoke of bewilderment and derision, mixed with questions and pity for me personally. I dreaded Peter's comments to the congregation too. Words that would bring back memories too difficult to handle with poise. To say the least, I felt emotionally brittle as I faced this day which my position as the vicar's wife obliged me to live through with all the dignity I could gather.

As I walked toward the entry, I saw Jean, one of the ladies in the parish, waiting inside. I remember thinking how nice it was of her to sit with me, so I wouldn't have to be alone that last Sunday. I smiled as I opened the heavy door.

"Mary, where is my silverware?" Jean demanded.

"Your silverware?"

"Yes. You used my mother's silverware for that wedding last Saturday. Now there are three forks missing."

Silverware? I wondered. Then I remembered, Jean had given one hundred place settings of stainless steel to the Church in memory of her mother.

"Three forks?" I asked, hardly aware that this could be happening on our last Sunday in the Episcopal Church.

"Yes, and you're not leaving until I get them back."

"Come with me, Jean, while I count them," I said.

Seething, I led Jean to the kitchen where several women were preparing a reception for us.

"I gave my borrowed key back to your daughter. Do you have yours with you?"

"Yes. I brought it. That's how I know you didn't return all the forks."

Jean opened the drawer and watched as I counted the forks. There were exactly one hundred.

"Well I just counted them and there were only ninety-seven," She insisted.

"They're all there now. You'd better lock it up before any more get away," I said smiling, though the entire episode seemed unreal to me.

It was only when I turned to leave that I noticed how silent the room had become. As I slowly ascended the stairs, two tears slipped down my cheeks. I should be glad to leave this place, I thought.

The liturgy began with one of Peter's favorite hymns: "The God of Abraham praise . . ." I became lost in the words I loved and the swelling organ music of Jim Brumbaugh, who'd come to help us out one past Advent and stayed for six years. The senior wardens who'd served Peter assisted in the service. Our beloved friend Jim Lowry, dying of a malignant brain tumor, vested and sat in his wheelchair. Earlier that week Peter and I had presented Jim and his family for reception into the Catholic Church. When he died two months later, Father Clark asked Peter to give the eulogy at his funeral.

The liturgy droned on around me, and I was hardly aware that it was over as I heard Peter's voice announce the name of the vicar pro-tem, the Reverend William Riker and his wife, the Reverend Barbara Riker. I noted dully that it was the second marriage for both. One of the new team ministries. How strange that the Church had never considered us a team, I thought.

The recessional music began, and I became aware of Peter at my side. He took my arm and we walked together down the aisle and out of the church we'd served for eighteen years. "Praise my soul the King of heaven; To his feet thy tribute bring."

It was our wedding music. Damn him, I thought, why'd he have to do that? I fumbled for a tissue, and as I dabbed at my eyes, an audible sob escaped from somewhere deep inside me.

16

I remember how in October the coastal storms would begin to beat the southern Oregon shores. I loved the mild summer months, but the excitement of the wind and rain together made the winter my favorite time of year. In the west, the black clouds vied for the winds that moved them quickly, angrily toward the land. Then with gathering force the gale would strike the rocky shoreline spraying the sea water onto the windows of houses along the beaches. In those days the greenish glass Japanese fishing floats washed up on our beaches, precious gifts, there for the discovery of sharp-eyed beachcombers.

Now, technology had replaced the beautiful glass ornaments with crude plastic fishing floats, functional, but no longer the treasures of the past.

We're too young to be called middle aged, they tell us. Nevertheless, we are entering into the autumn of our lives. Our children are grown. It could be a time of relaxation and peace. A time for just each other. I loved the summer of our lives, the years that saw our children grow into young adulthood. Now, like the onset of the seasonal storms in Oregon, it is our autumn, and might these years not be the most exhilarating time of all?

I asked the same questions that each of us has asked: Who are we? What is our purpose?

Today, I thought, we are the result of what we were yesterday, last month, last year, having created an environment of persons and events which translate into those things we value most. Those things which move us to caring and rejoicing. Our treasure.

What, then, is it for Peter and me to be called by God? Is it not simply the awareness that God has a purpose and a plan for each of us? And the courage for us to follow? To let go of our egos and allow our lives to be used in the hand of God? Is it not emptying in order to fill ourselves up with God's purpose? St. Augustine prayed: "Late it was that I loved You . . . and I burned for Your peace."

I thought of the surrender and assurance of the news clipping I'd taped to my refrigerator: ". . . like the seed that grows, the future is surprising . . ."

It seemed to me that we made all of our big moves in the fall of the year. It's strange how the directions and shapes of our lives wind and twist to finally mature and become. Yet they are never finished as humanly expected, but ever sensitive to the breath of the Spirit.

I looked back over the years since my early childhood, and once again it seemed that God intended some special task for my life. I thought again of the mother of our Lord. She knows what it means to be uncertain and confused about the future, to have thoughts and feelings that cannot be shared with anyone.

Now I would enter with Peter and our children that strange and fearsome power, the Roman Catholic Church, through whose door I had peeked from my earliest childhood on without understanding why. Strangely, even now I wondered if I would go alone.

All the time now, like a haunting parade, the hushed whispers assaulted me: Her parents weren't married in the church. No, she can't go. Mass. Confession. Sshh.

I recalled that my father had wanted to send me to St. Vincent's Hospital for nurses training, but I was afraid I would convert if I studied at a Catholic hospital. Stubbornly, I enrolled at a state university and sent my dad the bill. Captivated by St. Vincent's and the sisters, I recognized that because I felt attracted to the Catholic Church I was afraid of it. I smiled to myself, remembering. I was as Irish as he was.

Now this. It's not my choosing. Still, I'm here. And I wonder how it will be?

The kids all came home and we were received on the

Feast of St. Francis of Assisi. All of us, that is, except Theresa, for whom it was a matter of conscience. Painful as it was, she did not want to become a Catholic just because the rest of the family was doing it. We respected and supported her for her decision.

My aunt and sister and her husband came from Oregon. I wondered if any Episcopalians would be there. What could we expect? Recent months had held so many surprises.

Sunday morning we passed the strawberry fields on Cove Road as we drove the mile or so to St. John Vianney Church. The warm strawberry aroma had long since been washed away by early fall rains, bringing new life to the green plants. I noticed the freshly worked soil looked rich and loamy in the cool fall air. I thought about the growing process that reaches its peak in the summer's delicious berries. So it is with us, entering a new season in our lives.

At the door someone pinned a corsage on my dress while Peter watched. I looked at him and saw a stranger dressed in a white shirt and necktie.

Our sponsors were there: Bill and Cecelia Furlong, Ray and Edith Aspiri, Nancy and Paul Wallrof, Leslie and Steve Perry. In a daze, I followed them to the front pew they had reserved for us.

Strange emotions stirred in my head: fear, anxiety, anger, relief. They were all a part of this morning. I wanted to get on with our lives and face whatever had to be faced. The congregation sang. I heard Peter's clear voice above the rest. There was something else too. In spite of my shattered emotions, it seemed good that we had come. In my heart I felt a glimmer of the assurance and hope that I yearned for. Ours was a long journey, and today, I thought, the hardest part is over.

I turned and for the first time became aware of the full church. Catholics. Episcopalians. Their reassuring smiles of support and welcome. I knelt to pray.

Father Clark began the Mass, and we moved out of our pews. Peter took my hand in his moist one as we knelt on the altar steps, the children on either side. Our sponsors' reassuring hands touched each of our shoulders. I turned my head toward our empty places. Theresa stood there alone, straight and tall. So lonely, and yet remarkably courageous. She's a lot like her mother, I thought, and turned my attention to the words of the liturgy.

As we received the sacraments of Confirmation and the Body and Blood of our Lord Jesus, I was confronted with God's grace in a reality that was greater than anything I had expected. Having become a Catholic, I now embraced all of Anglicanism and more. I hoped not to lose the faith I loved, but to know it in all the fullness of his complete and total grace.

Nothing in this life could ever be more important than my "yes" to our Lord and his plan for our lives. United in the sacramental bond of marriage, Peter and I needed each other more than ever now. I felt glad that I had come with him.

I thanked God for somehow leading us here, and I asked him to help us to know him, to love him, and to serve him in the Catholic Church. These words became my most frequent prayer, the one that started off all my other praying, and it became the affirmation of my faith in God and his church. Years later I would learn that it is these benign prayers we've got to look out for. When God answers them, he often requires much more than we bargain for in the asking. I could not know that morning what God's answer to my prayer would mean. I did know that whatever lay ahead for us, we had come home, that the conversion of the will and mind we had experienced in our commitment to leave the Anglican Communion, to become Catholics, and to do so as husband and wife, was the beginning of a new and exciting relationship with God.

17

I felt excited as I drove to SeaTac Airport to pick up Peter after the meeting in Dallas with Bishop Law. It had been only one year since the first meeting with the Pro-Diocese, but we had lived a lifetime of events and decisions since. I thought of that first meeting, of its lack of cohesiveness, the confusion of goals and purpose, and I was anxious to hear what this one had been like. With a Catholic bishop present, this would surely be a more constructive experience for everyone. I could hardly wait to hear what had happened.

As we waited for the bags, I asked, "Well, how was it?"

"Great, just great! The night flight got me there just in time for Mass," Peter said. "Whew, I'm exhausted now, but it was fantastic. Bishop Law. Incredible."

"Okay. Tell me everything," I urged, delighted to see my husband obviously happy with the outcome.

"First of all, it was wonderful to finally be a Catholic and be able to begin by receiving Holy Communion. As I sat down in the chapel, I noticed two men in front of me with clerical collars. The others appeared to be seminarians. I felt out of place, even though I suspected that the men with collars were a part of our group. Then, when we passed the peace, a young man, hardly more than Kurt's age, turned to me and said, 'We're all glad you're here.' It seemed like a new beginning for me. I lost my nervousness, and I began to feel that we were meant to be there. Invited guests and not intruders, as I am so easily inclined to feel in all this."

Peter stepped forward to pick up his bag, and we

headed for our car. "This meeting was so different from the one a year ago in San Antonio. With a Catholic bishop present and the church paying the bill, we all felt the validity that the movement has taken on. I realize, too, that I'm not alone. Others have experienced the same treatment by Episcopalian bishops, as well as the reluctance of local Catholic priests. It's not been easy for any of us, and it was said over and over that those who have yet to make the break should not expect it to be easy."

As we drove toward the ferry in the early morning light, Peter talked and I listened eagerly.

"You'll love this," he said. "Each man was asked to share something of his background and the requirements of the local Catholic bishop. I told them that Hunthausen was asking for a favorable written recommendation from my former bishop. They all laughed." He turned to face me as we stopped for a red light.

"What?"

"Yeah. They thought it was hilarious. It became the joke of the conference."

"Were you embarrassed?" I asked.

"No. They know that any man leaving to become a Roman Catholic is not going to get backing from most Episcopal bishops. They know the archbishop's politics. They were really sympathetic that he happens to be my diocesan. It makes me wonder what to expect."

"Have all of them left the Episcopal Church?"

"No, only eight of us. I had to smile to think that in a Catholic seminary the continuing Anglicans took over the large chapel while Bishop Law celebrated in the small one. It was sad that we weren't together as a sign of intention and unity though. As the final Mass ended, Bishop Law began to sing *And I Will Raise Him Up*. It was a kind of spontaneous acclamation as the men's voices in the small chapel rose as one, clear and strong. Then from across the hall in the larger chapel, where the Episcopalians were finishing their liturgy, we heard their voices join in. It was a very touching moment, an especially beautiful way to end the conference."

I searched in my handbag for a tissue as our car approached the yacht basin in Federal Way. Across the Sound

I saw the familiar view of Point Robinson lighthouse on Vashon-Maury Island's most easterly arm. I recalled the summer day we'd sailed our twenty-one foot boat *Evensong* from Blake Island following a week of camping out with our kids. The water around the tiny island park was rough that morning as we left the marina at sunrise. The wind blew hard. I could only wonder at its actual velocity. As it caught both our mainsail and jib, we sailed wing and wing the entire length of Vashon-Maury Islands. Our boat was in the wind, totally at one with it, moving in complete harmony. It was eerily quiet too as *Evensong* cut cleanly through the water. There were no swells to ride because we were in them, moving with the tide as well. Monica and Tess sunbathed on the deck, and Kurt slept below in the boat's tiny cabin. Peter and I lounged in the cockpit, enjoying the illusion of complete calm.

We rounded Point Robinson for the final homeward stretch of southern Maury Island just before entering the mouth of Quartermaster Harbor. Peter was uneasy about what we would encounter there. We were likely to be caught up in whirlpools and crosscurrents that could easily prove hazardous to our tiny *Evensong*.

The next two hours were the most exciting of the entire trip as we tied our life jackets securely and held on tightly to the gunnels. Our small craft recklessly hurled past the jagged shoreline as though thrown by some imaginery catapult. Finally, propelled like a shot by near gale winds into the mouth of the harbor, we yanked our sails down just in time to keep from running aground. Once inside the sheltered harbor, I counted bodies. Kurt was missing. Hearing his name, he emerged from the cabin stretching and yawning. We tried to convince him that he'd slept through the best part of our vacation, and probably the most thrilling sail he could experience in a lifetime!

I felt the adrenaline just thinking about the excitement that day.

"What are you thinking about, Mary?" Peter asked.

I smiled and pointed toward Point Robinson. "I was just thinking about the day we sailed wing and wing from Blake Island. Do you remember how rough the water was and how Kurt slept through it?"

"Yeah," he said, laughing.

"I was so scared." I turned to Peter and smiled. "But I wouldn't have missed it for anything!"

As we talked about the meeting in Dallas, it seemed that Peter was just coming into the reality of what he had done, that now he was a Catholic seeking priesthood in the Catholic Church.

"Bishop Law is a unique personality, Mary. He has such openness. To welcome us the way he has."

"Of course, it's his job," I said.

"Well I know, but he gives it so much more than something we Catholics are supposed to do for you Anglicans.'" He turned to me and smiled. "I suppose that the openness I see is the result of men attempting to express God's love and his will in their own human terms."

"You know it must be painful for them. They have all sacrificed the desire for home and family, given up the opportunity for intimacy with another person, for a celibate priesthood. Now they're seeing the Church receive men from a Protestant denomination who've had it all, so to speak. I mean, you have a wife and four children. In their minds they must be thinking, what have you guys done for the Church? You've got everything they don't have . . ."

"Everything but priesthood," Peter said softly.

"Well yes, but that only says that you chose marriage and the Protestant ministry instead . . ."

"Granted, God calls us in different ways and in his time . . . but I have to admit, if I had found my way somehow into the Church of Rome, I don't know if I could have accepted a celibate priesthood."

"It's pretty humbling when you think of it."

"It sure makes my experience there even more heartwarming," Peter said.

"How could those seminarians, with all the natural drives and temptations young men are faced with, . . . how could they not feel their church has let them down? And what of the men who are older, who've been priests for fifteen or twenty years. They've sacrificed, and now the Church is opening the door to us . . . without so much as a backward glance at their condition."

"I have to admit, Mary, there was reluctance there. Oh, they made sincere efforts at openness and welcome, but still, there was reluctance. Almost a sense that we really shouldn't be coming among them."

"Just because the Holy Father says it's okay doesn't make us automatically welcome, or the whole thing any easier for the celibate priests," I said.

"Bishop Law is a strikingly charismatic personality and a well loved and respected episcopal authority. Do you know that in 1976 Jim Parker, then Provincial of the Episcopalian Society of the Holy Cross—"

"Who are they?" I asked.

"They were founded during the Oxford Movement by a group of high church Anglican priests as a means of mutual support during the persecutions they experienced from the accepted liberal low churchmanship of their day. Well, Father Parker was asked to get an appointment with Archbishop Jean Jadot, the Apostolic Delegate, to discuss the ecclesiastical status of many Episcopalians at this time. They hoped to explore possible avenues for entry into the Roman Catholic Church. Father Parker did not know how to get an appointment, since it seemed unlikely that the archbishop would see him without an introduction. He prayed about the matter for a time and decided to call a friend, a Catholic priest. Coincidentally, or more likely through the intervention of the Holy Spirit, Bishop Law happened to be sitting in that priest's living room. It was through him that Jim was able to get an appointment with Archbishop Jadot."

Goose bumps ran up and down my arms as Peter told me the story.

"Then to add even more mystery, there were other Episcopalians like myself, from all over the country, unaware of each other, who were writing letters to Archbishop Jadot at the same time. It was because of all of this that Jadot took the matter to the Holy Father and subsequently to the American bishops where it was eventually approved and then confirmed a year later."

"So that's how it happened," I said. At last I saw a pattern emerge. "You mean there were others like you writing to Archbishop Jadot at the same time you were?"

"Yes. You see it's all in the hands of God, Mary."

"Now that's spooky, like the breath of the Spirit moving across the land," I said, a sense of wonder washing over me like a tide. I thought of God's infinite generosity. His mercy. His peace. Undeserving as any of us might be.

"Bishop Law was then appointed by the Holy See to be the Ecclesiastical Delegate for the Pastoral Provision. I can't believe his openness and love. The concern for our families too. If any bishop can see this program through, he can do it."

"Oh, yes," I said.

"We need great humility. While we have knowledge of the Catholic faith, we really don't know Catholics; people who've never experienced anything but the traditions and practices of Roman Catholicism. I'm sure it's difficult for them."

As we arrived at the ferry dock, I looked across the Sound toward Blake Island, remembering that day several summers ago. "We're running with the wind now, wing and wing. Remember what it was like going at that speed, inside the pocket of the wind, feeling and hearing only stillness all around our boat? It was exciting. Unreal. We had to keep reminding ourselves what was really happening, what was really moving us along. That's what's happening now, Peter, but it's even bigger. In this greater "now" we're in the eye of the storm. And it's the breath of the Spirit that even now is moving us on."

18

We wanted to receive Holy Communion every day that it was possible. Each Saturday evening and Sunday morning we attended Mass at one of the island parishes. We would have gone daily if the Sacrament had been available to us.

Consequently, Peter continued as he had planned to celebrate the daily Mass privately in our basement chapel according to the Episcopal Church. He sought advice on the matter from Father Clark and his confessor. Both priests told him that since it had always been his practice, and the Catholic Mass was not available to him, it was permissible to continue this devotion privately.

"Their tacit approval is an insult to you, if you only knew it," I said one day as I brooded about it.

"Mary, it's what I've always done. You know that I would go to Mass at St. John Vianney if it were offered daily."

"Father Clark could give you a key and let you receive the reserved Sacrament if he wanted to," I countered. "He knows that you were a daily communicant in the Episcopal Church. He just doesn't trust us."

"Now don't be too hard on Father Clark. He's been awfully good about all this."

"You said you couldn't be an Episcopalian and a Catholic at the same time. Now you're trying to have it both ways."

"No . . ."

"If you ask me, it means nothing to them, what you

are doing now. They support you because they don't think you've ever offered a valid Mass anyway."

"Fortunately I didn't ask you, Mary."

"You wouldn't get so upset if you didn't think I was right," I said.

"You don't know what you're saying."

As we talked my anger grew, and with that I resolved not to say another word to him about it. I couldn't imagine why Peter would become a Catholic and continue to celebrate the Anglican Eucharist. The whole idea seemed a travesty of the principles for which we had become Catholics. I determined not to assist him in any way.

The next day Peter began the series of interviews with the Discernment Committee as outlined by Father David Jaeger, Vocations Director for the Archdiocese of Seattle. Peter looked upon the interviews as the beginning of a relationship with each priest and sister who would be a sympathetic support to his growth, both as a person and academician, in his journey toward priesthood in the months ahead, much like any Catholic seminarian.

During one of these interviews, I remember, a priest said, "We pray for vocations and God sends us you . . .? I can't help but wonder what it all means."

Peter was able to report to Father Jaeger on October 29th that the interviews had been completed. Father Jaeger indicated to the committee that he and Archbishop Hunthausen had already met with Bishop Cochrane, whom they told about the process of discernment and acceptance that Peter had entered into with the Catholic archdiocese. They said that Bishop Cochrane was "most gracious and cooperative." This both surprised and pleased us since clergy friends had reported that our former bishop had said he would "make sure" Peter was never ordained a Roman Catholic priest.

Caught up in our own pilgrim journey, Peter and I laughed at these contradictions and kept an optimistic outlook. Peter then began the course of study outlined by Bishop Law's office. It seemed now that events would move along quickly and that his ordination would occur within a few months, or at least no later than a year hence.

Father Clark asked Peter to participate in the parish as a Eucharistic minister and lector, but he declined. He felt that it was important for the people of the Catholic parishes to realize that we had come to experience the faith with them. So for the first time since his ordination in 1953, Peter sat in the pew. It was a first for me too, and I loved being there beside him. But it seemed unnatural not to see him at the altar, and I looked forward to the day when he would again have the gift of priesthood.

In spite of all our efforts, our place there was confusing and bewildering both to the people and to us. We slowly began to recognize that a part of conversion— for more and more we came to understand that it was truly conversion, not fulfillment, as we had so smugly touted in the beginning—was a pilgrimage that could only be found in dying to self, in the grace that blossoms when we give up something that is loved and dear.

We could not give up the life we loved without feeling a certain pain and loss. Just as God answers our prayers in the events and pressures of our lives, how we respond to them is our response to God. In those first weeks after our reception, we wanted to convey to our new Catholic brothers and sisters that our motives were open and pure, that we had not come among them to change their lives or to prove anything. Many of them had known us in the Island community. They welcomed us warmly. Others appeared to be unsure of why we had come and seemed to wonder how long we would stay. Each week we resolved to put them at ease, though at first most of them made little effort to be friendly. They were kind in their own way, but they didn't know what to make of our coming among them. They didn't know who we were. I could hardly blame them when we weren't sure of our own identity there. I knew that patience and friendly warmth were the keys to our relationship with them, but in my heart I wondered if things would change.

Sister Elsbeth wrote:

". . . this is the most difficult time for you as now
you are on the water itself, but just keep your eyes
on Jesus and he will lead you where he wants you."

It was all a part of the dying process, ". . . whoever
loses his life for my sake and that of the gospel will save it."
We needed to be patient, to simply be ourselves and love the
Lord. Everything else would take care of itself.

Father Jaeger wrote on November 4th acknowledging
the completion of the interviews and other requirements. He
said that the Discernment Committee would convene to
make their recommendation to the archbishop, who would in
turn report his decision to us by the end of December. In the
meantime Father Jaeger accepted an invitation to come for
dinner on December 2nd, to get better acquainted with me
and our children. We asked each of the children in the area to
reserve that evening for the occasion.

The evening before the dinner, John called. "Mom, I
can't make it tomorrow night. I've been invited to Susan's ski
lodge at Crystal Mountain. I don't want to let Dad down, but
I sure would like to go."

"Okay," I said, disappointed, but realizing that this
whole situation was really our problem not that of our children
who were well on their way to becoming adults.

Feeling a bit insecure about the other two, I asked
Kurt that night if he would be home for the dinner. He said he
just couldn't make it either. He had a big paper due the next
day, and he had to spend the evening at the Seattle library. I
was beginning to feel abandoned until I called Tess. She said
she would be coming home late in the afternoon to spend the
night with us. I thought, well, one out of four, not good, but
not too bad either when you consider they have their own
lives and responsibilities. And they were also a bit fed up with
the whole business, having by now their own interpretation of
the treatment their Dad had received from both the Episcopal
and Catholic hierarchy.

The following afternoon I went to the ferry to meet

Tess. She climbed into the car and said, "I've got a test tomorrow and a big paper due, Mom. I can't stay overnight. Can you or Dad take me to catch the 9:30 ferry to Tacoma?"

"Theresa, that's too late to walk through the park," I said. "Stay and study here. We'll take you to the first ferry in the morning."

There was hysteria in her voice as she said, "No, you're lucky I'm even here with all the work I have to do. I've got to go back tonight. If I stay, I'll be so worried about getting everything done I won't be able to sleep."

"Your being here really means a lot to your dad and me, but we can't let you go back tonight, Tess."

"I'll be all right. I've walked through Point Defiance before at night."

"But not when we knew about it. It's not safe. You could be mugged, and God knows what else."

"Mom, I'll be okay. I can take care of myself."

"No. You absolutely cannot." Peter raised his voice when Tess told him her plans.

"Dad, it'll be okay. You think I can't take care of myself, but I can."

"No. And that's final." He looked at his wrist watch. "If you have to go back tonight, you should go right now, before it gets dark," he said firmly.

Tess started to cry. "I wanted to be here for you and Mom. I went to all this trouble. Now you're making me go back without dinner."

"Theresa, you're exhausted," I said.

"We want your safety more than anything else. We can drive you to Olympia first thing in the morning, but we can't let you take the bus late tonight," Peter said.

I could hear her crying through the wall. So vulnerable, this Tess of mine, I thought. But Peter is right. It was the only thing to do if she could not wait until morning.

As the two left, I found myself alone to wait for Father Jaeger. He was coming specifically to meet our kids, who wouldn't be there. I felt deserted as for the first time it became clear to me that our children did not wish to be an intimate part of our pilgrimage. They had always been a part of our whole life in the Church. What was happening now? Was it just that they were growing up? Or was this a rebellion and rejection of us and the struggle we'd had . . . were now facing?

What would we tell Father Jaeger? We'd never played games when it came to our children. I didn't intend to start now. I knew that this could have a bad effect on our relationship with the archdiocese, even now, before we had a chance to establish any relationship at all.

"Come in, Father," I said as I invited him to sit. "I wish Peter were here now—he'll be back in a few minutes—to help explain all this, but, well," I fumbled, twisting my wedding band and nervously adjusting the sleeves on my blue silk blouse while I tried to explain what it was like to be the parent of four teen-agers. As I talked, I wondered if my words might be lost on this young man who could not possibly be more than three or four years older than my own John.

I smiled to myself as he relaxed in the easy chair, left foot resting on his right knee. With each child's situation, he laughed and countered with a story about one of his brothers or sisters.

It seemed an eternity before the back door opened and I heard Peter say, "Now I know why the Church believes in a celibate priesthood!"

"Oh, I don't know, Peter. Maybe having children would make us all a lot more human." Father Jaeger laughed.

After we ate dinner, Peter invited Father Jaeger to see the chapel with the icons he had painted. Kurt's bedroom was located in the basement opposite the chapel. He and I had an informal agreement that I would go into his room only if he became trapped in there by the debris. His room was a pit, a total disaster area which could set off a chain of nagging and ranting that would last for days, at the end of which I would become angry. Then in frustration I would declare that I had completely given up on him, much to his relief, of course. He knew I would, and he always waited me out.

I couldn't believe my ears when I heard Peter. Pointing to the closed door with the poster of an almost bare Farrah

Fawcett, he said, "That's Kurt's room, Father. Would you like to see it?"

"Sure. If he won't mind."

"I . . . I think he might," I said lamely.

Peter acted as though he hadn't heard me.

"Close your eyes, Father. I'll open the door and turn on the light," Peter said. He looked at me and winked.

I glared at him, but naturally he ignored me. I could only imagine what the room looked like, and what Father's reaction would be.

"Okay, Father, open your eyes."

Father Jaeger threw back his head and laughed, "And I'll bet when he walks out this door he is impeccably dressed and groomed," he said as he looked from one side of the room to the other.

"Yup," I said.

Neither of the men seemed to notice me, as they laughed all the way back to the living room.

As I turned off the light, I took one last horrified look. I thought, that kid is going to clean up this room if it's the last thing he ever does. Just wait til I get my hands on him, I thought as I pushed aside soiled clothing in order to close the door. Or were those the clean things I'd washed and folded yesterday, laying there on the floor?

19

As December, 1981 arrived we waited for word from Archbishop Hunthausen. Peter spent most of his time in his study, engrossed in the required reading, never far from the telephone. Then just before Christmas we received a letter from the archbishop. He said he would soon have the recommendation of the Discernment Committee, but he would not make a decision until late January when he returned to Seattle after a short break from his duties. He asked us to meet him in his office on January 22nd, more than a month away. Above all else his letter promised the results of his prayerful deliberation regarding Peter's request.

It was a characteristically sensitive letter filled with empathy for the wait that had become the focus of our lives. However, I could not help thinking that it had been an entire year since our first meeting. He seemed no nearer a decision now than he had been then. He had said he would make the decision by Christmas. Now we would have to wait another month. Well, at least, I thought, our Christmas won't be spoiled with uncertainty and the question of why we haven't heard.

In fact that Christmas was quiet and wonderful, freed as we were of our usual ecclesiastical responsibilities. How wonderful to have Peter all to ourselves on Christmas! To his sister in Jerusalem, he wrote:

It is a cold snowy morning. The island is a beautiful contrast, a white covered fairyland of shapes and winter mystery next to the deepening gray sky. Monica, her friend Valerie who came for the holidays with her, and I bicycled over to Maury Island to deliver a bottle of my blackberry wine to Sister Mary Frances, our organist at St. John Vianney, and one to a Slavic couple I've known for years. Old Mrs. Roncivich clapped her hands when she saw me and shouted, "I'm so happy! When you gonna be a priest?" We meet with Archbishop Hunthausen January 22nd . . . please ask your community to pray . . .

Sister Elsbeth's Christmas greeting brought:

. . . this Christmas will be a little difficult for you . . . on the one hand the sweetness and joy of having been received into the Church, but on the other hand you are in no man's land. You know that our Lord is guiding you, that your ministry is a shared one. Peter is the one who will be ordained, but his ministry is not complete without you, Mary. On the surface the waves break a bit, but for the time being you just have to roll with them. Before long you will know where our Lord wants you. Perhaps it will not be Seattle. Be assured, our Lord does have a place for you . . .

Peter, bundled in winter clothing, became a familiar figure walking up and down our driveway while praying the daily office. The frustration was there, he couldn't sit still for more than a few minutes at a time. Under the circumstances I felt he was handling everything rather well. Because of the numerous interviews and the uncertainty as to the next step, the archdiocese advised Peter not to seek interim employment. Though we had been thrifty, the three-month stipend from our Episcopalian congregation had come to an end, and now we would have only my secretarial salary to live on.

As I remember those days, I think of a quiet, unobtrusive man who lived two houses south of us. Pastor Herman Grimm, a retired Air Force Chaplain, a Lutheran, had become

Peter's beloved friend and mentor. A scholar of biblical Hebrew and Greek, Herman had tutored Peter as they studied together one morning each week for more than five years.

"Why, it just keeps Herman alive!" I could hear Bessie, his wife, now.

Those hours of study and friendship bore fruit in Peter's witness and love for the Scriptures. He found in Herman a quiet man of God with whom he could talk over his concerns and questions of faith. It was a rare friendship, seeming to have no ecclesiastical boundaries.

I didn't realize it at the time, but those hours with Herman were probably the one thing that convinced Peter that he could not be anything but a Catholic. Peter had found in Herman a timelessness and a truth that had to be lived if he were to remain true to the Body of Christ.

For years now I awoke early in the morning to find the place beside me empty, aware that Peter had been at his desk for an hour or more already, studying the Scriptures in their original Greek and Hebrew.

Of course, the day came when Peter had to tell Herman that he would become a Catholic. Pastor Grimm looked away, his face gray with shock. Then that smile. "You might become another Luther!"

Though he died a year before we left the island, I knew that whenever Peter walked that cold path or puttered in the garden, Herman Grimm was very much alive in him. Today his books, a gift from Bessie, are on Peter's desk, his friend and his companion.

Then three days before the scheduled meeting with Archbishop Hunthausen, Father Jaeger called to say that the archbishop planned to see us on the 22nd, but he did not yet have a decision. He would explain when we arrived.

We were puzzled and confused, but we naively expected the archbishop would have something good to share with us.

As our meeting began, the archbishop handed us a

copy of the three-page recommendation from the Discernment Committee. Their vote had been five to one that Peter
should be ordained, the dissenting vote being that of Sister
Dyckman who had been unable to meet with the committee.
However, upon reading the committee's report she indicated
that she agreed with it, and had she been present might not
have dissented. In any event, she said, she "did not dissent
strongly." There were several conditions attached to the recommendation, the first being that the archbishop not petition
the Holy See for Peter's ordination until he had served in an
internship for a period of one year. At the end of that time, if
all was satisfactory, the archbishop would then petition for
ordination on the condition that Peter would be assigned to a
special ministry with a part-time position as an associate pastor. If that was accepted and satisfactorily carried out, he
would then be allowed to serve in a full-time pastorate should
the personnel board judge that appropriate.

Archbishop Hunthausen told us he did not want to
make a decision on this basis. He wished to make an uncondi-
tional request for ordination or no request at all.

Neither Peter nor I realized then that no married
priest would be allowed to serve as a pastor, or even a full-
time associate pastor without special permission from the
Vatican. Their ministries would be used only in Catholic
institutions such as hospitals and schools, and they would be
assigned to one or perhaps various parishes on Sundays only.

Continuing, Archbishop Hunthausen said that in any
case if he were to ordain Peter, I must stay in the shadows at
all times. I wondered how I would manage that since a Catholic priest with a woman tagging along would be just about as
subtle as a wart on the end of your nose. However, I decided
to leave the shadows and their definition to the interpretation
of the archbishop and others.

So Archbishop Hunthausen said he would like more
time to think and pray about this matter of priesthood for
Peter. He expressed concern for the financial and emotional
needs of our family, which touched us deeply. Never before
had a bishop expressed this type of concern. He said it would
take only a couple of weeks before he would phone us with an
answer.

That day he told us of his involvement in the nuclear disarmament demonstrations at Trident Nuclear Submarine Base on Puget Sound. That he had made a decision not to pay his personal income tax in protest of United States' defense spending. He seemed preoccupied with his involvement, perhaps unable to adequately focus on other phases of his ministry.

As we walked away from the chancery offices for the second time in the late afternoon dusk of winter, Peter said to me, his head down and anger in his voice, "They are just playing games with us, Mary."

"He seemed honest with us."

"They don't want us."

"I don't know, Peter, we've come this far. I guess I feel we still have to hope. We have to have faith in him . . . and what he's telling us."

"They don't intend to do anything."

"Peter, I can't take this." As Peter opened the car door for me, I said, "We started this whole thing and we're not giving up. If they don't want us, they're going to have to tell us straight out. We're not going to quit and make it easy for them."

We returned to Vashon Island, analyzing and speculating as to what had really happened in our meeting, wondering what their next move would be. Then we learned that Archdeacon Hayman had told a mutual friend that he and Bishop Cochrane had read through Peter's entire personnel file with Archbishop Hunthausen. They had "really fixed Dally," their main focus being that he had a history of disobedience to his bishop.

Disobedience? If he was guilty of disobedience, it was not on a personal basis, but rather of conscience! The same convictions for which we had become Catholics now. Peter and a few others had often defended the sanctity of life and theological principles such as the doctrine of the Trinity. To simply accuse him of disobedience was not fair play. But it left us with no opportunity for rebuttal, because none of this had been shared with us by either Archbishop Hunthausen or Father Jaeger.

During these weeks the one person we had feared the

most, the psychologist, became our closest ally. Dr. Reilly bolstered and supported us in a way that was truly a gift. Our friends the Visitation Sisters were equally helpful.

Looking back, I realize that there must have been many who thought the Pastoral Provision was a token offering. Regardless of motives and feelings, the support and love we received was an heroic demonstration which sustained us as we were put off again and again.

Since we had not been told when we would next meet with the archbishop, Peter stayed near the phone and waited, but no call came. Finally, in late February, Archbishop Hunthausen asked us to come to his office again. He explained that he had reconvened the Discernment Committee, and all six members had been present. They voted a second time, the vote being six to zero in favor of ordination for Peter.

However, the archbishop could not yet decide what to do. He explained that he had called us in for the meeting because he knew it was a difficult time for us. He thought that he would have made his decision before now. He wished to inform us what phase he was now in, that he would have a definite decision within a very short while.

In the archbishop's office my chair faced the windows to the west. The low income apartment houses for the inner city people were now complete and occupied. I noted there was no longer a picturesque view of the downtown skyline and the Seattle harbor. There were only families living out their lives in quiet desperation, waiting for opportunities which, because of the circumstances of their existence, rarely came. And yet the Church—Archbishop Hunthausen—had done a good thing; these people would otherwise be among the homeless. Perhaps because of the Church's effort their children will have better lives, I thought. I reminded myself too, that this was the third time I had been invited to the Catholic prelate's office. In all the previous years I had been asked to the Episcopal bishop's office only once.

It was time to go. Our meeting had been short.

We returned once again to Vashon Island to wait. It

was now four months since Peter completed the interviews and the Discernment Committee had begun their deliberation. Though I didn't say so to Peter, I began to think quite a bit about their playing games with our lives and the lives of our children. We are fools, I thought, but what can we do? We are at their mercy. I felt intuitively that the outcome would not be good.

While we laughed at the rumors we heard about Bishop Cochrane and Archdeacon Hayman, we began to realize that they were probably all true. Certainly the Episcopal Church had received and ordained many Catholic priests in a relationship of trust and friendliness, priests who had left the celibate priesthood to marry. I asked myself again and again, why was this happening to us. I recalled that years ago, Peter's name had been submitted to a large socially, prominent parish. We were told that neither he nor I had the right family connections, the right background and education for that congregation. These were not our personal values. Yet it seemed they continued to control our lives, even though we were no longer attached to the Episcopalian hierarchy.

I had an overwhelming urge to throw open the window, to breathe deeply of the fresh air, but . . .

My anger grew. I would not talk to Peter about it, for in his silence I sensed that hurt and frustration were growing within him too.

There was something else. My old anger and depression began to haunt me again, directed toward my husband and the hierarchy of both religious bodies, but also toward myself. I began to loathe my reasoning as I had never done in the past. I told myself that I should have realized this would happen. I should have stood my ground and refused to budge. The more I tried to force aside my thoughts, the more they dominated me. I attempted to pray with a new concentration and meaning, but I felt empty.

From somewhere, an awareness of the unfathomable grace and love we receive in the sacraments took root within me as each week I went to Holy Communion. I prayed that God would forgive my unworthiness. That in this dark night of the soul, he would lead me to a greater realization of meaning and hope for the decisions of the days past and the days ahead. The words of Paul came to me, as they had before:

> What then shall we say to this? If God is for us, who can be against us?
>
> *Romans 8: 31*

20

Within a week the archbishop called and asked Peter to come alone to his office. Everything pointed toward a turndown, yet I could not believe that he would deliberate so long, only to say no in the end.

That morning Peter received a phone call from Jim Parker in Bishop Law's office. The archbishop had called Bishop Law that morning to say he would meet with Peter the same day to reject his request. The archbishop added that he felt Peter should be ordained, but not in Seattle. Jim and Bishop Law wanted to inform Peter of this before he went to the meeting. That already Bishop Law had spoken with Bishop Eusebius Beltran in the Diocese of Tulsa, Oklahoma. He would like to talk to us about coming there.

Unable to accept the meaning of Father Parker's words, Peter went to the meeting hopeful that Archbishop Hunthausen might still reconsider. It was almost impossible for either of us to believe that after eighteen months of conversations and investigation, we would be turned down in Seattle. After all, it was our home. People knew us there!

The archbishop began by saying that the Discernment Committee had met a third time, and now their vote had been three to three, tied. It seemed to Peter that he was also saying that the Archdiocese of Seattle, considered to be more liberal than most, would not be open to our papal conservatism. On these bases the archbishop had decided it would be best not to ordain Peter.

"Since this is the third vote, Archbishop, and each has been different, might your decision be negotiable?" Peter asked.

"I'm sorry, Peter. My decision is final."
The meeting lasted only a few minutes.

When Peter returned home, he called Jim Parker to ask about the possibility of applying to Catholic bishops in Oregon or Alaska. Jim indicated that these dioceses would not likely be open to overtures since they were in the same province as the Archbishop of Seattle. He felt that Peter's best chance would be with Bishop Beltran and that Bishop Beltran was waiting to hear from him, that a visitation had already been arranged if we wanted to go.

In my office at the school district the telephone rang. "How would you like to go to Oklahoma?"

"Oklahoma?" I moaned and wondered, why Oklahoma, Lord? I know I said I'd go anywhere. But it seemed a most unlikely place to me.

The following Sunday the first reading at Mass was the story of Abraham and Isaac. In those words I stood with Abraham before the altar. I tried to accept the story of Abraham's willingness to give to God all that he asked, even his most precious son, and God's goodness and the promise it implied when he said to Abraham,

> "I know now how devoted you are to God, since you did not withhold from me your own beloved son."
>
> *Genesis 22:12*

We arranged to fly to Tulsa on March 17th. After a year and a half of waiting, big decisions were suddenly being made for us at a moment's notice. I was skeptical too. Peter had told Bishop Beltran that we'd pay our own plane fare, but it was expensive, and we had no promise of employment for Peter. And I wondered, will this bishop turn us down too. I thought of our clergy friends in the Episcopal Church. How they'd said, "The word is they (meaning Rome) are only going to take a token two or three men who are married. Then it will be closed . . ." I knew we had to stretch ourselves, to be willing once again to risk our dignity and integrity, but it was hard. So hard. In the end I resigned myself to the fact that we had to try every possible avenue. Bishop Beltran had invited me to come along too. That had to be good for something, I assured myself.

We expected the Tulsa agenda would be similar to the one in Seattle. That we would be met by a young priest who would take us to a hotel, that sometime the next day we would meet Bishop Beltran.

When we arrived in Tulsa, there was a priest waiting for us. He's older than I expected, but he must be our ride, I thought.

"I'm Bishop Beltran," he said offering his hand.

Not only was this priest the bishop, but in his car we learned that we were on our way to his home where we would stay during our visit.

The following morning Bishop Beltran invited us to go with him to Our Lady of Sorrows Convent where he would celebrate Mass.

Without Puget Sound to orient me, I wondered in which direction we were headed that morning. After about twenty minutes we left the expressway. Turning into the sunrise, we drove past homes and farm yards, then we crested a hill and looked out across a wide prairie. The rising sun spread its rays all around the edges of a large domed building in the distance. I felt like a child again as I realized this must be Our Lady of Sorrows Convent. It spoke to me of the Jesuit Novitiate which stood on the hill my dad called "High Heaven," above the tiny farming community where I was born in Oregon. We turned up the winding drive and circled the large statue of the Sorrowful Mother at the main entrance. In a flood of childlike mystery and awe, I stepped from the car to see the birds swoop and dive around the stained bronze belltower high above our heads.

Almost unaware that I was not alone, I heard Peter ask, "Bishop, may we recieve Holy Communion at Mass?"

"You're Catholics aren't you?" was Bishop Beltran's simple, friendly reply.

The scene, as we entered the chapel, is one that will be printed in my memory forever. The massive alabaster crucifix, the gray marble cross, the spectacular crown of thorns encircling the symbol of the Holy Spirit suspended high above the altar. And solid chunks of marble—white, gray and pink—everywhere I looked.

A breeze played through the open windows, ruffling the veils of the nuns, while prairie songbirds raised their antiphonal songs to the sunrise.

The scene was a European chapel in a midwestern setting. It all seemed natural and yet somehow unlikely in the middle of this Oklahoma prairie. As unlikely as the two of us, I thought.

As Bishop Beltran began the celebration of the Mass, my breath caught the warm humid air. It was the scent of my childhood, my dad, "High Heaven," and the Jesuit Novitiate.

Strange land, this Oklahoma. We had stepped into the heartland of America. The land, the birds, the air, this convent. It seemed that we should be here.

As we entered the dining room after the Mass, Bishop Beltran went to the microphone, "Good morning, Sisters. I have two guests with me today. I'd like you to meet Peter and Mary Dally. They're from Seattle, and Peter is a former Episcopal priest. They're here to talk with me about Peter being a married priest in Oklahoma."

Unexpected as it was, the Bishop's openness would have been enough, but with a scraping of chairs the sisters all stood up. I smiled to myself and wondered what would happen next.

They clapped. Their wonderful German smiles spread across their faces.

Peter and I were touched beyond words. In that place, so far from home, it seemed that at last we had been welcomed, not only to Oklahoma, but to the Catholic Church.

During the breakfast Bishop Beltran said in a way that would become so familiar to us, "Now we're going to the chancery where you will be interviewed by a number of people."

"What should Mary do, Bishop?" Peter asked.

"She'll be interviewed with you."

"Oh my!" I said. My voice caught in breathless surprise. The yarn I had hastily stuffed into my luggage to knit a sweater for Monica flashed through my mind. I hadn't expected this.

"You don't mind, do you? I want people to get to know both of you. If you decide to come, you'll be serving here together," Bishop Beltran said.

"No. I don't mind. I just thought that . . ."

"Mary's quite willing to stay in the background, Bishop," Peter said.

"I'd like her to be interviewed with you, if neither of you mind."

"I don't mind at all. I just thought," I stammered.

As I walked down the hall, my heels clicked on the marble floors. Through the windows, lawns stretched into acres of early spring yellows and purples, of forsythia and hyacinth. I had not expected the warmth of these old nuns and this man, their bishop. And I wondered what the Lord really had in store for us here. I thought of Sister Elsbeth's letter, ". . . and it will be better than anything you can imagine."

I thought, too, of the other Mary. She had traveled by donkey to another town to give birth to her child. Then to protect his life, the family had gone to Egypt and stayed there until it was safe to return home to Nazareth. If we come here, I thought, this will be home. There will be no returning to the evergreens and the clear blue water of Puget Sound.

"Sister Theolinda," I heard Bishop Beltran saying, "did you meet the Dallys?"

"Welcome," Sister said. She sat at the switchboard, her sweet smile gleaming under her thick eyeglasses. In front of her lay an ordinary-looking book.

"What are you reading, Sister?" Peter asked.

"Oh, this is a book about the South. I'm a Southerner, you know." Her voice was gentle.

"Isn't Oklahoma considered the South?" I asked. "Or is it the West? Or the Southwest?"

"Oklahomans fought on the side of the Confederacy

in the War between the States. Of course we were Indian Territory then," Sister Theolinda smiled.

"So we are in the South then," I said.

"Well, yes. But some of us do have skeletons in our closets." Sister's mischievous smile spread across her face. "We don't talk about it much, but, well, Mother was a Yankee." She chuckled.

"Ready?" The bishop had his coat, and we were on our way, waving and smiling as Sister Theolinda leaned out the window of the reception room above the main entry.

"God bless you," she called after us.

That evening from the top floor of the Petroleum Club in downtown Tulsa, the city and the space-age architecture of Oral Roberts University streched out to the south as far as we could see. To the north we saw the shadows of the Osage Hills. Bishop Beltran explained that from the dining room in his house one could see a beautiful view of the city at night.

How can we tell this man of the place we've come from? Of the tall evergreens and snow-capped mountain peaks all around us? Of the icy blue waters of Puget Sound? And yet I've been happy wherever we lived. I knew I could be happy here, too.

The next morning found us on our way to St. Mary Church for a school Mass and more interviews.

"You'll be meeting with Father Stephen MacAulay, pastor of St. Mary's, who is also on the Personnel Board. Then I want you to talk with Sister Virginia Lane who is in Pastoral Care there," Bishop Beltran said. "She isn't on the Personnel Board, but I think you should talk with everyone possible."

Sister Virginia invited us into her tiny office. As we sat facing each other in a cramped triangle, she began, "Now tell me all about yourselves. Why do you want to be a priest, Peter?" Sister Virginia rested her elbows on the arms of her chair, folding her lovely manicured hands loosely in her lap. She seemed mildly conscious of herself in her pretty print blouse and blue cotton skirt. I self-consciously looked down at my own reddened hands, as though they might have something to do with hers.

Peter talked candidly, as he had to the other interviewers. She interrupted.

"We don't have a lot of time. I have to drive a lady to a doctor's appointment soon." She turned her swivel chair toward me as she asked, "Mary, do you want to be a priest?"

Though Sister Virginia smiled, her question did not seem friendly.

"No," I said simply, surprised.

"Why not?"

"Why?" I paused, once again surprised. "Well, I feel called to be a priest's wife. I have a vocation also, different but equal to my husband's." I laughed as I tried to say lightly, "Eve may have been created from only a rib, but she walked beside Adam, not behind him."

"Peter, are you in favor of women's ordination?" Sister Virginia asked.

"No," Peter said, "Though I'm not against women. I just personally feel it is a Christological issue. Besides, men need to take their rightful responsibility in society and in the Church."

I looked at sister's hands again. They were firmly clasped together now, her fingers curled inward toward her palms, her knuckles drawn.

"But certainly you must believe that women can be priests?" She looked impatiently at her watch. "I'm sorry, our time is up. I have to go."

"I love women. I married one." He laughed. "It's not a matter of whether women would make good priests or whether they are worthy. If anything, they're probably a lot more worthy than men." Sister Virginia seemed distracted, so he simply offered his hand. "I've enjoyed talking with you, Sister."

"Yes. Well, it's been nice meeting you both."

Shaken from the interview, I didn't know what to make of it. Her questions seemed overly aggressive. But why, I wondered. Does she want to be a priest? And why did she direct her anger at us? I didn't understand the politics in the Catholic Church, and I wondered what her questions had to do with my husband becoming a priest.

It was the Feast of St. Joseph, husband of Mary, and the bishop was scheduled to celebrate Mass at St. Joseph Convent with the Benedictine sisters who ran a school in the center of the city. This was their motherhouse, and they greeted us warmly and supportively, just as the Sisters of the Sorrowful Mother had.

The next day we drove south on the Indian Nations Turnpike with Bishop Beltran. The two men talked, while I absorbed myself in the gently rolling green hills around me. Green Country, the TV news had said. Lacey thickets of trees scattered around grassy pastures and cultivated fields marked the creek beds and rain run-off areas. I learned that the curious grasshopper-like contraptions I saw along the roadway and in fields were oil wells.

"This is where it all began," Bishop Beltran said, referring to the gas and oil industry.

We left McAllister and drove southwest toward the Kiamichi Mountains and the Glenmary Missions where we'd visit. The patches of purplish lavender bushes blooming along the roadsides were gently spectacular in their abundance.

"The flowers here are beautiful," I said.

"That's red bud, Oklahoma's state tree. It grows everywhere."

"When will we reach the mountains, Bishop?" I asked.

"You're in them now. Don't you see the forest?" He smiled.

"Oh, ah, yes," I said, hoping to conceal my surprise. "Our mountains have snow. And they're much bigger too."

The bright yellow forsythia bursting forth here and there was a kind of resurrection in the frequent front yard rubble of discarded washing machines and rusting cars. It seemed to me that the whole outdoors of Oklahoma felt like a hot, sticky greenhouse. Yet it was only the middle of March.

Bishop Beltran told us that if we came to Oklahoma, we would be committed to the diocese for the rest of our lives. That Peter would be expected to function as a priest for as many years as his health would allow. We should expect to bring with us only our personal belongings, because our housing and everything we needed would be furnished for us by the Church. There would be a small stipend for living expenses.

I thought of our Lord, walking along the shore of the Sea of Galilee. Now he beckoned to us, as he had then to Peter and Andrew:

> "Come after me, and I will make you fishers of men." At once they left their nets and followed him.
>
> *Matthew 4:19-20*

We are called along with Peter and Andrew, and James and John, who were asked to leave their father, Zebedee.

We will leave our children.

We have already made the decision to go where the Lord leads us, I thought. That benign prayer I'd been praying, 'Lord, help me to know you, to love you and to serve you' crossed my lips now. It's really all we'd ever wanted in our ministry together, all I really ever had in mind when I married this man, though I too have had my moments of doubt and my attempts to manipulate God.

'But Lord, I never thought of giving up all my possessions. My antique furniture. My home. Of leaving my children and friends, or the cool Northwest summers with their lazy days on Puget Sound beaches.

I have to ask you once again, now Lord, take your will and make it mine.'

"This is a nice little town. What do people do around here?" Peter asked a boy outside the storefront church in Clayton.

The boy's shoulders comfortably slouched, and his hands rested deeply in the pockets of his high-water trousers. "Naw-thin'," drawled the kid.

I liked him. I loved the natural charm of people comfortable about themselves and the culture they were a part of. I guess I envied them a bit. His "naw-thin" would stay with me even longer than I suspected.

As we drove north the next day, I realized that our visit to Oklahoma was nearly over. Our five days with Bishop Beltran had been enlightening and exciting. We had one more interview that evening when we returned to the bishop's home. We were tired and talked out, glad this would be the last one.

"Whatta y'all think a' Oklahoma?" the young blond priest asked as he flipped open a can of beer and unbuttoned his clerical collar.

"The people are wonderful," Peter said. "I like it. Don't you, Mary?"

"Yes," I said to Father Daigle. "It's so different from the Pacific Northwest, but I've always wanted to live in another part of the country."

"Why'd y'all become Catholics anyway?" he asked Peter.

He'd given us the cue we'd become accustomed to, and we tried, once again, to tell this man in words which had become inadequate to the task what we were all about.

"Well, I'll tell you a little story," Father Daigle said as we concluded. "When I knew I was gonna talk to ya, I called my folks up an' I said, Mama and Daddy, I wanna ask you a question, and I don't want you to give me an answer right quick. I want you to think about it, and I'll call you back tomorrow for the answer. How would you like to have a married priest? Don't tell me now. I'll call you back. So the next night I called 'em back, and I said, okay, have you thought about it? Mama said, "Why Chris, I think it would be just fine to have a married priest, but I don't think he should be allowed to hear confessions." I said, "Why, Mama?" She said, "Cause a married man, his wife'd get it all outa him." Father Daigle leaned back and laughed wildly. "I think you'll do all right."

That evening Bishop Beltran talked about key factors of doctrine to make sure we understood and agreed with Roman Catholic theology.

"Now Oklahoma is very different from the West Coast. You need to consider carefully if you can adjust to such a different climate and area. You'll be leaving behind your families, perhaps even some of your children."

"We like what we've seen, Bishop," Peter said. "However, we need to think about it. It would be a tremendous change."

"I want you to understand that I believe in a celibate priesthood," Bishop Beltran said firmly. "I do have two other married men to interview who are in situations similar to yours."

"Does this mean that you will select one of the three men to sponsor, Bishop?" I asked.

"Oh, no. I will sponsor all three of you if that is what works out. I don't know though at this point. I haven't even met the other two yet."

"It would be wonderful not to be alone in this," Peter said.

"I'll say," I agreed.

"I'm doing this because the Holy Father has said we should, as an exception to the rule of celibacy. It is not intended to change the Church's tradition and practice. If you decide to come, I would like you to move down here after permission to ordain you has been received from the Holy See. You would then be assigned to a parish staff where we would get to know you and you would get to know us. After a period of time, probably not a long time, you would be ordained a deacon and of course eventually a priest." He turned to me, "I would want you, Mary, to be a part of the parish too. People need to get used to seeing you together in order to become comfortable with the idea that the priest has a wife."

"Bishop, one thing I feel uncomfortable about is our interview with Sister Virginia at St. Mary Church. She wasn't terribly interested in hearing why we became Catholics . . . which is fine, but that was the focus of nearly all of the other interviewers. She asked me if I wanted to be a priest. Perhaps I was too sensitive, but it seemed almost an attack," I said.

"What did you tell her?" the bishop asked.

"I said no, that I believe my vocation is that of priest's wife."

"Did you ask her if she wanted to be a priest?"

"No." I laughed. "I was too startled by her question. Is there a lot of feeling here against this program?"

"Her approach was what I might have expected. She's not on the Personnel Board. I just wanted as many people as possible to get to meet with you. I think the exposure is good for you and for the people here. Some have said that those men leaving the Episcopal Church are conservative reactionaries. My feeling is that you are all pre-Vatican II men." Bishop Beltran turned to face Peter. "I feel that naturally, since you have not been through Vatican II as our priests have, we must bring you up-to-date with the changes that have occurred since then."

"I can only assure you that if we come here, I will, with God's help, do everything in my power to be a good priest, Bishop," Peter said.

"What will you do now when you return to Washington?" Bishop Beltran asked.

"Well, the first thing I'm going to do is look for a job."

"Good. I think you need to do that."

"And I'll continue to study and request books from St. Bede's Library in Bishop Law's office. I'll wait on you, Bishop."

"Now if there are any problems, I'll write or call you. I will begin the process as soon as I get everything together, but these things always take a long time. I'll be in touch with you from time to time, and if you have any questions you can call me."

As we visited, Bishop Beltran directed our attention to the handmade rug in the center of the living room. It was a gift from the people of Santiago Atitlan in Guatamala, a mission of the two Oklahoma dioceses. He told us about Father Stanley Rother, who had struggled in the seminary with the required Latin. Finally he was asked to leave the seminary. When Bishop Reed asked Rother if he wanted to be a priest, he replied that he did indeed feel called. Given another chance in a second seminary, he was eventually ordained a priest, and he then asked to be assigned to the mission in Guatamala. Father Rother's life seemed blessed again as he struggled and successfully learned Spanish. And eventually he learned the even more difficult dialect of the Indians in Santiago Atitlan.

Then because of the dangerous political climate, he was called home to Oklahoma. But he felt that he could not simply leave his people, so without regard for his own personal safety he asked to return.

On July 28, 1981 three masked men armed with guns entered the rectory and went directly to Father Rother's bedroom. He was not there. They awakened another young man who was staying in the rectory and told him they would kill him if he did not take them to the priest. Frightened, the youth led them to the room where the priest slept. Father Rother could have escaped, but he realized that if he did they would kill the boy. He deliberately opened the door to his room. There was a violent struggle before they shot Father Rother.

Somehow, in the Bishop's brief telling of this story, I felt I had known Father Stanley Rother. I was deeply touched by the young man's life and death. His call to priesthood. His struggle. Finally the Church's wisdom and acceptance.

Oklahoma was a hard land. A generous land. Short of priests. Yet willing to give her own for the spread of Christ's Kingdom.

I left Tulsa feeling that it would be all right to be human there. That the fears and doubts I had experienced earlier were a normal part of the journey of the servant discerning the Lord's call. That it would be all right to experience and work my way through them again if need be. Human perfection was not a requirement in God's infinite wisdom and mercy. The greater condition was simply the desire to love and to serve God in this place. Oklahoma.

Bishop Beltran's generosity and understanding were a most touching example of the Church there. If he decided to sponsor Peter, I felt sure we would come. How could we not?

21

I noticed that the pink bark of the old cherry tree was nearly hidden by the mass of springtime's white blossoms. Each new season brought its own mood for the big tree which stood just down the grassy bank outside my office window. In summer its leafy branches shaded our office from the hot sun. By Halloween the leaves had fallen to reveal limbs so pink that visitors asked if the windows were tinted. This morning the blossoms were filled with the hum of bees from a nearby apiary.

I felt tempted to daydream about the future on this spring day, beautiful and sunny as it was, though my desk was full of work. The footsteps of the bearded young man waving a small piece of paper in front of me returned my thoughts to the present.

"Pete doesn't wanna do that," Richard said quietly. He stopped in front of my desk and hooked his thumbs in the pockets of his Levis, as he traced the design of the floor tiles with his shoe.

"Yes, he does," I said. "He needs to be busy, and besides that we really need the money."

"Yeah. I know. But I can't see a minister doin' janitor work." He looked at me for a moment and shook his head from side to side. "Naw, it's not right."

"Well, there just aren't any jobs, and he can really only do temporary work. He can't get into anything permanent because we'll be moving to Oklahoma. That could be two months from now or next year."

"I'd be glad to have him, but, well, geez, Mary, I don't know if I can do that to him, or to you. Let me think on it a few days." Richard leaned back on his heels. "You're sure?" he asked a second time.

"Yes, I'm sure. There's nothing wrong with honest work." I assured him, though inside I wasn't at all sure that it would be good for Peter. But I only said, "Wait. You don't think the other custodians would be threatened because of my job here, do you?"

"Oh, they probably would. You know how they are, but I know Pete would get 'em over that fast. He has a way of puttin' people at their ease." Richard turned to go. "Naw. That's not it. I just hate to see a man like him—you know, a minister for so long—do that kind of work." He shook his head as he walked toward the entrance.

Peter wanted badly to contribute to the support of our family. Since our return from Tulsa, he'd worked a little as a substitute dispatcher for the Island Volunteer Fire Department where he was well-known as a volunteer fireman and EMT. But he rarely got to work more than sixteen hours a week, for the minimum wage. So he really wanted to do substitute custodial work in the school district if Richard would hire him. We were constantly looking for men who would fill in for the regulars, so it was a logical solution.

Leaving the Episcopal Church and the year and a half under Archbishop Hunthausen had taken its toll on Peter, and I felt a certain unease about his doing custodial work, as well as concern about the reaction of the other school district employees. There was always a certain amount of jealousy directed toward the administrative office staff. Since I was secretary to the superintendent, I felt sure they would complain loudly. But I really didn't care about that. My job was one that gathered a certain amount of criticism anyway by its very nature, so a little more gossip didn't bother me. The thing that did concern me was Peter. He'd been through a lot, and I wondered if it would be good for him to clean toilets. I knew he didn't mind the work, but I felt uneasy about how it would affect his sense of self-worth. True, he'd worked as a janitor years ago, but that was as a college student not as a man who'd been a minister for nearly thirty years. I felt intuitively that the work wasn't worth the small amount of money it would bring, but I decided not to stand in his way if he wanted to do it and Richard was willing to hire him. Peter had begun to do occasional work in the currant fields for Peter Shepherd. One day a neighbor woman saw him and asked if he would be willing to do some yard work for her mother. As she talked, she recognized Peter, and embarrassed she said, "Oh, I can't ask you to do that, Father Dally. What are you doing out here anyway?"

While the incident amused us, it was also frustrating, because it pointed out that temporary employment for Peter was almost impossible. His profession had been that of an Episcopal minister, and now he needed interim employment. There was really nothing he could do. Or rather nothing people who knew him would allow him to do. They loved him and they simply could not bring themselves to watch him lose the identity he'd always had in our community.

At Peter's urging, I asked Richard a second time to let him substitute. While he was still reluctant, he called Peter a week later. It was difficult for the teachers, too. At first they looked away when they saw him coming, embarrassed that he was now cleaning the school buildings where he had once visited as a minister in the community. But his apparent peace of mind and extraordinary sense of humor soon put them at ease.

At first the other custodial employees seemed defensive and suspicious. They were reluctant to assign him the dirtier tasks. However, he insisted that he not be treated differently, and within a few weeks he'd won them over.

Our daily lives settled into the rhythm of juggling Peter's three part-time jobs. Whenever he could work it in, he studied the materials from St. Bede's Library in Bishop Law's office. Always there was the waiting.

Sometimes the planning and preparation for three jobs seemed hardly worth the small amount of money Peter brought home, but we both felt it was important to stay busy. And we couldn't deny that we needed every penny we could scrape together for the family's needs, while we were trying to add to our savings for the move to Oklahoma. We didn't talk about it much, but we both wondered when we would hear from Bishop Beltran, and if he would sponsor Peter.

We had returned from Tulsa on March 23rd. Bishop

Beltran had said he would be in touch with us if there was a problem. He had also said that within the week he would receive letters from the people who had interviewed us, and he would have a decision as soon as he returned from his pilgrimage to the Holy Land and Rome. It was the middle of May, and we should have heard from him by now. What was happening this time? Facing another long silence, it appeared that we would be turned down again. Dare we even hope otherwise?

Late in May Peter's old impatience returned. He telephoned Bishop Beltran, who explained that he would meet with the interviewers in about one week. At that time he would have a decision.

"I don't mind the waiting, Bishop. It's the isolation that gets to me. I have no one to talk to here, and . . ."

"Peter, please call me anytime you feel like it. I'll be glad to talk with you. The rates are low at night. Call then."

Peter hung up the phone and turned to me. "I can't just . . ."

It would take more than that to convince my husband he could pick up the phone any time and call his bishop, but we both realized that Bishop Beltran was sincere. In our few days with him, we'd come to know him as that kind of man.

"All the same it was good of him to offer," I said.

22

In our beautiful little basement chapel with the icons he had created, Peter said the daily prayers of the Catholic breviary and continued to celebrate the Holy Eucharist according to the Episcopal Church and the priesthood that was still so much a part of him. Though he had received Catholic approval from his confessor and others, Peter felt ill at ease with the practice. Shortly after we returned from Tulsa, he asked counsel of Father Greenfield, our oldest and dearest friend who was now a monk in the Episcopalian Cowley Society of St. John the Evangelist.

"You cannot have it both ways," Father Greenfield wrote. "You are now a layman in the Roman Catholic Church. It is your duty to abide by what their canon law and tradition offers. You must, therefore, desist from saying Mass until you are ordained a Roman Catholic priest."

So it was that Robert Greenfield, a devout and learned Episcopal priest, reverently and respectfully—in the deepest sense of those words—assisted Peter in another important decision within the Catholic Church. Father Greenfield's wisdom and his love for the whole Body of Christ transcended ecclesiastical boundaries to bring his friend and fellow Christian a measure of understanding and peace.

Peter never offered Mass again until he was ordained a Roman Catholic priest.

I had strong reservations about his offering the Anglican liturgy as a lay Roman Catholic and never joined with him. However, after Peter stopped offering Mass, it became our practice to pray the morning office together in the chapel before I left for work.

I grieved far more than he appeared to. Each day when I went there to be with him, I mourned the loss of the faculty that I knew meant more to Peter than anything else ever would. The lamp burned no more for the presence of the Blessed Sacrament, for he had removed the handmade oak tabernacle. In its place stood only the empty table with its offering of flowers. I had never before known him without the expression of his priestly life, and in a vague way I felt responsible for his loss of it. Yet in that room with its simple homemade altar, the beautiful icons he had painted, the bamboo shades and simple rugs that served to mark off the areas of the chapel, we shared his loss together. In a new and unexpected dimension we grew closer than we had ever been in our married life. While not being physically united in that room, we became more completely one flesh than ever before. Through our suffering and the derision we had experienced, God had brought us into a closer unity with him and with each other.

True to his word, Bishop Beltran called on May 27th to tell us of his decision to sponsor Peter for ordination, that he would prepare the paperwork for Rome. In the letter which followed the phone call, he explained that the time lines would be indefinite since he did not think he could complete the paperwork before the end of the summer. Then he reminded us that Jim Parker's case had only recently been approved after an entire year in Rome.

Jim, Bishop Law's assistant, would be the first married former Episcopal priest to be ordained a Catholic priest in the United States. The date had been quietly set for June 30th. Peter and I rejoiced with Mary Alma and Jim, indeed with all of those who, like us, were waiting for this landmark demonstration. Up until this actual "first," skeptics in both religious bodies had taken a wait-and-see attitude. Now with the ordination of Father Parker we all knew the Catholic Church was serious about its invitation. It was a great day, indeed.

Though it might take a year or more for Peter's ordination to be approved, we both felt that we were now on our way. The waiting, no matter what the time lines, would be tolerable because we knew that in God's time our prayers would be answered. In Bishop Beltran we had found a man unafraid of risk, dedicated to God and his people.

It was the signal we'd been waiting for to get busy with our lives. We continued to add to our savings account for the move to Oklahoma, and I wondered what we would do with those rugs that meant so much in our relationship to each other and to God. They were beautiful. Not expensive, authentic oriental rugs but nevertheless beautiful. I was glad Peter had insisted I buy them with the money I'd saved more than a year and a half earlier. Over and over again they boosted my morale, and in their ordinariness they symbolized my hope in the future.

There were moments that spring when depression got the better of me. I tried to keep my eyes on the future, content in knowing that all of creation is in God's loving hands. Believing that ours was the fulfillment of a vocation to which Peter and I had been called together, I made a concerted effort to focus on the new richness we had found in our love for each other. We began to feel, too, that this was not only important for the fulfillment of God's purpose for our lives, but for the Church as well. Others in our small Catholic community expressed similar thoughts.

We weren't fooled into thinking that our lives would change the Catholic Church, but who could know what the experience of a few married priests might mean to the Church of 2030? And what about us? Our ministry in the Episcopal Church had not been easy, though the issues there were entirely different from those we expected to face now. Those had been the issues of papal authority, the sanctity of marriage, indeed of all human life; the magisterium of the Church, and most importantly the reunion of all Christians. It was our need to find more positive ways to respond to these issues that had drawn Peter to the Roman Catholic Church. To fill the void he hadn't been able to fill in any other way.

In the new ministry it would be enough to simply share in the Body of Christ. We could not want or expect more than this.

I was not in much of a mood for a party, but the

children and Peter pushed for a celebration of our twenty-fifth wedding anniversary, June 14th. After days of discussion and debate about expense, we finally decided on a German-style yard party with a few close friends. We would serve sausages from the German meat market in Seattle and that wonderful rye bread you could buy only at the Three Girls Bakery in the Pike Place Market. And beer. It sounded simple and fun.

During the week before the big event, we worked hard to prepare our yard and garden, so much so that Peter managed to twist his back, pinching a nerve and causing numbness in his hands. Our family doctor prescribed a cervical collar which in turn caused an allergic skin rash around his neck. To make matters worse, the chemicals he used in the school caused more skin irritation until he was a mass of red swollen rash, hardly able to move comfortably. Still he insisted on mowing the lawn on Saturday as we all pitched in to get ready for the party the following day.

The day of our anniversary it rained a bit, as is normal in June, so the kids put up the yellow and blue striped canopy, which created an even greater air of festivity. The people came and we had a good time. Someone brought a huge heart of red flowers and took our picture sitting in the middle of it. I remember that Mike and Nita Pottinger gave us a pair of antique silver candlesticks, the finish was worn and the tin underneath showed through. We loved them because they were a symbol of our friendship, and I felt sure they had belonged to Nita's mother. They'd given us a part of themselves.

Within a few weeks Peter was offered a full-time dispatching job, and he accepted the position, agreeing to take the required two-day class in Tacoma in mid-August. He particularly liked the dispatch work. Through it he was able to perform a service to our community, and it allowed him time to study for the theology examinations required by the Catholic Church.

We spent a lot of time that summer enjoying the island, certain that we would soon be leaving for Oklahoma. We swam every day in the public pool, bicycled and took long walks on the island roads. We got the sailboat and the canoes out of storage, determined to enjoy our last summer in the Northwest. It was a particularly peaceful and happy time. The first, it seemed, since that day in August, 1980, when we'd heard the announcement.

I was engrossed in the usual busy summer schedule of the school district office, and it appeared certain that the remaining months on Vashon Island would be characterized only by a small degree of impatience, anticipation, and a lot of talk about when to put our house up for sale, what to move, and what we would leave behind.

Late in July, friends asked us to be godparents for their new baby, Rory Elizabeth. We went to Salem, Oregon, where our friend and former colleague, Father Kent Haley, baptized Rory. I remember we took a long weekend and had a wonderful, refreshing time visiting my family as well as many old friends.

The day after we returned home, the phone rang in my office. It was Peter. I knew immediately that something was wrong.

23

"Mary?"

"Yes? What's wrong?" I asked.

"I'm trying to tell you. An accusation. She says . . ." Peter's voice broke.

"Peter, what is it?" I sensed something terrible had happened. "What is it?" I demanded again.

"The business card. The one in the door when we got back from Oregon. The detective. I thought it was the Ames kid, the one who's been in trouble with the law."

"Yes?"

"I called her. She says it's me. They—they say I assaulted someone."

"Who? Did you ask her who?"

"I asked, but she wouldn't tell me. She said I have to come to Seattle, to the courthouse this afternoon." Peter's voice was almost catatonic. "Mary . . . they say I'm accused of *sexual* assault."

"Who? Who accused you?" In disbelief I said softly to my husband, "She, whoever she is, can't just call you up and accuse you of doing something to another person and not tell you anything else about it." I sputtered as I talked, filled with disbelief at this conversation. "It must be a joke."

It can't be happening, I thought. Who would say a thing like that? It *had* to be somebody's idea of sick fun. Obscene phone calls in the middle of the night flashed through my mind. Years of them. Sickening and frightening us and our children. We never knew who the caller was.

In the next second I knew it wasn't a joke. Peter was dead serious.

"Her name was the same as that on the card in the door. Will you go with me, Mary?"

"Go in there? When they won't tell you anything about it? They're crazy," I stammered.

"They may be crazy, but I don't think I have any choice. I think I have to go. They say today."

Silence.

"Do you mind if I ask Stu about this? It doesn't seem right, they're not telling you anything. It almost seems like a trap."

My mind raced in circles, trying to think clearly, to remember what little I had ever heard about legal requirements, what choices we had. Instinctively I felt that Peter was not emotionally up to a confrontation with a female detective in the Sex Crimes Division. I had known innocent people accused of sexual misconduct whose professional lives had been destroyed by another's sickness, simply because it's nearly always assumed that the accused person is guilty.

"I wish you wouldn't go," I heard myself say. "I'm afraid they will twist your words and make anything they want out of them. Do you mind if I talk to Stu, Peter?" I asked a second time.

"No." He hesitated. "I don't mind. I just don't know what to do. They say I have to come in today," he said, his voice a monotone of shock and fear.

With Stu's common sense and experience with personnel in the school district, I felt he would know what was best now.

Helplessly, my thoughts turned to the waters of Puget Sound at the south end of the island where converging tidal currents made dark angry whirlpools competing for debris and small craft caught unawares. I felt like I was drowning in a churning pool of angry water, trapped in the deepening cone, as the centripetal force increased and finally swallowed me. Evil. Around and around. Then down. To nothing. All that we have faced. All the pain. The putdowns. Hurt. Sorrow. Rejection.

Finally accepted; now this.

This.

All of it for nothing.

Nothing. My emotions screamed.

It seemed to take me forever to walk into Stu's office only a few feet from my desk.

"What?" Stu stood up abruptly.

My words tumbled out.

"Who? Didn't they say who?"

"He says they wouldn't tell him anything."

"Who called Father Dally?"

"He was so upset. I don't know. Some detective. He thought it was someone asking him for a reference for some kid. Stu, I'm afraid for Peter to go in there."

"Yes."

"Even an accusation by some crazy person." I started to cry.

"You're right. It would not be wise for him to go. Even a *question* of immorality, and the Catholic Church would never have another thing to do with him. Pete should call them back and say he'll have his attorney get in touch with them. Get Dave Boylan to do that for you." As I dabbed at my eyes, Stu put his arm around my shoulder to comfort me. "Don't worry now, Mary. Dave can find out what it's about. You just go talk to Pete, and try to reassure him."

Another long walk to my desk and the telephone again. "Peter?"

"Yes?"

I told him what Stu had said, and I asked him to call me back after he talked to the detective and to Dave. "Are you all right, Peter? Do you want me to come home?"

"No. I'm okay. I'll call you back in a few minutes."

I hung up the phone. I felt terrified. My mind refused to function as I feebly tried to go about my office tasks. Buried in my fear, I felt it had to be a mistake, at best a misunderstanding or some terrible, cruel joke. I thought again of the phone calls, of all the "crazies" we knew. This island is full of them. Over the years every one of them had come around at least once, it seemed. The flower children of the sixties. The addicts and dropouts. The Viet Nam casualties. Poor guys. All of them. They came to our door. Peter never turned anyone away. We listened. We fed them. We tried to send them on their way with a little more dignity, a little more hope and courage than they had come with. Now what were we facing?

Today, years later, I have to force myself to think about the events that followed, for I feel more inclined to resist the pain and anger resurrected by the memories than to accept the reality and joy that is the triumph of good over evil. And I try to remember once again that when we receive great gifts, it is often at enormous cost. And that makes the gift all the more dear.

Even now I cannot grasp the import of our decision, and the decisions of others like us. Choices made in conscience that catapulted us into a public arena we'd never before experienced. Whether we liked it or intended it to be that way or not, we found ourselves on the cutting edge of life, caught in the eye of the storm, running wing and wing. Should we not have expected to draw attention to ourselves, to trigger prejudices and hatreds long buried?

Looking back, I wonder whether the Lord allowed this evil accusation to make us more completely dependent upon him? Could the purpose have been to prepare us for the more difficult witness we would have to make in the Catholic Church? Any situation ahead of us would require personal integrity as well as a sensitive spirit. Or was this simply a message that regardless of how right, how moral our lives, there would always be evil ready to attack and devour, to bring down and destroy God's purpose in our lives and the lives of others. No matter what, we had to go on believing in ourselves and in Peter's call to priesthood.

As the nightmare unfolded before us, I felt touched in yet another way, that the drama of my role as priest's wife rested simply in that most threatening of all conditions, *being* there.

That day I felt scared. So scared.

24

"See you in court? What does that mean?" I asked.

"I don't know," Peter said to me over the phone. "But those were her words when I said I'd have Dave call her."

"And she didn't tell you what it was about?"

"No. I asked her again too. But Dave said not to worry. He'd take care of it as soon as he gets back." Peter was calm and seemed reassured by his conversation with Dave.

"Then, I guess that's it. We should try to relax and not worry about it." I looked down at the scratch pad on my desk, alarmed to find the word, "H E L P" scrawled every which way in a variety of shapes and sizes, a hint of the growing panic inside me.

"Yes. But to wait a week? I just can't imagine . . ." Peter's voice faded, but did seem to have some of its resilience back. "Well, he did say it's probably just a misunderstanding of some kind."

Peter had intercepted our friend Dave Boylan just as he was leaving for a week-long fishing trip. Dave instructed him to tell the detective he'd call her when he returned.

"I know, dear, it seems strange, but Dave knows what he's doing. Do you want me to come home?"

"No. I'll be all right."

"H E L P," I scribbled once again.

The day Dave Boylan was expected home came and went.

"I think you should call Dave, Peter. We should have heard from him by now."

"Yeah, I know." I could tell from the phone conversation that Dave had forgotten. He promised to call the detective first thing in the morning.

Two more days passed. Nothing. Then the phone rang. It was Dave.

"I had a heck of a time finding out anything. Nobody knows about it. The assistant prosecuting attorney who would be assigned to it isn't there for a few days, and there doesn't seem to be any paperwork. I think it's over, whatever it was, but I'll keep trying to get her, just to make sure," Dave said.

Peter turned to me. "Dave says he thinks it's over. Nobody in the prosecutor's office knows anything about it."

"Thank God," I said. Strange, I thought to myself. The detective's threat. Weeks of uncertainty and fear, and nobody knew anything about it? Oh well, just thank God it's over, I told myself.

Then we heard from Father Morgan in Tulsa. He and a priest friend would arrive for a visit any day. The decks were clear. We could both relax and enjoy showing them around our beautiful island and the city of Seattle. I put the uncertainties of the past weeks behind me and looked forward to their visit.

The following evening—
"Father?"

"Yes. What is it, Dave?" I heard the sudden tension in Peter's voice as he answered the telephone.

"Can you come to my house? I'd like your permission to have Ted Hale meet with us too."

"What is it, Dave?"

"I'll talk to you when you get here. It's very serious, Father."

"I'll be right there. Yes. Call Ted."

Peter turned to me. "I'm going to Dave's house. Be back as soon as I can."

"What is it?" I asked.

"He wouldn't say—be back soon." His lips brushed my cheek on his way out the door.

As I watched Peter leave our driveway, I leaned on the porch railing. It's just a technicality, I told myself. It'll be settled in no time, especially with two lawyers on it. I went to the cupboard and took out the plastic bowl I used when I picked raspberries in our garden. They were hanging rich and juicy on the vines, and picking them in the cool evening air was good for the soul. As I closed the kitchen door behind me, I relished the quiet of the garden and the plump raspberries I would find there.

Peter returned from Dave's house several hours later. Devastated, he told me what Dave and Ted had found out.

"Well, it's Fred Hode."

"Who's that?" I asked.

"He lives here on the island. I remember Kurt and I gave him a ride from the Tacoma ferry once. Well, this is the story. He says he came into our yard to ask me for a drink of water, and as we were talking, I forced him down on the ground and sexually assaulted him." Peter looked at me, seeming to disbelieve his own words.

"That's ludicrous!"

"Dave says the police report is a little vague too."

"When was this supposed to have happened?"

"It was about six weeks ago, that Saturday before our anniversary. Remember, I was in the yard mowing the lawn to get ready for the party. I'd pinched a nerve in my back and I was wearing that cervical collar. He stopped by, and I noticed he was hot and sweaty. I thought he had come in for water, so I offered him a glass, and he turned it down. We talked for a few minutes, but I was impatient to get rid of him. I didn't feel well, and I had a lot of work to do."

"I remember someone coming into the yard, now that you mention it. The upstairs window was open, and I heard you talking. I remember wondering who it was, but when I looked, I didn't recognize him." As I thought about that afternoon, the circumstances and events slowly came alive in my memory. Now after weeks of agonizing and blind speculation, this was what it was all about. I leaned against the kitchen sink and thought of how bizarre the accusation seemed.

"Well, that's it. I have no idea why he would accuse me of assaulting him. Ted and Dave say that if I worked on the road crew or at K-2, I could just punch him out. Or my friends would." Peter smiled. "And that would be the end of it. But since I am a minister, he can accuse me, even by innuendo, and most people would accept his word against mine." Peter shook his head.

"A morals charge? Why they don't have to prove anything! You'll be through with the Catholic Church. Out."

"And now Dave says the complaint has been filed without so much as the assistant prosecutor's answering his phone calls. I should have gone in there that day, Mary. If I had taken care of it right away, this wouldn't have happened. You see, I didn't go when the detective said I had to, then Dave forgot to call. One thing on top of another."

"Filed? What does that mean?"

"Once it's filed, it is available to the press."

"Oh, no!" I gasped. "Not the papers!"

"They're going to call in another lawyer to talk to the prosecutor. His name is Mike Levit, and he knows the prosecuting attorney personally, so he'll have access to him. Mike will explain my situation to him and why I didn't go in that day. He'll ask the prosecutor to withdraw the filing pending investigation." Peter sighed. "But . . ."

I had never seen him look so broken and sad. We both knew that if it got into the papers, it would be the end of everything for us.

". . . there's not much hope." Peter's voice was a mixture of fear and sadness. "Dave and Ted say they absolutely *never* withdraw a complaint once it has been filed. It will take an act of God to do it."

Those were frightening words, and as our eyes met, neither of us dared to expect a miracle.

I had urged Peter not to go that day, because I had been afraid for him. Now look what has happened, I thought. Somehow I felt responsible.

"I've volunteered to have a polygraph test tomorrow morning. Will you go in with me?" Peter asked, interrupting my thoughts.

"Yes."

"They say it will help. Then we're supposed to meet with the lawyers. They're going to call in another one too, Ernest Harris. They say he's an expert in these cases."

These cases? What does that mean, I wondered.

The following morning we met Dave Boylan in front of the polygraph office. He was grinning from ear to ear. "You needed a miracle, Father. You got it. Somehow Mike convinced the prosecuting attorney to withdraw the filing."

"Thank God," Peter said. He turned to me.

I fought back the tears of relief. My first in days. Said nothing.

"I didn't think we'd get him to do it, but the assistants on the case didn't answer any of my phone calls, and they should have. I've never heard of any other case where the complaint has been withdrawn like this after filing. It's really a miracle! I can hardly believe it myself. Do you realize this will give us a chance to get the entire incident straightened out?"

Once again I felt that the ordeal was nearly over. Dave sounded so sure.

I was nervous sitting at the large conference table in the law firm's library. The attorneys, Dave, Ted, Mike Levit, and Ernest Harris sat across from us.

"First of all, Father Dally," Mike began, "I believe in your innocence." His dark eyes were direct, and a reassuring smile touched his lips as he spoke to us. Behind him on the credenza stood a photograph of a beautiful dark-haired young woman and two children.

"You know that polygraph tests are not considered conclusive," Ernest said. "They are useful only when all the other factors agree with what the polygraph indicates."

"The results of your test this morning will be helpful in getting them to drop the complaint now that the filing has been withdrawn," Dave explained.

"When I go to the prosecuting attorney, I'll explain further about your situation. That you've applied for priesthood in the Catholic Church in a special program for married men. If they're going to bring charges on the strength of what they've got from this guy, they won't prove anything, and they might as well tie a rope around your neck and knock the chair out from under you. I only hope he's listening." Mike said.

They asked us many questions about our lives, our family, and the weekend of the alleged incident. I sat quietly, speaking only to answer questions directed to me. It all seemed like a bad dream.

"Mary, what do you remember about the day Fred came into your yard?" Ernest asked.

"Peter was working in the yard, and I was upstairs in our bedroom with the windows open. I remember hearing voices." Suddenly I felt self-conscious.

"Well, our yard is so public, there isn't any place to do anything hidden. We're on the main road going into the village. One of my complaints has always been that we don't have any privacy for social gatherings. The kids were in and out of the house too."

As I talked, Peter got up from his chair and began pacing back and forth in the room.

"Try to relax, Father," Dave said. "You're an explosion about to happen, you're so tense. Try to realize we're doing everything we can for you now."

They were wonderful, these men; especially Dave and Ted. I wondered how we could ever thank them for their help. I knew that without them we would have no hope.

"I don't get it." Peter looked out the window. Then he turned to us helplessly and said, "He waits weeks before going to the police. They wait weeks to contact me. They've seen our yard, know how public it is. They believe this?"

"They're out to get you, Father. That's all," Ted said.

"Were your kids in the yard at this time?" Ernest asked me.

"I don't remember that they were, but they could have been. It was a nice day, and there was a lot of neighborhood activity."

"Okay," Mike said, soothingly. "Is there anything else?"

"Our neighbors who lived in the rental house just a few feet from our driveway were moving out that weekend. They were coming and going all day. The people next to them were around too, working on their cars. It seems like this could easily be cleared up just by talking to the neighbors," I said.

"I don't think that's a good idea. Anyway, you could have gone around behind the house out of the neighbors' view," Mike said to Peter.

"There isn't any place in our yard where a person cannot be observed from the street or another house," Peter explained, more calmly now.

"I'm afraid that if this is not kept absolutely confidential, we'll attract Fred's attention and that could blow the whole thing wide open," Ernest said. "We want to avoid publicity."

"What motive would he have for doing this?" I asked.

"I don't think Fred did this because he hopes to have you convicted. He just wants the notoriety. The small town fame, so to speak," Dave said.

"You are a public figure on Vashon Island, Father. Particularly now that you have applied to be a Catholic priest. We think he could be after the thrill of being the one to stop you," Ernest said.

"You mean like John Hinckley?" I laughed nervously at the incredibility.

Our decision had drawn attention to ourselves and triggered other hatreds. I thought of my own past feelings of prejudice and contempt toward Catholicism. I remembered the smashed statue of the Blessed Mother Peter had discovered the week after his resignation.

Then, too, there was the Marian statue at the back of the church. It had been there for nearly twenty years. An entire generation of Episcopalians had become accustomed to its reminder of our Blessed Mother's gift of the Savior. It had been a gift from a Greek family, a gesture of friendship between Anglicans and Orthodox. We were no sooner out the door on that last Sunday when someone removed it from the church.

"Exactly. Hinckley wanted to call attention to himself. The same could be true of this guy. He just doesn't think as big as Hinckley did," Ernest explained.

"Confidentiality is our only hope. We don't want to give him any publicity," Mike said.

"What you're saying sounds as reasonable as anything else about this nightmare," I said as I turned to Peter. He had told me a dozen times how sorry he was that I had to go through this. Our eyes met, locked in the sure knowledge of commitment to our marriage, to each other. If our relationship can survive this, I thought, that will be another miracle.

Mike's secretary opened the door.

"Transfer the call in here," he said to her. "Hello, Alice." We sat quietly as Mike listened for several minutes. "Yes. Yes. I'm sure of it. Good. I keep telling you guys all my clients are innocent. Thanks, Alice." Mike laughed as he hung up the phone.

"That was the supervisor of the group handling your case in the prosecutor's office. She's a fair person. I used to work with her. She has pulled her assistant off the case because she is prejudiced against you, Father. It seems she was acquainted with the man who hit your kids in that car accident a few years ago. She remembers you, Father, and according to her you behaved in a disgusting self-righteous manner toward him."

"I—" Peter began.

"No matter, Father." Mike smiled and waved his hand. "We're all human. The point is she made the mistake of saying that you need to be made an example of, as a warning to other ministers and priests to keep them from sexually molesting children."

"She was out to get you, and because of her prejudices Alice took her off the case." He looked at each of us around the table and smiled broadly. "Another miracle. That's great.

Just what we need." He turned to Dave. "Those women down there are all steamed up about the recent article in *Newsweek* too, the one about ministers and priests who molest the kids they work with. They think they've got a live one here to make an example of."

"But Fred Hode isn't a child. He's an adult," Peter said.

"I know, but you're a minister who wants to be a priest. To those women you're a real prize."

"They know that even the publicity would destroy you," Ernest said. "And the publicity alone, without a chance at conviction, would accomplish what they want."

When we were in the car, Dave said, "Father, you've been under a terrific strain for a long time." He waited a moment before he continued. "I've been doing some inquiring, and I'm going to make a suggestion. I think you need someone to talk to, get your feelings out in a neutral environment where you can understand what's been going on with you. I've learned about a psychiatrist who might turn out to be a real help in facing all that has happened these past few weeks. They say he sees a lot of ministers and priests. Here's his name and phone number. I hope you'll call him. I know that money is pretty tight for you guys, but Ted and I won't be sending you a bill, so that will help a little. You need someone to help you put the whole thing in perspective. Okay?"

Dave explained that the following week the attorneys would sit down with the prosecuting attorney and present the case.

Another week of waiting, I thought. Would it ever be over? And what of Oklahoma? Would Peter still have a chance? His petition had already gone to Rome, but would Bishop Beltran want him after this? If the district attorney doesn't drop the complaint and Peter is charged, what would there be left for us? We are at our most vulnerable, and people always believe the worst.

And what of our marriage? Could I pick up the tattered pieces of my emotions? It wasn't just the accusation against Peter, but the humiliation, the final insult on top of everything else. Torn from my faith community. Ruptured by scorn and ridicule. Then finally turned down by Hunthausen. For what?

Nothing.

A new bitterness and anger was growing inside me like a cancer. I tried to think of the other Mary, but what did her life have to say to me now? She never had to face anything like this, I told myself. And myself answered: Or did she? She was pregnant out of wedlock. Her son was said to be crazy and a drunkard. She saw him convicted by the legal authorities. Finally, she stood at the foot of the cross . . . Enough. Enough.

The lump in my throat. Was it a permanent obstruction?

25

"Well, what do you think of Dave's suggestion?" I asked as we drove onto the island.

"About seeing the psychiatrist, you mean?"

"Yes."

"I think it's a good idea. But can we afford it?"

"Well, I think we have to," I said. "God must still be in this somewhere. If things work out for you in Oklahoma, he'll see us through. I mean through everything, including the money situation." I looked out the window as we passed Dean Miller's house. We have so many good friends here, I thought. I wonder how they would react if they knew what we are up against now? I turned to see Peter's strong profile. "God knows what the attorneys are going to cost."

"I'll call the doctor for an appointment when we get home," Peter said.

I thought to myself, I'm the one who needs a psychiatrist. I felt devastated and abandoned. There was an element of unreality about everything again. It was hard to believe that I would not wake up and find the entire episode had been a bad dream.

Why? Why would he do this? What about the island deputies? And why had it not gotten out on the island? Surely we would have heard if it had. What defense was there, anyway? Only Peter's word against his. It seemed that around every corner we would meet an old friend, a former parishioner, or a Catholic who would believe the worst. I wanted to hide from everyone.

Well, both of us could not afford to go to a psychiatrist. It was more important for Peter to go. I had never seen him so beaten down as he was now. I wanted healing for him, though in my heart I knew I needed help too. We would face that later. I would be all right if Peter was.

The attorneys had pointed out the recent publicity in the newspapers and on television, about the congressional page who accused United States senators of sexual misconduct. A special investigation had been started immediately. Across the nation newspapers and magazines carried stories about moral decay among our nation's most prominent leaders, only to have the eighteen-year-old alcoholic page admit that he had made up the whole story. Each time I picked up a newspaper I wept. For their families. For them. For the boy. For the trouble we humans visit upon one another.

Was Fred Hode like the others? What evil and destruction. Motives I could not comprehend. There had to be profound sickness and anger. A perverted desire for personal acclaim. A hatred of the Church.

I tried to find out what I could about this young man and his family. Someone said he hung around the college one of our kids attended, but he wasn't a student there.

"They used to be Catholic, and he hates them. He thinks all priests are perverts. He doesn't like me, and he really gets angry when I talk about your wanting to be a Catholic priest, Dad," one of our kids said when we asked if any of them knew him. "He just hangs around a lot. Everybody jokes about the athletic contests he says he's going to win, but he never does. He tries to be real macho, but some people say he's got sexual problems."

"I don't remember him in our high school," I said.

"I think he dropped out before we came here."

The weeks marched slowly by. Time. It grew larger in its unreality. It was almost as though we had been forgotten. Somewhere in my psyche I kept returning to the idea that Peter's ordination must be very important for the Church. It was the only explanation I had. And I thought, great gifts at great price. Lord, how we need your saving strength and grace.

The apprehension we lived with was paralytic, a part of every moment of each day. A blanket of saddness had fallen over our lives. Like the first snow of winter, day-to-day living covered us over, held us in frozen suspension as we waited.

There were long hours and days alone for thinking and for talking. In my anger I said things I should not have said.

I knew that Peter had to be under great stress. I was very sensitive to my husband's vulnerability and the guilt I knew he must feel, even in his innocence. Questions raged inside me as we talked about Fred Hode. Over and over again I asked myself: Why? What could he gain? Yet through it all I knew there was no gain. Only destruction.

As the situation worked on my mind, our marriage relationship became more difficult for me. I knew I must not allow the stress to destroy us. Still, I couldn't help it. I had been through too much. Confused and hurt, the anger grew inside me like a cancerous tumor, fed by the evil accusation. I drove at him again and again. But I had to vent my feelings to someone. We were trapped. He was trapped. Everything in our relationship, everything about him told me that the accusation was the work of another person's sickness. But what if they didn't drop the charges? What if they said he was guilty, and he wasn't? What then?

It would all be for nothing.

I needed perspective, but there was no one I could talk to. I asked myself over and over why this had happened. I hoped desperately that the attorneys would find out it was a miscommunication of some sort.

In the past months, as we had faced the challenges brought on by our decision to become Catholics, our marriage relationship had grown deeper and stronger. Only through complete trust and commitment could our love survive this new trauma. We became reclusive; not wanting to go about the community or face our friends, not wanting to answer the inevitable questions about Peter's future in the Catholic priesthood. We'd never been very good with glib answers, and now we felt even less sure. The days dragged on endlessly, and it seemed the nightmare would never end.

One day at the post office I saw Laura Hale, Ted's wife. She wanted to hug me but didn't. It was there in her eyes. I knew Ted had told her, and I turned away.

Dave Boylan kept in close touch with us, calling almost daily. His warmth and support, his complete faithfulness was a gift that I will carry in my heart as long as I live.

Somewhere in the middle of all this Father Morgan and Father Gallatin arrived from Tulsa.

We wondered if we should tell the two priests about the accusation. The four attorneys counseled that we should not; that once the matter was cleared, there seemed no reason to discuss it with anyone. The important thing now was to keep the entire situation absolutely confidential, so that Peter's chances for the future would not be harmed.

On Saturday morning Peter went to the fire dispatcher's training session. Betty Stone, a former Tulsan now living on Vashon Island, and I took the priests to Seattle to see the sights, all as a matter of routine. As we lunched at the top of the space needle on that sparkling clear day, we saw the Cascade Mountains to the east, Mt. Baker miles to the north, the spectacular Olympic Range to the west, and the outline of Mount St. Helens' crater in the south. It was beautiful, almost as if God had given me this miracle of beauty and normalcy in the midst of the bizarre nightmare we were living through.

It is difficult for one who is not a native Pacific Northwesterner to realize that such clear days are surprisingly rare. Betty and I were amused by the two priests who marveled at the panoramic view they thought was the norm for Seattle in August.

On Sunday morning Father Gallatin celebrated Mass in our basement chapel. I served the priests breakfast, and they left. There were promises of reciprocation when we arrived in Tulsa and shouts of praise for our hospitality as the dust from our driveway rose behind their little car, and they turned north toward the Seattle ferry.

I could not help but wonder if we would ever see them again.

When Mike Levit returned from his vacation we did not hear from him. Another week went by. Peter called Dave.

"I haven't heard from him either, Father, but no news is good news. We can be sure of that."

"The stress is killing us. Isn't there any way we can find out what's going on?" Peter asked.

"Yeah. Well, let me call Mike and see what's happening. I know he wanted to take the results of the polygraph test to the prosecuting attorney, but I don't know if he's done it yet."

"Father, Mike says he has delivered the results of the polygraph to the prosecutor," Dave said when he called back. "He says that the assistant prosecuting attorneys are trying to get in touch with Fred Hode to bring him in for an interview. They have no case unless his testimony becomes definite."

"And he hasn't come in yet?" he asked, puzzled by Dave's statement.

"No. They've left telephone messages for him, and written him letters, but he doesn't respond. If they don't hear from him, they'll naturally assume the accusation was false. I've even tried to hunt him up here on the island. He doesn't answer the messages I leave, so I guess he's avoiding me too."

"Dave, are you saying that they've never actually questioned Fred?" Peter asked.

"That's right, Father."

"All of this and they haven't actually talked to him face to face? Ever?" It seemed impossible that Fred could have caused so much hell in our lives, and none of them, not the detective, not the prosecutor's assistants—*no one*—had talked to him face to face.

"Nope. All they've ever had is the original complaint he made to the local deputies," Dave answered.

"You're kidding." Peter laughed, incredulous of our friend's statement. "Does this mean it's over?"

"Well, not yet. They're still trying to get in contact with him. He could still come in to the prosecutor's office and say anything he wants."

"He doesn't have anything to say." For the first time Peter allowed himself the luxury of unrestrained anger. "I don't know what this was all about, but look what it's done to us! There could have been such terrible consequences for me and my family. Thank God I have a wife and children who have stood by me."

Peter's anger was that of a man who had experienced the prolonged pain and frustration of a false accusation, one that could easily have destroyed us all.

"I know, Father," Dave said quietly.

"It's bewildering to me that all of this could happen, and now they can't even find the guy."

"I know, Father. All I can say now is it looks like it's over, but it won't be final until we get the word from the prosecutor."

"Is there anything we can do? I want to put this behind me as fast as I can."

"No. We just have to continue to be patient and keep our fingers crossed. When the complaint is officially dropped, you'll be the first to know, believe me."

On September 27th we received a letter from Ernest Harris:

> . . . the prosecutor's office has declined to file any charges against you at this time. The prosecutor's office has chosen this method of terminating their investigation, rather than admitting they made a mistake, as a way of "saving face."

So ended a nightmare that had begun three months earlier.

The bill from Mike and Ernest totaled $4,568.63.

We sent them the $4,055 we had saved for our move to Oklahoma.

$508.63 remained to be paid. We had no idea where we would get the money.

How many of us have experienced tragedy and loss only to find that when it has passed the only tangible reality is a number in a check book?

Fred Hode didn't have to prove anything. He had only to *suggest* perversion to destroy us. Had it not been for a few people who knew us and recognized the stakes, I tremble to think what might have happened.

The ordeal was over and we had survived, but I wondered if we could go on.

26

Still there loomed the fleeting ghost of Fred Hode. But we heard nothing, and Dave Boylan assured us that nothing would come of the allegation. Just as the prosecuting attorney's office stated, the entire matter had been dropped.

We scraped the money together for Peter to continue his twice-monthly psychiatric appointments, and slowly we began to notice signs of recovery from the emotional stress of the summer. From somewhere we received the wisdom to realize that we would find the healing we needed in our response to friendship and to the gestures of warmth around us. We needed time to dispel our fears. Without the experience of God's grace at work in our lives, it would have been impossible for us to achieve the normal patterns of the past. We stumbled blindly, finding our way as best we could, facing each day as it came, neither wanting nor expecting perfection or an easy path. One step, one day at a time, we gradually accepted the fact that the ordeal was over, that it would not return.

As I watched Peter's former energy and enthusiasm return, I was comforted by what I saw. Little did I realize then that my own healing was only surface, that sooner or later I would have to face myself and the anger I felt.

Not only had we received God's abundant grace and love, but our faith had matured and deepened during the trials we'd faced. We found ourselves stronger, more faithful, more at peace, and more loving of other people than ever in the past. We enjoyed our life together in a new devotion to each other's needs, an unexpectedly rich dimension to our marriage. We shared simple pleasures and tasks in a more meaningful way. Having experienced that nightmare, it seemed that nothing would ever be the same again.

A part of each of us died that summer. In our shock, we did not fully understand all that had happened. It was as if we had been protected from the absorption that would have destroyed us if we had been capable of real comprehension. We felt we had been victimized too, a part of a puzzle, the answers to which we might never know. And we would have to be content with the unknowing. Gradually we understood it was over, and that was enough. It was time to forgive, but could we ever forget?

I now added a new line to the prayer: Lord, help me to know you, to love you and to serve you, and in Jesus name heal our hurts and sadness.

Though Bishop Beltran had agreed to sponsor Peter, we didn't know when he had sent the petition to Rome, nor did we know how long it would take to get the answer. There was still the outstanding legal fee of $508.63, a lot of money from our small resources: there were the childrens' continuing education needs, and we had to set aside funds to pay for the move to Oklahoma. We needed time. Time to pay the remaining fees, time to save for our moving expenses, and time for the summer's wounds to heal.

It seemed that once again, I needed all my energy just to live from one day to the next. Peter needed my assurance and love now more than ever. Months, or was it years, had passed since August, 1980 when we first read about he Pastoral Provision in the *Seattle P.I.* While I felt drawn toward the challenges of the future, many of my old feelings of loss and hopelessness, the self-deprecation and guilt I thought were buried, and the devastation of the summer, all emerged to assault me again in a new and more destructive way. I felt desolate and lost. We had won. Good had triumphed over evil, but for what? Instead of looking forward to the future, I wondered where evil would befall us next. On what field would we face the next battle? There had to be an answer for me somewhere, or was it just my sin and weakness that kept me from joyfully embracing what I knew to be my vocation as well as my husband's. Unlike the other Mary's affirming love in her words, "Oh yes, Lord. Your will be done." I found only weariness in my heart.

I rejoiced that Peter was regaining his old sense of self, but what was happening to me? My feelings of hopelessness were overpowering at times. I needed healing in my life, but there was no one to whom I could turn.

From somewhere—I don't know where—I discovered the words of Cardinal Leo Suenens, one of the great minds of the Second Vatican Council:

> To hope is a duty, not a luxury,
> To hope is not to dream, but to turn dreams into reality.
> Happy are those who dream dreams and are ready to pay the price to make them come true.

27

I began to face a gnawing realization that a married priest in the Roman Catholic Church represented an intrusion which, even in the most friendly circumstances, would be largely unwelcome. However, we noticed that as the congregation of St. John Vianney on Vashon Island awaited each new development of our journey, we were certainly accepted by them. At first reticent, the Catholic congregation gradually displayed a warmth and friendship toward us. They had grown from wondering what we intended to do there to rooting for Peter, who now occasionally served as lector and Eucharistic minister at Sunday Mass and frequently helped with the men's club wood-cutting project on Saturday mornings. I recall, with an inward smile of affection for them, that a Sunday rarely passed without someone asking if we'd "heard from Bishop Beltran or the pope."

The gestures of friendship served as food for our starving egos, but behind the warmth and joy hung the fear that the innovation of a married priest might be too close to the familiar tensions caused by the recent changes in the Episcopal Church. Because of this, we had to examine our own feelings whether we wanted to be the focal point of the same kind of tensions in the Roman Catholic Church.

There were other crosscurrents going on inside me. I asked myself repeatedly why we were doing this. Somehow there had to be an answer to that question for me personally as well as for Peter. As I questioned, I grew in my own conviction that the task ahead would be a fulfillment of God's will in my life, without detracting from the importance of Peter's call to priesthood in the Catholic Church. I began to feel ready (as ready as I ever would!), and I grew increasingly aware that the Church had to be ready too. I sensed intuitively that our role, Peter's and mine, would be found in patience and prayer. I felt touched by the support and prayers of so many other people during the past months. The power of intercessory prayer in the Mass had become a firsthand experience for me in the Catholic faith to which we now intimately belonged.

Overriding everything was the miracle that we had survived the accusations of the summer. I felt a vague sense that Peter's ordination was *very* important. What other reason for such demons? And the miracles that could only have been the working of the Holy Spirit! Then I would ask myself, but why? Why is it so important? It wasn't possible to understand, but I thought about these questions constantly, praying that the Lord would give me a loving and grateful heart.

The Visitation Sisters in Federal Way, across the Sound from us, wrote or phoned us frequently. Their prayers sustained us through the summer's hardships, though we lacked the confidence to share with them openly. They loved us enough to pray for our intentions, not knowing or even caring what our specific needs were.

One day Mother Anne called to ask if Peter would come to the monastery in November to teach a series of Scripture classes. They wanted them in the evening so I could come along. Peter agreed.

Peter's self-confidence was at its lowest ever, and he found it almost impossible to go before this group of women contemplatives whom he felt had far more to offer than he. Literally trembling with fear, he persevered, giving little of his usual depth of spirit and lighthearted humor to the task. By the end of the series he felt he had failed miserably and wondered how he could ever make it up to these women of such great spiritual depth.

As the last session drew to a close, the sisters told us that Father George Maloney, of the Society of Jesus, would be with them for the first week in Advent to conduct a retreat, primarily for religious women. They invited me to come, and they suggested that Peter could stay at Palisades, the men's retreat house down the road. He could then attend the conferences with Father Maloney. The retreat was a gift to us. We gratefully accepted. As we left the monastery that evening, Mother Anne gave Peter an envelope which we expected to contain a letter of thanks for the classes. It contained not only a thank you but a check for $500.

It was exactly what we needed to pay the remaining legal fees. We could now put the entire summer behind us in every way. We would truly begin anew with the gift of the week-long retreat.

As the time of the retreat drew near, I found to my surprise that I felt increasingly nervous about a week of silence in a monastery. What would it be like? Could I keep silent that long? Would the other retreatants, sisters and laywomen, welcome us? How would Father Maloney react to Peter and me?

Then we learned that Peter could stay in the priest's apartment next to Father Maloney's quarters. He would have to return to work at the fire station on Thursday evening, then come back to the monastery for me on Sunday. We both thought of backing out. The retreat was becoming too complicated for us.

I forced myself to go through with it, even though I wondered if I could emotionally handle a week-long retreat.

During the free time on the second day, I decided to walk down to the waterfront. It was December and the air was chilly, but not too cold to enjoy sitting at the edge of the water listening to the gentle lapping of the waves. They touched the huge gray boulders that guarded the shoreline against the onslaught of winter storms, and alternately served as favorite spots for retreatants to sun themselves. I looked across Puget Sound to the eastern shore of Maury Island, the southeastern appendage to Vashon Island. Faintly in the distance to the northwest was Point Robinson Lighthouse, reminding me of family picnics and parish celebrations on its grassy beaches.

Directly across, the bare cliffs of Sandy Shores rose out of the Sound. Above the neat, fashionable homes lay the stark reality of the gravel pits. I was shocked to look across the Sound to the place where my friend, Mary Ellen, a doctor's wife, had stopped her car and taken an overdose of tranquilizers just four months earlier.

"You're gonna love Oklahoma and they're gonna love you." I remembered Mary Ellen's soft Tennessee accent that day we'd lunched together to celebrate our offer from the Bishop of Tulsa. Looking now at the place of her death, I felt stunned by the sadness of it.

Why had she done it?

She was beautiful and intelligent. She seemed to have everything.

Why?

It might have been me, I thought. Had I given in to the evil temptations and thoughts that came thundering upon me these past months. It might have been me. I thought that my life had been uprooted, taken out of my control without any consideration for the way I felt. Then even worse things happened. 'Now here I am, Lord, safe on the shore, by your grace alone. I know that now.'

I thought of Father Maloney's meditation that morning. Of God the Father working in every event and in all kinds of people. In me. Of his Son Jesus, truly God and truly man. Of his childhood and growing up in the little village of Nazareth, playing around the carpentry shop. He must have used every moment, I reflected, to discover who he really was, to grow and prepare for the purpose for which he was sent by the Father. It was good for me to remember that Jesus, too, was tempted. This morning Father Maloney talked of surrender to the divine will. Are these words for me, I wondered?

Surrender. Not resignation.

Simple abandonment.

Openness . . . like the sea.

In that few moments on the shore of Puget Sound I knew that even though I'd faced the past's terrible temptation of wanting to end my life, I could do what I had to do. Here was a part of the answer in my constant prayer: To know you, to love you, and to serve you . . .

28

On the last day of the retreat I waited eagerly near the main entrance for Peter to come for me. A gentle northwest drizzle fell on the planters of bonsai trees in the sisters' courtyard. I was eager to share with my husband a gift I'd received just a short time earlier.

At the end of the morning conference, the retreatants came together for Mass before lunch and departure to our homes thoughout Washington and Oregon. I received Holy Communion and returned to my place—near the back of the chapel, as I had done throughout the week of retreat. I thought of Sister Magdalene, a widow and mother of grown children, who always said when she offered me the cup, "Mary, dear. The blood of Christ." As I knelt in my place I closed my eyes to pray as usual. Then I opened my eyes, and suddenly they were wide open. There, coming out of the head of Father Maloney and several retreatants kneeling in front of me were tongues of fire! It was magnificent, yet alarming. It was not like any experience I'd ever had. As I watched, the flames continued. In a strange mixture of fright and a deep sense of peace, I closed my eyes again, afraid to open them for fear that I would see the tongues, yet yearning more than anything to see them once more. I remained kneeling as Father Maloney gave the blessing. Somehow, I simply could not move from that position for a moment. Then I could hear the others around me leaving the chapel. I stayed there a long time with my eyes tightly shut. The week-long silence had ended, and there were muffled voices just outside the chapel door.

As I became fully aware of the people talking, I remember thinking I must get up and leave. I can't stay here forever with my eyes closed. I felt an overwhelming desire to share the vision with the others, but I really wasn't comfortable with that inclination. Instead, moved by something other than my will, I hurried past the other retreatants to my room where I quickly closed the door.

I picked up the book I'd been reading before Mass. While I'd never been an "open the book and God will speak to you" sort of person, I received the guidance that I needed in that moment through the words on that page. It advised that a spiritual experience such as this is not an end in itself. It is not the purpose of our faith to generate such experiences, that the tongues of fire were a gift to me for my needs at that moment. The passage seemed to warn not to play with or flaunt the gifts of the Spirit. Nor need we seek further revelation and proof. My understanding led me to feel that I should not become preoccupied with the gift, but simply to accept what God had given me. That it is enough to get on with the business of loving God and serving him, living out our lives in fulfillment of his holy will.

I thought about it. Tongues of fire. The overwhelming presence and power of God's Holy Spirit. As in calling out his church at Pentecost. Now me. What could it mean? It would have to be enough for me simply to accept that it had happened.

Even then, as the thoughts ran through my mind, my body, yes, my soul, everything about me filled with a peaceful joy. I knew that it was the end of my fears and uncertainties. The Holy Spirit had given me his most powerful symbol, his message of grace and unfathomable love.

All the thoughts, the feelings I'd experienced with Mary, my Mother, completed themselves in that moment of new beginning, in the acceptance and understanding of the gift I had received.

Mary in Nazareth.

Mary with Elizabeth.

Mary in the last months of her pregnancy,
     riding on a donkey.

Mary and Joseph.

The birth of the baby.

Mary in the Temple.
Mary at Cana.
Mary at the cross.
Mary at the resurrection.
Mary with the beloved disciple.
Her life.
My life.

I went to lunch. Those who had smiled assurance to me all week introduced themselves. We exchanged addresses and promised to pray for each other. I packed my things and waited for Peter. It would be all right to share these things with him.

As I stood by the entrance alone, I watched the silver strands of falling rain outside the window. Across the drive the evergreens stood primly erect, their graceful arms extended decorously, as though they had just entered a great ballroom. Then, standing very still, they waited for the orchestra to begin the pure strains of a Strauss waltz. Around them, the gardener's rainwear glittered as he stooped and puttered in the rhododendrons and azaleas growing at their feet. Already the retreatants were leaving and there were few cars left in the lot. The raindrops slipped from the covered breezeway, washed the bonsai, and made tiny, star-shaped splatters on the sidewalk. It reminded me that soon we would embrace a new home. Oklahoma. A throw-away section of our country, historically good for nothing, and so it was given to the Indians. The Trail of Tears. The Five Civilized Tribes. Hot, humid, dusty. That's where we would live. It would be our home. We would leave this emerald land behind. How I would miss it.

I looked up and saw Peter across the parking lot. He was tall and straight as he walked toward me.

29

Peter saw me through the window. He smiled as he ducked under the covered walkway to get out of the rain.

I thought about the relative meaning of time. Of the few instances during our marriage when we had been apart, stretching as it always did into a strange eternity. I was again seeing him for the first time, his youthful grin spread across his face, telling me without words how much I mean to him.

Never again would I analyze and question whether we were doing the right thing. Never again would I be filled with doubts about God's will for our lives. Unsettle the Catholic Church?

The problem was not ours.

We had received the gift of faith. Like Noah's rainbow, the Holy Spirit had given me a new promise of God's love for us. Though I did not recognize it that day, a peace beyond anything I had experienced began to characterize my relationships with other people.

Earlier I had wondered how Peter would respond to my experience. Charism. Gift, favor, grace. Am I now a charismatic Christian, I had to ask myself. Well, it had never failed, had it? Every time in my life that I had said, "Not me. I'll never do that," I found myself in the middle of all that I had said I would never do or be.

Never leave the Episcopal Church? Never be a Roman Catholic?

Yet, here I am.

Oklahoma?

It seemed the last place on earth that day eight months ago when Peter called me at work.

I had visualized a windblown, barren land of dusty unpaved roads, and cowboys with red and blue bandanas tied over their faces to shield themselves from the dust that blew around them.

Now we planned to live in that land of real Indians and backward small towns whose poverty contrasted sharply with stately mansions and chauffeur-driven limousines of the cities.

What will Peter say? I had to tell him. There was something inside me that said he was the one person with whom I should share the vision of the tongues of fire, this promise that the nightmare of the past summer was over. It was as though God had placed his 'seal of approval' on our vocations together—one flesh in his name. Was it a sign that the evil allegations and the miracles which answered them were proof of Peter's vocation to the Catholic priesthood?

I recalled that once or twice when I prayed I had said, "I know I'm not supposed to ask, but Lord, if you could just give me a little sign. So we'll know it's the right thing we're doing?"

And what a sign it was!

There were some things I just couldn't talk about, I thought. And like the other Mary, there were many things I would hold in my heart in the months and years ahead.

As we left the convent driveway, Peter looked straight ahead and listened without comment as I described the tongues of fire. I talked nonstop, the words tumbling over each other, not wanting to hear his reaction. I could not help feeling like a child who felt embarrassed to find she'd unexpectedly come of age.

"Well, do you believe me?" I concluded abruptly.

"Yes," he said simply. "I believe you."

"What do you think caused it?" I asked, thinking he would say it was the fried egg I'd eaten for breakfast, his usual explanation for such experiences.

"I think it was the Holy Spirit, Mary. I believe you saw the tongues of fire, like the apostles at Pentecost."

He's using the same words, I thought. "I'm sure no one else saw it," I assured him. It had not occurred to me that anyone else there could have seen it. Surprisingly, that fact didn't detract from the reality of the experience either.

"Do you think you'll see it again?"

"I hope not," I said. "It was incredible but not something I would want to happen every time I receive Holy Communion. Even the possibility is frightening."

Peter laughed and turned to face me for the first time. "I believe you, and I agree with you. It was the Spirit of God speaking to you. And there is something else too, there were a lot of people at that retreat, including Father Maloney, who are truly filled with the Holy Spirit. I don't mean that they speak in tongues, although I'm sure some of them do have the gift of tongues. I mean the Holy Spirit is using their lives in a very holy way."

We settled into silence, enjoying the drive south along Puget Sound.

From that time on I never again questioned the place of our ministry within the structure and tradition of the Roman Catholic Church. I think I realized more than ever that it would not be an easy life. But one thing I knew for sure, we held a special place in God's plan for his Church on earth. And it all seemed to be connected in some indefinable manner: the nightmare of the summer, the Visitation sisters, and the gift of the tongues of fire, as at Pentecost.

In the weeks that followed, a quiet calm overtook our lives. I reflected on the words of Edith Stein, a brilliant Jewish philosopher who, converted to our Lord, became Sister Benedicta of the Cross, O.C.D., and was eventually martyred at Auschwitz:

> Whatever did not fit in with my plan did lie within the plan of God. I have an ever deeper and firmer belief that nothing is merely an accident when seen in the light of God, that my whole life down to the smallest detail has been marked out for me in the plan of divine providence and has a completely coherent meaning in God's all-seeing eyes.

30

That Christmas two things happened that were memorable. On December 23rd, Bishop Beltran called to say that he had mailed Peter's petition to the Congregation for the Doctrine of the Faith in Rome, as well as two other petitions for married men to be ordained in the Diocese of Tulsa: Patrick Eastman, a Church of England clergyman and Gary Sherman, a former Lutheran pastor. Both were unprecedented. Patrick would move to the United States to be ordained, and perhaps most dramatic of all three, no married American Lutheran had ever been ordained a Catholic priest.

Obviously, we were overjoyed that at last Peter's petition was actually on its way. At least, I think we were, because we thought it had been sent months earlier. Bishop Beltran had said he intended to send the three in the summer. While we were disappointed to learn it had not gone earlier, that did not detract from the new knowledge that now, for sure, it was on its way. We told ourselves that it would be a long time in Rome. After all, Father Jim Parker's petition had been there for more than a year before it was approved. We resigned ourselves to pray for the Congregation for the Doctrine of the Faith and for the gift of patience for ourselves.

The other thing that occurred that Christmas was somewhat less momentous. One day as Peter helped me put away our faded, chipped dinnerware, I recalled how I had bought three sets of service for eight from a Sears Outlet sale flier, sight unseen, at $19.95 each fifteen years earlier. I smiled to myself as I stroked the worn silver-colored rim of the dinnerplate in my hands, and I remembered the parish groups I'd served buffet-style as well as many family holiday dinners.

"I wish we could afford new china. You know, just enough for the family this Christmas," Peter said on a sudden impulse.

"Yes. I'd like that too, but it's not really all that important . . ." I smiled and closed the cupboard door.

The next thing I knew we'd talked ourselves into it, and we were on our way to Frederick and Nelson in Seattle to buy six place settings of Blue Danube, a facsimile of the antique Blue Onion pattern of which Peter's mother had given us several serving pieces.

"This is ridiculous. We can't afford china. Not these kinds of dishes. We're moving to Oklahoma. We don't need new china now, and besides we have to save our money."

Peter listened quietly as I protested and gradually talked myself into this sudden impulse. He never waivered. He thought we should have them no matter what.

I'll always remember that day in Frederick and Nelson. It seemed that buying those few dishes was the first normal thing we'd done in nearly a year, though we had to charge them to our account and pay a little each month. We were still trying to save money for our move to Tulsa. The whole thing was crazy. Still, we did it.

On Christmas day the children and I proudly arranged the white linen tablecloth and grandmother's fine linen napkins, and the new blue and white china dishes. As we stood beside our chairs and bowed our heads for Peter's prayer of thanksgiving, I looked down at the new dinner plate in front of me. As we said "Amen" together, one shining tear splashed into my plate. Brushing away the moisture with my fingertips, I looked around the table and realized that Peter and all the children were watching me. Their smiles seemed to say, "She's crying . . . it's a success!"

The seeming luxury of the new china and the material sacrifice it symbolized served in a small way to bring reality back into our lives.

In February I wrote to Sister Elsbeth in Jerusalem:

I almost feel suspicious that things are going so smoothly these days. I say suspicious because St. Frances Cabrini (and Father Greenfield!) used to say, "When things are going well, look out!" Well, I for one am going to enjoy it. These months have been a good time for us, a time of adjustment and cleansing. A time to look back, to be thankful, and a time to anticipate the wonderful things our Lord has in store for us. It has been a time to concentrate on and live for the "now"; we all need to be reminded to do that more fully.

On St. Patrick's Day, one year after we had boarded the plane to Tulsa, Peter left for the Josephinum Seminary in Columbus, Ohio where he would take the academic assessment examination. We were told that these interviews were to assess the candidate to determine deficiencies. A committee would then make recommendations for further studies.

At the airport Peter missed his connection with the young priest who was sent to pick him up. He got a cab and ended up making the twenty-mile drive with a green-haired, husky-voiced female driver who seemed unsure of where Peter wanted to go. When they finally arrived, the seminary was dark and appeared to be deserted, but Peter persistently rang the doorbell again and again. After a long time, the door was cautiously opened by an ancient, slippered priest who absent-mindedly assigned Peter to the suite of rooms reserved for the Papal Nuncio. He graciously accepted the hospitality, chuckling to himself. This was the Pontifical Seminary in America!

When Peter returned to Seattle, he continued his studies and waited for the committee's recommendations. When the results arrived, Peter settled into a more focused kind of study pattern. The certification exams would be scheduled after Bishop Beltran received his decretal from Rome.

On April 18th we wrote to Bishop Beltran asking for his advice about the sale of our home. We were concerned that our house might not sell easily because the lagging economy of 1983 had brought real estate sales in the Seattle area to a near standstill. We also asked the bishop what he expected our housing needs to be in Tulsa. Did we need to move our large appliances, furniture, etc.? Because we had not been able to save much money after paying the summer's legal fees, we would have to sell as much as we could to pay our moving expenses. We hoped to put the house on the market during the spring and summer months, the time of year when mainlanders were most attracted to our beautiful island. We grew uneasy when several weeks passed and we did not receive a reply from Bishop Beltran.

Then in the latter part of May, Bishop Beltran wrote to say that we should sell our house and everything that we could. Our furniture and everything needed for day-to-day living would be a part of our housing in Tulsa. He also said that we should plan to move to Tulsa in the fall, that Patrick Eastman and his wife Maureen would arrive at the same time. He planned to set up a program of study for both candidates.

Bishop Beltran said nothing to us about the third candidate, Gary Sherman, and we wondered if he had decided not to pursue priesthood in the Catholic Church.

We had our house appraised and the real estate people planted the *for sale* sign in our yard. It was a signal that our life on the island would soon come to an end. I began to prepare myself as best I knew how to think about what we would take with us, and which of our possessions we would sell in yard sales. I encouraged the children to come home to go through their things, but I was unable to get their attention, or perhaps they simply refused to hear me. Each of the children resented our move halfway across the country by ignoring or declining every invitation to be a part of the disposition of things they'd grown up with. I was at a loss for how to enlist their cooperation. Our move to Tulsa was a fact we'd lived with for more than a year. It was going to happen. We all had to face decisions about the accumulation of twenty years of living in one community.

As I assessed the situation, I couldn't help but wonder

what my life might have been like in the summer of '83 had we remained in the Episcopal Church. I would certainly not be facing dramatic, nearly irrational changes. My thoughts screamed: It's not necessary! You don't have to do this! Called by God? Step out in faith? Okay! But sell everything? Give away all your possessions? The accumulation of an entire lifetime?

Any way I looked at it, there was an element of insanity in what we were about to do. Or perhaps, I told myself, this would be the most sane thing we had ever done. I set my mind on the fact that we were called, and we had answered yes. We had a choice; we could have said no.

I wondered if the other Mary had felt torn with questions and doubts, with difficulties in carrying out her commitment after she had so eagerly said yes. If I might know the secrets of her heart, Lord. As a woman, I can imagine how she might have felt as her body swelled with the Holy Babe. Of how she left her home in Nazareth to travel to Bethlehem with Joseph, and their flight into Egypt to save the child. To see the man Jesus, her son, die on the cross. It had cost her everything. So much more than I will ever be asked to give.

Once again I fought the paralysis of depression. It prevented me from gathering the enthusiasm and momentum I needed for our move. It was as if each task begun and then completed brought us closer to the leaving, and to whatever awaited us in Tulsa. In my mind I wanted to throw myself into our new life, to look forward to the exciting adventure I believed it to be. But I was afraid. We were starting over. The sale of our furniture and other possessions was the reality of what starting over means for a woman whose children are nearly grown and who has just begun to think she's due for rest and relaxation. Preferably on an island in the South Pacific, just about as far removed from being the wife of a Catholic priest as possible. I wanted to turn and run as memories of those days and weeks in the autumn of 1980 came crashing in on me. The fears. The doubts. The questions and feelings of anger assailed me as I faced the task ahead, the outgrowth of that decision made two-and-a-half years earlier.

Then June 14th, our wedding anniversary, arrived again. I could not help the sadness I felt, remembering the events of the previous year. Unfair as it was to Peter, somehow our anniversary would never again be the completely happy remembrance it had been in past years.

On June 20, 1983, Bishop Beltran phoned us to say he had received Peter's decretal from Rome. It was the permission needed to ordain him. He suggested that we continue with our preparations to move and plan to be in Tulsa in the fall, probably October. Peter would continue the study program there before taking the certification examination. Once that was completed, the bishop would proceed with ordination.

We sent letters to all our friends and family with the good news. Congratulations flooded in to us from all over the country. All those friends and relatives who had encouraged us and prayed for us over the long haul cheered us on now to the happy future they all seemed sure awaited us in Tulsa.

31

It was the emptying out of a five-bedroom family home. The lives of six people. Moving on in that ever-present growing process. Turning away. But not forgetting.

As I walked slowly around the large table in our basement, I was conscious that my friends Ellie Lowry and Leslie Perry watched me pick up one thing and then another, returning each to the table.

"That's it," I said, placing the tennis rackets and cans of tennis balls together. "It's all got to go." I smiled. I wanted to be decisive. To let them know that it was all right, though I couldn't hide the fact that it wasn't easy.

"Are you really sure?" Ellie asked again. "You know how big my attic is. You can store as much as you like with me." We had raised our children together. Ellie knew that the things on that table symbolized my whole life. She understood this even better than I that day as I looked from one to the next, fatigued and in a mild state of trauma with the changes our lives were so rapidly taking.

"Now let us do the haggling, Mary." Leslie laughed as she said, "Just keep Peter in the house so he won't give everything away!"

I stopped and picked up the little handmade table in the dollhouse that Peter and Tommy Tomlinsen had made for Monica and Theresa one Christmas when they were small. The chalet-style dollhouse held tiny pieces of furniture that Peter had painted in brightly-colored Norwegian designs. I thought of how Peter had spent his day off for weeks secretly building the toy. Of how we'd searched Seattle for just the right doll family to live there.

My eye passed over, then came back to a dusty shoe box. I lifted the lid. Inside were small cups and saucers, and a chocolate pot. I remembered the day I'd come home to find Peter sitting with Monica and Tess at their child-size table sipping hot chocolate with miniature marshmallows and reading *Winnie The Pooh*. Little Tess squirmed as Monica sneaked more marshmallows her way with one hand, while she earnestly sucked the thumb on her other hand.

The silk plaid-covered book of Robert Burns' poems. Percy Perry. Thanksgiving dinners from Frederick and Nelson. Roast turkey. Dressing. Pumpkin pie. All "specially" packaged for Mr. P.J. Perry. The hand-painted papier-maché turkey place card for each small guest. Toast upon toast with raised glasses of wine. The blazing fire in the library fireplace with the collie asleep on the rug. Another toast. "And up until now, your children have been better behaved than ever before!" Finally, the parade to the bathroom after dinner to wash little hands. Then back to the library to open the cover of the newest treasured acquisition. Free to turn each page. Look at picture books. Read. Turn and look and read.

My beloved Captain's chair with the broken rung. The well-rubbed arm rests. Thoughts of my upstairs bedroom window with the view of the patio below. Homemade ice cream in an electric ice cream maker. Dear friends left behind.

"Only material possessions," I said, with a sigh. "Only things."

What memories these tables hold!

"Now, tomorrow, let us take the money, and we can be the ones to stand firm on the prices," Leslie said. "We don't want you to be tempted to give things away either." She must know we need the money to get to Oklahoma, I thought.

We laughed, but it was nervous, tense laughter; not the fun we were used to having together.

"It's all so dusty and dirty from being stored in the attic. I'll be glad when it's gone," I said, with an effort to sound casual. I looked through the open basement door into the backyard and blinked away my tears.

This was the first of three yard sales we had carefully planned. I hoped this would enable us to get rid of things in stages, making the sorting and decision-making easier, and leaving the most necessary pieces of furniture available for use until we had to move.

I had begun by selling family antiques and furniture to dealers early in June. What the dealers did not want we would sell in yard sales.

As Peter and I sorted through mementos and other symbols of our lives, the decisions of what to keep, what to sell, and what to throw away spread endlessly before us. We discovered yet another category too. What we could not take with us and could not bring ourselves to sell or throw away, we gave to friends, gifts of ourselves and the years we'd shared with them.

Peter wrote to Bishop Beltran on July 15th, bringing him up to date on our moving preparations. We planned to leave Vashon Island sometime in September, visit relatives in Oregon and California, and plan to arrive in Tulsa in mid-October. He asked what arrangements we should make for moving our things, which would mainly consist of his library, our dishes, great-grandmother's two antique chests and table, some paintings and personal possessions, and, oh yes, those rugs. We'd tried, but we just couldn't get them to fit into any of the leave-behind categories.

Bishop Beltran wrote back immediately. He confirmed that our time lines would work out well with his schedule and what he had planned for us. He could not tell us where we would live or where Peter would be assigned. With a number of clergy reassignments being made before August 28th, he would let us know what parish Peter would be assigned to before we left Washington. He explained that while the diocese would not be able to pay our total moving costs, they would assist us.

On August 30th the Bishop wrote to say that he was leaving for Rome and that Father Dorney, the chancellor, would be in touch with us to let us know where to have our things sent. There was no word of an assignment to a parish.

His letter was followed the next day by one from Father Dorney in which he said Father Greg Gier's rectory had a large basement where we could store our things until we arrived.

Peter wrote to Father Gier at Christ the King Church, giving him the approximate arrival date of our books, which we sent parcel post, the cheapest way, and our other things which would arrive by moving van. Father Gier did not respond to the letter.

While the vagueness of our arrival in Tulsa was puzzling, we were so busy with the details of our move and saying goodbye to friends that we did not think very much about it. Our faith in Bishop Beltran seemed to carry us beyond any doubts we might have felt. In the brief moments when I did allow concern to creep into my thoughts, the idea that we had sold everything and were going to move halfway across the United States, not knowing what the next step would be, was overwhelming, if not completely insane.

One day at work, Cecelia came into my office.

"Mary, are you sure everything is going the way you want for your move to Tulsa?"

"Yes, I think so," I said, my back to her.

"Where will you live? Where will Father be assigned?"

Cecelia, a devout Catholic, had never stopped calling Peter "Father," and at that moment it touched me deeply. As I turned to her, I could not stop the tears which came to my eyes.

"I don't know, Cecelia. I don't know where we are to be assigned, and I don't know where we will live. It could be a back bedroom in some rectory, for all I know."

As I talked, her dark Basque eyes grew larger and larger in her lovely oval face.

"Oh Mary." Tears filled her eyes, as together we struggled not to lose control.

"How will you live? Do you have savings?" she asked, her voice barely audible.

"We have a little money from selling our things. We

don't know what the bishop plans, but I can't imagine them paying Peter anything before he is able to function as a priest. I don't know what we'll do."

"Oh, Mary."

"We can trust Bishop Beltran. Maybe he . . ." My voice drifted off as I realized we had absolutely no idea what lay ahead for us in Tulsa.

"Oh, Mary. To leave all that you have and . . ."

"I know we'll be taken care of. And I don't care where I live. I don't have high expectations. We'll make do with whatever." I turned away again. "I'm not worried." But we both knew that in my heart I was.

Our house hadn't sold during the summer. In the last weeks we were able to lease it to a teacher and his family, welcome assurance that we would be able make the monthly payments. To our amusement, a number of people told us how relieved they were that we hadn't sold the house . . . so we'd have a home to come back to!

We moved our last few things out and waxed the kitchen floor on our last trip through the house that rainy morning. We were alone and the house was quiet. Empty without emptiness. There were ghosts everywhere. I comforted myself thinking of the new young family that would be moved in by evening.

Just as we climbed into our loaded old blue station wagon, Katie German, a friend from our summer swims, drove into our driveway.

"I don't want you to forget us," she called, reaching into the back seat of her station wagon. Katie ran over to our car and handed us a handmade pottery bowl crafted by her husband, Forrest, a well-known Northwest potter. She had filled the bowl with chocolate chip cookies.

"Oh, Katie," I stammered. "Well, what can I say? Thank you so much!"

"God bless you! Keep on swimming!" Peter called after her, as he reached into the bowl for a handful of cookies.

"Oh no you don't," I said pulling the bowl away. "Not until lunch!"

We were on our way at last, leaving behind twenty years of memories, of days well lived. The community, the people we had worked with in the school district and the fire department, and our Catholic friends at St. John Vianney had all wished us Godspeed with dinners and gifts of cash.

As we drove onto the ferry that rainy September morning, we felt well loved, indeed.

32

It is the Feast of the Visitation, May 31, 1985.

The good wine. It's there in Peter's face as I stand beside him in the front pew of this beautiful old cathedral. Tears fill my eyes, but now they are tears of joy. As I study my husband's strong profile, he turns and our eyes meet in a loving embrace. The music swells around us. It seems that this moment is meant for us alone.

Though I know it is the three new priests we celebrate. Not me at all.

Still, it is my triumph too.

They cannot take that away from me. Ever.

In this moment of joy I think of our first days in Tulsa. Autumn, 1983. Christ the King Church. Our new home.

I can see myself as I walk to the front door and look out through the torn screen. I don't know what to make of this house. Everything. Tears of sadness that day filled my eyes and spilled onto my cheeks. Beyond the porch a playful breeze runs back and forth kicking the dry leaves, rattling, creating the illusion of echoes as they tumble about the bare front yard.

"Peter, do you realize there's no grass in this yard?" I ask softly, looking from one side to the other.

"What did you say?" he asks.

"Not a flower."

"Well, of course there are no flowers, Mary. It's the middle of October." Impatient with me, he turns away.

"The leaves. What is there about this place?"

I turn to my husband, but he is engrossed in examining the closet in the front bedroom. He is already thinking of how the room can be converted into a study.

"It reminds me of the street in *To Kill A Mockingbird*." The American South. A culture so different, and yet the same.

"Huhh? Wha'd you say?" Peter asks.

No point in repeating myself, I think as I lean heavily on the dilapidated screen door for a long time, breathing deeply of the humid early morning air. There is an unreality about the moment as my head spins with the brown figures the leaves create as they turn and whirl. Their sounds seem to blend and then compete with the shouts of school children not far away. All around me. What is there about this . . .

How can I face this house?

Everything.

Already my clothes are damp and clinging from perspiration. It is an effort just to breathe.

In and out. In and out.

Rusty, broken air conditioner. (Probably can't be fixed.)

No electricity.

No water.

No furniture.

Dirty, stained carpet. (Smells of urine.)

Greasy kitchen walls.

Uneven floors.

We didn't have high expectations, but . . .

Forget it, I say to myself. Make the best of it. It's the way things are.

I turn to the small collection of boxes in the dining area. Our things. Not just the material symbols of our lives, but all that we have committed ourselves to, this *experiment*, as the bishop called it in his last letter.

Only now do I see the large arrangement of fresh flowers. Brilliant flash of color. Remarkably out of place in this dull, gloomy house. I smile as I think of the delivery person who, inspired by the obvious incongruity, had perched the bouquet almost whimsically on the highest packing carton.

The bright array of flowers seem like a mirage, and as I move toward them I half expect them to vanish.

But they are not a mirage.

In all of this, they are the only reality.

I touch them. Yes. They are real.

I open the card.

"Welcome home. Love, Don and Annie."

Our friends. They knew we'd have to face a new kind of struggle.

Will we ever have friends like these again?

I think of our island home. Nestled in the icy blue waters of Puget Sound. Lacey shoreline. Green forests. Fragrant strawberries.

"Did you see these, Peter? The flowers?"

No answer.

I look away. For the first time I notice that the windows in the house are bare. Through the bedroom window I see a row of rusty, broken rain gutters hanging from the edge of the roof like neglected strings of beaded curtains in a backroom doorway. Outside, a bent rain spout rests against a pile of asbestos shingles from the house.

"Bet this place leaks like a sieve."

"Now Mary, it's not so bad. We can scrub and paint and . . ." Peter says. His steps spring jauntily as he enters the room.

"And what?" I ask. "No amount of scrubbing is going to get the smell out of this carpet. You'll never find paint to cover that awful aqua color in the front bedroom, unless you're going to paint the walls black."

"Well, what do you want me to do?" Peter asks defensively. "The bishop's office said that the pastor, before he left on vacation, told them the house was ready."

"It just doesn't seem like Bishop Beltran would put us in a place like this."

In the church office.

"I'm so glad you're here, 'cuz I'm an Episcopalian," Susan, the church secretary, drawls in her friendly way.

"That's wonderful. We'll feel right at home," I say to her. To myself I think: Great. Just what we need. A secretary who's not a Catholic, but an Episcopalian.

"The movers brought your stuff about a week ago. We didn't know when you'd get here," Susan says. She sits at her desk, resting her chin in the palm of her hand.

"I wrote to the pastor and gave him the date of our arrival," Peter explains. For the first time he seems puzzled.

"Boy, you should have seen us scramble when that big movin' van drove up out front. We wondered where all your stuff would fit in that house." Penny, the other secretary, laughs.

"Then they didn't wanna leave your things in there," Susan says. "I think it was a toss up—whether they were afraid someone would break in and steal everything, or whether it was really the house you were going to live in." She turns to Penny and shakes her head, laughing. "I wouldn't wanna live in that dump, would you?" She drawls the last word, separating it into two syllables.

"Then when we went over there. Well, I was just sure they hadn't left it all. Those few boxes? Is that all of it?" Penny asks.

"We sold everything else. Bishop Beltran said to bring only our personal belongings. And actually, most of those boxes are Peter's books," I explain.

"Well, it sure isn't much of a welcome, is it?" Susan laughs nervously. She seems embarrassed.

"Sure am having a tough time with that old hot water heater." Bill the janitor enters the office and checks his mail box. "This here the new fella?"

"Yes, Bill. These are the folks for the house. Ready to move in," Penny says. She is warm and motherly.

"Say, Bill, when do you think we can get the water and lights turned on?" Peter asks.

"I'm a'workin on it," Bill drawls over his shoulder as the door swings shut behind him.

"Oklahoma! It's a great place if you can cope with Tulsa time." Susan laughs again.

To myself, I think, her accent. I love it.

"Say, why don't you two come over to my house for

dinner?" Penny asks. "We're members of the parish, and I'd love to have my husband and sons meet you."

"You're gonna love this parish," Susan says enthusiastically. "And our new pastor is just a riot. Why, when I took him to the airport to leave on his vacation, he was so excited he just went 'round and 'round. His arms all spread out, makin' sounds like an airplane!"

"Thanks, Penny, dinner sounds wonderful," Peter says.

"Here's my address." She scribbles on a piece of scratch paper. "Don't dress up. Just come when you're ready. Oh, five or sixish. Okay?"

"Sounds great. Thank you, Penny," I say, grateful for this welcoming gesture.

"We'll be back tomorrow morning to see what we can do with that house," Peter says as we leave the church office. "See you."

"Bye, now."

Once outside, I ask, "What kind of a priest would go around a public place pretending he's an airplane?"

We easily found Penny and Gary Victor's home. It was a frame house across from the synagogue on Owasso Street, typical of so many modest family homes we'd seen while we were driving down the streets of Tulsa. Two stories. Air conditioning units placed outside of windows. Large screened front porch.

We opened the screen door to the porch and stepped inside.

"You must be the Dallys. Come in," Gary said as he held the second screen door open. "Have a seat."

"Hi, I'm so glad you're here," Penny said, beaming. "It's Peter and Mary, isn't it? Boys, come here. I want you to meet these folks."

Four boys reluctantly filed into the small living room and stood beside the oversized tropical fish tank. Even the youngest appeared tall and husky, and as I looked from them to their father I felt as though I'd been surrounded by a band of Indian braves.

"What tribe are you?" Peter asked.

"I'm Osage and Choctaw," Gary answered with pride.

"Well, it's sure good to meet you guys," Peter said. "I'm part Chippewa."

"The Dallys are going to live and work in our parish. Peter's going to be a priest," Penny explained.

"We have a fifth child. Actually, she's the oldest. She's a student at Yale," Gary said proudly.

As we turned to sit down, the four boys filed out of the room as they had entered. "How long have you lived in Tulsa?" Peter asked.

"Just about all our lives." Penny laughed, a bubbling kind of laughter that seemed to come from somewhere deep inside.

We spent a pleasant evening with Penny and Gary talking about their kids and our kids, about why we had become Catholics. Why Oklahoma. What our lives would be like in their parish.

At the end of the evening Gary said, "I'm glad I got to meet you this way. I think what you're doin' is goin' to be hard, and I'm glad you're here with us. I think we're goin' to be good friends."

Penny and Gary were typical of Tulsans. Proud of their Native American heritage, they shared their unique culture and everything they had in a loving and accepting way.

These will be our people, I thought. So different, and yet very much the same as those we left behind.

"You're not staying there now, are you?" Bishop Beltran asked across the table at dinner the next evening. We had come to the Petroleum Club in downtown Tulsa to meet our bishop and Gary and Mary Sherman. The former Lutheran, now a priest candidate, and his wife had moved to Tulsa a month earlier.

Bishop Beltran had asked about the house, and I had

told him. I hadn't meant to say it all, but suddenly there it was.

"Yes. We checked out of the hotel this morning. We thought we could get the house ready faster if we were right there," Peter explained.

"How were you able to shower and get ready to come for this dinner?" the bishop asked.

I told him how I had gone across the street to the rectory to ask the associate pastor for permission to use one of the bathrooms there.

"Don't go over there, Mary," Peter said. "I don't think we should bother them."

"Bother them? They've put us in a dirty, filthy house without furniture and hot water. They could have had the utilities turned on. They knew when we would arrive. Anyway, we've been in town for three days now. I don't care if I do bother them." I brushed the hair out of my eyes and wiped my wet hands on my jeans. "I'm going to ask if we can use their shower." The sagging screen door scraped as it shut behind me. "What's the assistant pastor's name?" I yelled from the porch.

"I don't know. Just go. Bet he's not home!" He laughed.

I returned a few minutes later with the key and the older priest's directions to the second floor guest suite. Once inside our house, I surprised us both when I suddenly burst into tears.

"Why Mary, what's the matter?" Peter asked, putting aside his paint brush.

"That house. The furniture. Those carpets. Suites of rooms upstairs. I don't feel welcome here." Suddenly I was overcome with homesickness and a sense of degradation. I buried my face in Peter's chest as he folded his arms around me and held me. "How can they live like that and ask us to . . ." I sobbed, ". . . live like this?"

I didn't expect to live in a place like the rectory or even a nice house filled with new furniture, but I hadn't expected to be treated this way, either. And I wondered what kind of a priest would be so insensitive. I wondered if he wanted us here at all.

"The assistant pastor was kind enough to let us use one of the guest bathrooms in the rectory," I explained to Bishop Beltran. I looked across the dining room in the Petroleum Club, north to the Osage Hills. I thought of Penny and Gary Victor. They weren't really sure what was going on in the pastor's head. Others in the parish would be embarrassed if they knew, too.

"Do you mind if I come by tomorrow morning?" Bishop Beltran asked. "You could probably fix up the house, Peter, but you'll have a busy schedule of instruction and study as soon as we get the program under way. It's not the time to be involved in extensive cleaning and painting. I think I can find a better place for you to live. It won't be anything fancy, but at least you'll have furniture and hot water."

The following day Bishop Beltran moved us into a house owned by the Sisters of the Sorrowful Mother near St. John Medical Center. They were the same group of sisters who had welcomed us at their motherhouse when we first visited Tulsa in March, 1982. It was no surprise that they welcomed us now.

33

That happened a year and a half ago. Our friends on Vashon Island were right. We faced a different kind of struggle in Tulsa.

Many here in the cathedral church tonight have supported and affirmed Peter's vocation from the beginning. Others who first greeted us with anger and hostility have now received us in a spirit of openness and love, recognizing that God gives his children a diversity of gifts. That Holy Church moves with great mystery and in her own time. That she is the Catholic Church, and if all of us are a part of the Body of Christ, we must find within ourselves the humility and grace to embrace all that our membership implies. Sadly I realize there are still others whose faces I do not see at all, for they have chosen to stay away, unable to reconcile themselves with any exception to a celibate priesthood. I've learned that I am not responsible for their lack of openness. I feel sad for them, that we aren't here together. But I've learned that I am not the cause. It is their problem, and I pray for them. For all of us, in spite of our differences, are united in the Body of Christ.

Now we have persevered, and Peter will be a priest. Whatever comes next, that one precious gift can never be taken back. As I stand here beside him, my hand reaches to touch his, for he knows how important a part I feel in his priestly vocation.

As strains of the *Gloria* fill the Gothic arches of the cathedral, my thoughts wander to the legacy of the past months, an atmosphere often petty and hostile on one hand, supportive and affirming on the other.

"I want the people to get to know you so they will be aware that the priest has a wife," Bishop Beltran had told us. "Participate in parish life as often as you can. Both of you serve as lectors and Eucharistic ministers. Spend time with the staff as much as possible. Let them get to know you, and you get to know them."

The bishop had a program of study and development in mind that required the cooperation of the pastors to whom the three priest candidates were assigned, and their staffs as well. Other priests in the diocese were responsible for the candidates' preparation for the certification examinations.

That Bishop Beltran had arranged for housing and stipends for the three priest candidates upon their arrival in the diocese was not only heartwarming, but it made us feel a part of the diocesan family right from the start. Especially so, since it soon became clear that the Church would not realize any substantial return on this investment until the men were ordained priests at some time in the future. We were all deeply touched by this gesture of the Church's support and affirmation.

Together with our bishop, we broke new ground almost daily. As the months passed, Bishop Beltran would say again and again in answer to our questions, "Well, we don't know. You must remember, this is an experiment."

As in Washington, we found that the prospect of a married priest was not easy for the laity. However, the people did not seem to be threatened now, but only slightly reserved toward married former Episcopal ministers coming into the Catholic priesthood. As husbands and wives and parents, their understanding of our sacrifice for the sake of the Catholic faith touched Peter and me deeply. Indeed, their response moved us even more than any *sacrifice* we had made. Moreover, we found that they wanted to know everything about us. We tried to share our story with them in a completely open and forthright way.

But we soon understood that we were a constant reminder of their recent grief over the loss of many loved priests

in the years after Vatican Council II. Many priests had left
their vocations for various reasons, one of which was the
mandatory rule of celibacy. We found that our relationship to
the laity, and the whole question of priests who had left the
priesthood to marry, required our most heartfelt sensitivity
and warmth. Indeed, this became a heartbreaking symbol of
the 60s for Peter and for me as well. Through this bond, lay
men and women seemed to warm easily to us.

We did not think we would be accepted by the laity.
But we found the priests and sisters at Christ the King, from
whom we had expected support and encouragement, filled
with pain and anger over the Church's gesture to give outsiders what she would not extend to her own. This small
diocese, where only four percent of the population is Catholic, had lost nearly half of its priests in the years following
Vatican II. The pain of that loss was still very much a part of
their lives. We were looked upon as undeserving outsiders,
and there seemed to be no thought that we, too, might be
sensitive to the loss of so many of their brothers and sisters in
Christ.

Or perhaps we did not try hard enough to let them
know that we understood.

Naively, we thought we had come among priests and
religious who would surround us with love in a sanctuary of
friendship and appreciation for the journey we had made, if
not for the place from which we had come. A refuge where we
would be spiritually and emotionally strengthened and nurtured in an environment of mutual support for the demands of
Peter's future ministry, and the unique gift of my sharing it
with him.

Instead, as we found our every action watched and
judged in an atmosphere that was unexpectedly brittle and
volatile, we seemed to go into a state of shock.

Weren't these the same religious whom I had secretly
admired as a child? Who had won the deep respect and love,
the profound admiration of the entire Christian world? The
same priests and sisters who joyfully loved and served those

who most needed their love and support? Or were those just my own fantasies and dreams, not found in the living Body of Christ?

Puzzled and bewildered, we attempted to please them, often not knowing what it was they expected of us.

"I don't get it, Father Gier says not to tell any of the laity who we are. No one is to know we're here. He doesn't know whether he or the bishop will announce the program. He seems friendly enough, but there's something wrong," Peter said, as he had several times in those first weeks. We often walked to Christ the King for daily Mass, and he brought it up again that morning as we started for home.

"He doesn't seem to have the openness we experienced with Bishop Beltran and so many of the other priests. Maybe we shouldn't even be going to Christ the King for daily Mass. In so small a group, people are bound to wonder who we are."

"They said for us to go there," Peter said.

"It's hard not to talk to anyone. It's been weeks, and still Father Gier says he doesn't know if he or the bishop will announce our assignment here," I said.

"The bishop will be here for his visitation on Christ the King Sunday. I guess we should assume that he will announce it," Peter concluded.

"If Father Gier doesn't want us here, it would be better if he just said so," I said.

As we walked south on Trenton Avenue that morning, we talked over the things we had come to wonder about. Trees lined the street on either side, their bare branches forming a kind of canopy overhead. Once again I heard the echoes of the leaves on the empty street as they rattled against each other in the gentle breeze, pushed along by our shuffling feet. Somewhere a dog barked. Then another answered a few houses away. Or maybe it was just the echoes—

These are the sounds of loneliness, I thought. They seem to be everywhere.

Yet in another sense, these weeks were retreat-like.

The renewal in our lives of daily Mass. The opportunity for me to spend time reading after so many years of working and child-rearing. Peter's studies, uninterrupted by the telephone and the door bell. Walks in nearby Utica Square, and through the Rose Garden in Woodward Park where I wondered at the awesome beauty of roses blooming in late November. The fountain at Utica National Bank and Trust. Water. Precious water. In this dry land. The grotto of Our Lady of Fatima in front of St. John Medical Center. The warmth of the sisters and priests there. The sunshine! In winter. Unheard of at home. The Sun Belt, they told us. Unquestionably, there was an awe and a mysticism about our first weeks in Tulsa. For in spite of everything, we felt filled with wonder that God had called us to this place. We were eager to make this city and her Catholic community our home.

On the feast of Christ the King, Bishop Beltran announced at all the Masses that Peter would be on the staff as a married priest candidate. He carefully explained the program of the Pastoral Provision. However, it was decided not to introduce us personally to the congregation. I doubt that we would have met anyone if it had not been for Sister Patrice, who was herself new in the parish, and those lay men and women who made the effort to find out who we were, to welcome us on their own.

"Well, what did you think of today?" I asked Peter.

"It was very nice. A bit awkward, but I'm glad they didn't make a big fuss over us. Aren't you?"

"Yes," I said. But to myself I thought, it seems so strange. The reluctance I felt. As though there's really no heart in this program. This experiment.

"I'm glad for the time to study for my exams, Mary," Peter said defensively. "Next week I'm to go to the staff meeting and observe. Father said I could have a place to keep my things, though I don't think I'll be spending much time at the church."

"Well, at least we're moving ahead," I said, but instinctively I felt uneasy. It seemed to me that what was happening at Christ the King was not entirely in tune with what Bishop Beltran had planned.

Peter's space turned out to be a cupboard in the corner behind Susan's desk. He kept a few things there, his coffee cup and a notebook. Susan gave him a poster which he taped inside the door. A dogwood tree blooming in a huge forest of tall evergreens with the words: To be different is often a wonderful thing.

Susan became our friend and support in a situation that had to be difficult for her. A loyal Episcopalian, she must have felt betrayed, as others had, by our leaving the Episcopal Church. One day, after a small incident, I remember her saying in her friendly Southern way, "That's why I didn't become one!" I learned again from her that the most cherished treasures of friendship are often found where we least expect them.

"I asked Susan for a parish list today so that I can pray for each person by name. It's a huge parish, of course, but I thought I could break the list down into groups and take a few each day. You know, like I used to do in the Episcopal Church?" Peter said.

"That's great," I answered. "How did the staff meeting go?"

We sat at great-grandmother's table in the sunfilled corner of the kitchen. The sunshine, I thought. I hope I remember never to take it for granted.

"Okay. They wanted to know what I intend to do with the list, and when I explained they seemed to think it was sort of old fashioned. One of the sisters laughed and said, "Why don't you just pray for *the people of the parish* and forget all those names?"

"It probably just isn't her custom." I brushed it off.

"Well, I think it's important for me to fit in. But I don't see why there should be any objection to an intercession list. Father says I can have a Bible class. We'll start in Advent, and I can use the small library next to his office."

"That's wonderful!"

I felt happy and relieved for Peter. It had been a long wait, and he needed to feel useful now. But somewhere inside me, fear found its place. A subtle apprehension that I was unable to let go of.

One day as we explored the old part of the city, we discovered an historical marker telling of the oak tree where the Creek Indians, one of the Five Civilized Tribes, had brought the tulsi (ashes) from their village fires when they were forced by the government to leave their homelands in Alabama. They had rekindled their village fires under the giant oak in a sacred mingling of the past with the present. Tulsi, a symbol of the past, from which the new city of Tulsa would later take its name.

We easily found the Council Oak, as the tree is called. It was the biggest one around, but to two Pacific Northwesterners it didn't seem as large as its reputation had hinted.

Still the branches were thick and gnarled. It had seen a lot of history. The Indian. Then the white man. The oil boom out of which grew the new city of Tulsa. Many people had passed under it on important and ordinary missions alike. The tree had something to say to me. Straight and strong it grew, its roots going deep into the soil of Oklahoma. Not an easy task for any living thing in this dry land. But it was imperative if the oak was to have vitality and growth, for deep in the hard soil would be found the life-giving water. Precious water.

So it is with us, I thought.

The small room was filled to capacity with the six or seven people who came to the Bible class that first Sunday. Sister Gretchen, one of the staff, came too.

"Now don't you pay any attention to me," Sister said as she laid her pen and steno pad on the table in front of her. "Father asked me to be here to take a few notes."

Surprised by this, we could not help ourselves. In the

atmosphere of reproof we had come to expect at Christ the King, this seemed a threatening gesture on the part of the pastor.

"We didn't invite you here. No one asked if we would have you. We were forced to take you," Sister Gretchen said one day as we were leaving the church office after an awkward moment. Her words hurt, and I wondered why she had said this, even if it were true. Years later, with Susan's helpful understanding, I would realize that this holy sister was telling us in her own way why things were the way they were for us at Christ the King. Her words had been meant to comfort, not to hurt us.

They asked us questions about our children. We told them ours were normal kids who had their ups and downs like any others. As stories came back to us that our children had lots of problems, we laughed at their misinterpretation of "normal kids."

"We'll see if you're good enough," they all seemed to say.

The road was bumpy and full of holes, and we fell into them with all human frailty. Unable to see the whole picture, we tried to turn to the tasks at hand with charity and love for our brothers and sisters. I believe that they, more often than not, tried to do the same.

In December we moved into the second house owned by the Sisters of the Sorrowful Mother. Susan and Penny got the staff together and gave us a surprise house warming. It was a gesture of welcome, and it meant a great deal to us. They were really trying to make us feel welcome. Maybe we were over the rough part, I hoped.

In January someone took our photograph and Sister Patrice wrote an article for the newsletter to introduce us to the congregation. As I looked at the little publication, I hardly recognized the two frightened people huddled there, squinting in the Oklahoma sunlight. Something was happening to us. I felt almost as though somehow we were slipping away, losing ourselves in a sadness and apprehension that we had not known before.

I thought of the years since 1980. We had been through a lot as Peter tried for one entire year to get Archbishop Hunthausen's permission to leave the Episcopal Church. Then the somewhat anti-climactic trauma of finally leaving. We had expected the archbishop to sponsor us. Then that had slipped away. Oklahoma was offered. We were grateful and so happy when Bishop Beltran accepted us. Then that awful summer. Everything seemed washed clean when I received the vision of tongues of fire. Our plans moved forward smoothly. But it was not easy to break up a household of so many years and sell our possessions, each representing a part of our very selves. Still, when it was accomplished, we felt so much peace about it. Free at last, it seemed. But we had to leave our children and friends behind, and that was far more difficult than the letting go of material things. And there was no freedom or peace to follow.

As we eagerly drove across the country, we looked forward with excitement and anticipation to Peter's new ministry in the Catholic priesthood.

What to make of it? What was it that was happening to us now? We were too anxious. Too eager to make it happen. We hadn't expected it to be easy, but . . .

Peter went to Dallas in January for the oral certification exams. He did not do well and was told by the committee that he would have to retake three of them.

He realized that if he was going to pass the second time, he had to enlist a competent tutor. He would have one more chance. He went to Father Thomas Casey, a Jesuit priest at Holy Family Cathedral. Father Casey, formerly a professor at Creighton University, knew the academic environment and what would be required to pass the exams.

"When I told Father Gier today that I have asked Father Casey to tutor me, he was furious," Peter said.

"Why?" I asked in surprise.

"He says Casey is too conservative," Peter said as he chuckled out loud.

"Do you think you've done the right thing?" I asked.

"Yes, I do. Father Casey is behind me, and I know he'll help me. I don't think I can pass without him. I don't understand what the examiners want. This is the first time the exam has been given at Holy Trinity Seminary. I can't help but wonder if the priests there have any idea where former Anglicans are coming from, or why we're here to begin with, and what it is we need to know to be good Roman Catholic priests. But I know Father Casey can find out what they expect. He will tutor me on the material so I'll understand what they want and they'll certify me."

I couldn't understand why Father Gier wouldn't want Peter to get Father Casey's help. It seemed that he should be glad another priest was helping him, especially since he himself was always too busy to talk with either of us. Could it be that he really doesn't want Peter to succeed, I wondered. No. I just couldn't accept that.

Father Casey repeatedly called the examiners at Holy Trinity Seminary until he found out just what studies Peter must have to pass the exams.

He helped us in another way too. Living and believing as he did in a celibate priesthood, he was comfortable enough to openly discuss its strengths and weaknesses, and our relationship to it as married people. Father Casey knew it was critical for us to talk about this. We needed to talk with him in a supportive and open atmosphere about what we were experiencing in the Catholic Church. Most importantly, Father Casey believed Peter should be a priest, and he wanted to help him to be a good one.

"I couldn't have survived as a priest if it had not been for the support I received from my sisters and their families," Father Casey said to us one evening as we sat around our living room.

That's why he feels comfortable around me, too, I thought.

"I went into the Jesuits because I wanted community, and yet because of the needs of the modern Church I often found myself living and serving alone. So I had two families to fall back upon, my religious order and my own family."

"I don't know if I could have been a celibate," Peter responded. "My life with Mary is just so complete. I don't know if I could have lived with the loneliness of celibacy. On the other hand, Father Greenfield, our close friend who is a celibate priest in the Episcopal Church said that he loved God so much that he couldn't make room for a woman in his life. I don't think that anyone but a man or woman called to celibacy can really understand that lifestyle. By the same token, from a cultural and historical point of view, Holy Matrimony has always been safeguarded and protected in the Catholic Church where celibacy is held in highest regard. The two go hand in hand," Peter said.

"Yes," Father Casey agreed.

"Sometimes I wonder why we ever did this," Peter said as he smiled. "I mean, let's face it. We're not wanted. We've come into a situation where we may never be accepted."

"It's not easy for you. It's not easy for us." Father Casey set his coffee cup aside and leaned forward, turning to Peter. "Still, I believe you have a vocation to priesthood. And in that case, it doesn't matter whether a priest or anyone else likes you personally or the fact that you have a wife. The Church has made a decision. In this case to receive married former Episcopal ministers. It is important for all of us to remember that these decisions are not made without a great deal of prayer and deliberation. We don't have to like it. But when a man is *called* by God, as you have been, each of us must respect his vocation. It is presumptuous of *any* person, priest or sister or layman, to interfere by imposing their own prejudices."

As I listened to this man, tears filled my eyes and I looked away. How could I show him how much I loved him for saying that?

How do I show a man who is a celibate priest that I care for him as a brother? Not to be misunderstood?

Father Gier planned a three-day sensitivity training retreat for the staff to be held at Our Lady of Sorrows Convent. Peter had participated in sensitivity training both in the Episcopal Church and with the National Guard, so he was familiar with the different types and processes. But he soon became uncomfortable with the development of the program at this conference when he and others there saw that it lacked all positive reinforcement.

It was at this point that things seemed to go from bad to worse for us at Christ the King. Still, we kept trying to make something good out of this experience that had become both uneasy and bewildering for us.

On Easter Sunday we left on pilgrimage to the Holy Land and Rome with the bishop and a group of lay men and women. When Bishop Beltran asked if we would like to go, the money seemed impossible for us to raise. But we had seen other financial miracles, so in faith we made our reservations. Not only would we visit the holy places, but we would also visit Sister Elsbeth in Jerusalem, whom we had not seen for more than ten years.

When it came time to pay the balance needed for the pilgrimage, our savings and a portion of my retirement fund made it possible for us to go.

What a gift! The visits to the holy places. The walks across the hills and along the Sea of Galilee where Jesus had walked. To be with Sister Elsbeth again and to meet the other sisters. The same sisters who had prayed us into the Catholic Church and sustained us now with their prayers.

To go to Rome where Peter and Paul had brought the Gospels of Jesus to the pagan world. To receive Holy Communion at the tomb of Peter, and to walk through Michaelangelo's great basilica, meeting all those saints we'd read about in Church history. The Pieta. The Sistine Chapel. To learn that the bone fragments of a woman had been found in the crypt next to those believed to be the bones of Peter, the first pope. Tradition said that he had a wife. No one knew for sure if they were her bones, but their proximity to his original tomb seemed to reinforce the belief that she was martyred beside him on the Vatican hill.

Then to visit Assisi where St. Francis received his call and began his ministry to the poor. To pray near the tomb of this saint who seemed to pop up again and again in our lives! To recall that day in 1981, on the Feast of St. Francis, when we had been received into full communion with the Church of Rome. In spite of all that had happened to us, we realized more than ever that reunion with the See of Peter was God's greatest gift to us on our pilgrim journey in faith.

Feeling like our heads had been heaped with grace, our faith grew. Enriched in a new and infinitely more powerful way by our visit to the holy places and the affirmation of Peter's vocation we experienced in our friendship with the other pilgrims, we returned to Tulsa filled with awe and hope, never more sure of Peter's call and the truly remarkable gift of my sharing in it with him.

Peter was scheduled to take the certification exams the following week in Dallas. On Tuesday, after our return from the pilgrimage, he went to Christ the King for the weekly staff meeting. On his way into the meeting he stopped to get the updates for his parish intercession list from Susan.

During the staff meeting he quietly applied peel-off labels to the pages of his intercession book.

"What are you doing, Peter?" Father Gier impatiently stopped the meeting to ask.

"Updating my intercession list," Peter answered.

"Well, stop it immediately."

"Okay." Peter put the book away.

That afternoon as Peter returned to the church after making hospital calls, Father Gier hurried out of the rectory. "I'm extremely displeased. You were very disturbing at my meeting this morning. We need to see the bishop immediately. I simply can't take any more of you."

"Do you want to call him or shall I?"

Father Gier called the bishop and made arrangements for the two of them to meet with him that afternoon.

"What seems to be the problem?" the bishop asked.

"I want him out. Now." Father Gier said.

"What did I do?" Peter asked.

"You ruffled papers during my staff meeting."

"Is that all? Is that what's bothering you?" Peter asked, irritated by what seemed to him sheer pettiness.

"Bishop, I've never been so angry in my whole life. I—well, he made me extremely angry." Father Gier said.

"What about my other duties? The Bible class?"

"Well yes, that was successful."

"What about the lenten program?"

"I would like to have seen more uh . . ." Father hesitated.

"I don't understand. What have I done that is so wrong? Can you be more specific?" Peter was impatient with the priest.

"Well, I don't know . . ."

"I can see that we have to terminate this situation," Bishop Beltran quietly interrupted. He had listened and watched throughout the exchange. "Peter, if you were in my meeting, I would not want you working on something else."

With a few parting words to Bishop Beltran, Father Gier left the office.

"Peter, why didn't you come to me before things reached this point?" the Bishop asked.

"I didn't think I should. I'm the outsider. I—well, I just didn't think I should come tattling to you."

"In the future I want you to come to me. You should have this time."

"What about my exams, Bishop? What's going to happen now?"

"Don't worry about this right now. We'll work it out. Just go to Dallas and take your exams. Do the best you can. We'll talk about this when you return."

Bishop Beltran was so completely reassuring that when Peter came home from the meeting he felt as though the bishop understood how we had been affected by our experiences at Christ the King. We knew we weren't blameless, but neither were they. Unrealistically, I think, we hoped and expected that there would be a reconciliation. The matter simply didn't seem to be an obstacle to starting over with mutual love and acceptance. Naively, I suppose, I thought that to clear the air and continue at Christ the King would bring about healing and a healthy relationship between us and Father Gier and the staff there.

This time Peter satisfactorily answered all the examiners' questions in Dallas. In so doing, he had completed all the canonical requirements for ordination to the priesthood.

Almost four years had passed since that day in August, 1980, when he had first asked to be considered under the Pastoral Provision.

34

"Congratulations, Peter," Bishop Beltran said as he greeted Peter at the door of his office. "You've passed your exams and I'm happy for you." They shook hands and he invited Peter to sit down in the spacious third floor office. The windows caught the morning light adding to the sunny atmosphere of the room where Western art hung on two of the walls. The bishop's working desk was that of a busy pastor. The rows of bookshelves told of a man whose love for the Catholic Church expressed itself in his great love for the people of God.

"Thank you, Bishop. I don't have to tell you it's a big relief to have them behind me."

Since they had overcome all the obstacles to ordination, the bishop's decision to ordain Peter and Patrick Eastman seemed to involve only the formality of setting an appropriate date.

"I'm concerned about what happened between you and Father Gier," the bishop began. "It has come to me that you have gossiped all over town that you were fired."

"Gossiped?" Peter was stunned by Bishop Beltran's accusation. He couldn't think of having even mentioned it to anyone.

Then he remembered.

"Oh, I know. Mary and I went to a house blessing where I joked to the priest: I lost my job at Christ the King. Why don't you let me work for you? But, Bishop, he knew I was only kidding. Gossip? I don't know anyone to gossip to." Peter couldn't believe the bishop had actually thought he had gossiped about Father Gier.

"First of all, he didn't fire you. Secondly, he couldn't fire you. You were assigned there by me. I am the only one who can change that assignment."

"I see," Peter said.

"There were problems, and you didn't come to me." He stopped and waited a moment. "You're nervous and excitable. Uptight. Though I don't even like to use that word. I would like to do what I can for you, but I cannot ordain you now. You lost your temper with the pastor I assigned you to work with. I must see more self-control on your part."

"I don't . . ." Peter was shocked. It seemed clear to him that the priest's behavior in Bishop Beltran's office was an indication of the prejudice we had experienced as part of the Pastoral Provision program. "Bishop, I did everything I could to get along with Father Gier. I haven't gossiped about him or any other priest."

Peter's eye fell on the icon of the Blessed Mother. She alone in her effort to live out her vocation as the Mother of our Lord is the model for the Church, he thought. "What do you want me to do?" he asked the bishop.

"I would like to see healing between you. If you're going to be a priest in this diocese, you must work with all the other priests. In this small diocese these kinds of situations can be very bad. Has there been a reconciliation between you and Father Gier?"

"No, Bishop."

"I want you to take the initiative and apologize to him for your behavior."

"But, I haven't—"

"It will be your responsibility to go to him, Peter."

Bishop Beltran abruptly stood up and crossed the room. Thoughtfully, he looked out the window. It seemed a long time before he spoke again.

"You're nervous and tense. I don't know that you can get along with the other priests. I'm told that you're dense and thick-headed, that you have a dislike for Episcopalians, your former brothers. I can't have you going around causing trouble for us ecumenically. I'm going to have to put you on probation. Probably not for too long. Maybe six months. That is, provided I can find another priest to assign you with.

Ordination. I don't know. We'll just have to see how things go. If all goes well, and I hope it will, we'll plan the ordination at the end of the probationary period."

Peter was stunned. He had not expected this. The situation had seemed so obvious that day in the bishop's office. And Bishop Beltran had seemed to see it then too. He wondered what had happened in the meantime.

"I've been placed on probation, Mary," Peter said over the telephone.

"What?" I couldn't believe my ears. "Probation? Why?"

"I lost my temper with Gier."

"What? Don't tell me that wasn't a tantrum he threw in Bishop Beltran's office that day," I said, furious at our helplessness.

"Someone, a priest, told the bishop I gossiped all over town about Father Gier. They don't want us, Mary."

"Come on! Who is the gossip, anyway? No one is that naive."

"He's a priest. I'm not."

"So what? Right is right. He didn't want us in his parish in the first place. Surely the bishop knows that."

"The bishop says I'm like a little boy, showing-off all the things I can do. Inviting everybody to dinner."

"I thought we were supposed to get to know people. The priests and sisters. Showing-off? Who says so?" I had enjoyed making a sincere effort at hospitality and friendship. This unexpected impression about our motives was painful to me.

"Well, the bishop says it'll be at least six months, *if* he can find a priest who will take me into his parish."

"What does that mean?"

"I've heard somewhere that once a pastor turns against a seminarian, a candidate in my case, the other priests—well, who knows what will happen."

"What will we do? We've given up our lives in Washington. We've sold everything. We have nothing to go back to. That is, if we had the money to return," I said, as I thought of how we'd used our savings for the pilgrimage to the Holy Land.

"I know," Peter said. "It's me. I'm so sorry I've done this to you, Mary."

A few days later the bishop asked Peter to bring me to his house. It was kind of him to be concerned for me, but what could I say? What could either of us say? Petty or not, I could not bring myself to tell the bishop about all the things that had happened to us. In all of this we were only two human beings. Not perfect. We had tried, and apparently we had failed miserably. We would simply have to live with his decision.

He told us that now each priest candidate would be moved toward ordination on an individual basis. Patrick Eastman would be ordained deacon as soon as possible, and priest before the summer was out. Since he had been received into the Catholic Church just before coming to Tulsa, only eight months earlier, he would be given a special dispensation to be ordained before he fulfilled the Vatican's required waiting period of one year.

Truthfully, I have to say that the situation, as it had developed, was very difficult for us. While we rejoiced with Patrick and Maureen, a further wait, so unfairly imposed, was devastating to Peter and me.

In all of this, we fumbled and searched for a thread of assurance that this was not, in fact, the end of everything we had hoped for. We could only hold fast to our faith in God, his Holy Church, and our belief in Peter's vocation to the priesthood.

It was now the spring of 1984. After more than three years of preparation, Peter had passed all the exams for ordination, and now the Church had told him he would not be ordained.

Probation would take the place of priesthood for now.

Peter continued his theological studies on his own,

with Father Casey's guidance. Once again his hours with Herman Grimm came to his aid, as he turned to his beloved study of the Scriptures in the Epistle of James. Had it not been for this, he would have nearly lost his mind, as he sat around the house waiting for the bishop to let him know where he would place him next, for we had to believe that there would be another chance. He continued to care for Catholic patients at Hillcrest Hospital, though with some awkwardness, because he no longer had the support he needed from the priests at Christ the King for the administration of the sacraments to patients. We felt alone, as now more than ever Peter was the outsider.

During the weeks that followed we did several things as Peter immersed himself more deeply in study and prayer. We attended daily Mass with the Sisters of the Sorrowful Mother in their chapel at St. John Medical Center. They supported us in a way that was warm and reassuring. On Sundays we went to Holy Family Cathedral to participate in their beautiful sung Masses. I made the decision to meet as regularly as possible with my confessor.

We thought and talked a lot about the months at Christ the King. The rejection we experienced by the pastor and most of the staff. We had not heard from any of the staff except Sister Gretchen since the morning of that fateful staff meeting.

Our lives were like open wounds, lacking the reconciling grace we both craved. But in this new and alien environment, we didn't know how to approach these priests and sisters on our own. Or perhaps we were afraid we would only make things worse.

It was a welcome gesture when Tom Layman, the director of the diocesan Adoration of the Blessed Sacrament Program, called me to ask if I would like to participate, I said that I would like that very much.

"You can't do that. Who has time to go there every week, anyway?" Peter said.

"It's something I want to do. I'll make time," I said.

The first week, as I was getting ready to leave the house, Peter decided to go with me. Later Bishop Beltran appointed Peter to assist Tom with the program, and when he was ordained he became the priest advisor. Now, years later, Peter would not think of missing his daily holy hour, no matter how full his priestly schedule might be. But back then we went weekly, and sometimes more often, to pray before the Blessed Sacrament in the Chapel of Peace at St. John Medical Center. I never went alone once. Without his understanding why, our Lord seemed always to draw Peter there with me.

There were surprising friendships with lay people we had met at Christ the King which rekindled and grew in a loving, supportive companionship. These served to blunt for us the painful rejection of the staff there.

We bought bicycles. Every opportunity we got, we rode the River Parks trails together. We watched the magnolia trees bloom and smelled their fragrance up and down our street. And when the oppressive summer heat came upon us, we listened to the song of the crickets that greeted the sunset each evening.

We tried to keep a forward look as we planted flowers in our backyard and placed hanging baskets of begonias and geranium ivy on the front porch. The day I hung them there, a passing car slowed in front of our house. The driver appeared to watch the addition of the hanging baskets. With these flowers I'm telling all of Tulsa that we're here to stay, I said to myself. I felt more assured and determined than ever, as we waited for some word from our bishop.

One day, more than two months after Peter's meeting with Bishop Beltran, we were at the Benedictine Convent of St. Joseph. Two different priests congratulated Peter. They had heard that he'd been assigned to St. Pius X Church under Father Dorney, the chancellor of the diocese.

To say that we were surprised is an understatement. No one had told us. Gossip. Rumors. I was furious. Why did we have to hear this from others?

"Now, Mary. At least we know," Peter said to me. "Actually, I think it's kind of funny. I get accused of gossip about Father Gier. Now this. Don't you see? It's hilarious!"

"Oh, I suppose it is funny. But you'll have to admit that it's a double standard," I said as I turned to him and smiled. "And I guess I'm really just sick and tired of always getting the blame for everything. Aren't you?"

"We're the outsiders. There's nothing to do but take it."

"Are you going to call Bishop Beltran and ask him about it?"

"No. He'll be in touch with me."

We waited another two weeks before the bishop called Peter to his office to tell him of the assignment.

Again Bishop Beltran said, "I want people to get to know you. I want you to be visible so they'll know you're going to be a priest and get used to seeing you with a wife. Take your turn greeting people at the door so they'll know who you are. Sign up to be lectors and Eucharistic ministers. Then in about six months we'll see how things are going."

Again, it seemed to me that Bishop Beltran's attitude was completely wholesome and direct. Just as we had experienced him earlier. What then was the problem with the priests and sisters? We had been told that the Church feared that the married priests of the Pastoral Provision would be a scandal to the laity. Clearly though, in our experience at Christ the King and at the hospital the laity didn't have nearly the difficulties that the priests and religious had. I asked myself, could it be that sisters hoping for women's ordination saw their dreams fade in the wake of the few married former Episcopalian ministers who would be ordained to the Catholic priesthood? While it was important and necessary for us to love and appreciate their vocations, the question of women's ordination was in God's hands. It wasn't a question for them, or for us. We had simply responded to a call that Peter had felt for a number of years. It had never occurred to us that the Pastoral Provision would take the place of possible ordination for women in the Catholic Church.

At St. Pius X, Peter sat in the congregation for ten

months. Not once was he scheduled to read a lesson. Only twice did he serve as a Eucharistic minister. Father Dorney asked him to greet people, and he usually took one of the side doors. But it was not easy for him, as he went there each Sunday, to face the quizzical looks of the lay people as they arrived for Mass. He explained that he was a member of the staff, a priest candidate, but it was not clear to the parishioners who he was or what he was doing there, since he was never seen as a participant in the Sunday liturgies. By now we had come to recognize liturgical participation as the normal pattern of preparation for men entering the priesthood. Nor were the men of the Pastoral Provision allowed to wear their clerical collars here, as was the practice in some other dioceses. This would have identified Peter to lay persons both in the parish and in the hospital where he worked.

Father Dorney had introduced us to the parish by way of an appropriate but lengthly letter in the news bulletin. I doubted whether many people had taken the time to read it and make the connection between the message and Peter. We had long since given up on ever being introduced in person to a congregation as a priest candidate and his wife.

I began to wonder for the first time if Bishop Beltran and the Tulsa Diocese were sincere in their consideration of Peter for priesthood.

As the experiment at St. Pius unfolded, I realized that the sisters and employees knew little about the Episcopal ministry or the men who were part of the Pastoral Provision. In their minds we had come from a small Protestant sect, having little knowledge of the practices of the historic Catholic Church and the life of the Church since Vatican II. The sisters here and those we'd worked with at Christ the King were for the most part women who had been born into Catholic families and attended Catholic grammar and high schools. They had then entered Catholic religious communities and received academic degrees from Catholic colleges. There was nothing about their appearance which hinted that they were members of a religious community. Moreover, while they considered themselves liberal and well-rounded individuals, their attitude toward Peter lacked a sense of cooperation. Some appeared angry and haughty, negating any suggestion that their lives, much less their physical appearance, conveyed to the world that they had been set aside to serve the Lord Jesus.

The weeks and months passed. As a convert to Catholicism, I felt more the outsider than ever, as the old feelings of devastation and depression pressed in upon me. I could not understand their lack of openness, their hesitance to include us in the life of the Church in any meaningful way.

Was this the way it was to be? Is it possible, I wondered, that these consecrated women, whose contributions to the Church had been a matter of awe through the years, had come to this? It almost seemed they were jealous of Peter and me. Never before in our lives had we been rejected this way. In my anger I blamed them and some of the other women employees for the devastation I felt. I found it next to impossible to love them. In my hopelessness, I wanted to give up even trying to understand. But there was something in me that would not let me give up, and I determined almost daily not to take them seriously or personally. My anger grew in spite of my good intentions.

As the pattern of our life became clear, I could not imagine what the Church planned to do with Peter. If my husband was going to be a priest, why did he only sit in the congregation? No liturgical experience. Nothing, for that matter, which would prepare him and the people of St. Pius for his future priesthood.

Peter asked to teach an adult Bible class, which again was successful. Father Dorney asked him to begin a monthly wedding anniversary Mass. But any layman could have done these things. And while he experienced more freedom than at Christ the King, the programs at St. Pius X were closely monitored by one of the sisters.

It almost seemed to me that they wanted to see how much he could take before he blew up completely.

Or were they simply hoping we would become discouraged and return to Washington state? I began to think that perhaps Bishop Beltran had kindly supported Peter after the situation with Father Gier because he thought Peter would fail his second try at the certification exam. They could have said they had given him a second chance. It would have been an easy out for the Church.

But he hadn't failed. He had passed, and we were still here. If the time was now to be used for training, that would explain it, but clearly that was not the case.

Each staff member helped with the evening adult education classes by rotating the responsibility to teach. Peter was assigned to the one week we were scheduled to be in Seattle for our older son's wedding. It could have been a coincidence, but it seemed unusual that the Director of Religious Education didn't reschedule Peter to another week, since it was normal to switch other staff members around.

In another instance, Peter asked a sister to approve a letter he wished to send regarding the anniversary Masses. She scratched out the title of Priest Candidate and told him not to use it. What title should he use? She didn't know.

And what of my participation? I signed up when we registered in the parish to serve as lector and sacristan. In the early fall I signed up again and attended the training workshops where I placed my name on each list for the third time. When months passed and I had not been called, I asked Peter if the new people were being used yet. When he inquired, he was told that I had not signed up. No one ever called me to participate. I wanted to believe that it could have been an oversight, but somehow that didn't seem likely.

All of these incidents were too petty to mention or even to think about. But when taken together they began to tell a story that could only be interpreted as rejection, or at best a reluctance to involve either of us in the life of the parish in ways that would have been entirely appropriate.

I had become an angry, bitter person and I knew it. I was no better than they. What had happened to the love and grace which meant so much to me in the Catholic Church? I asked counsel of my confessor. I continued to go to daily Mass. I prayed for forgiveness and healing, but I felt no relief from my depression. What of our Blessed Mother, Mary? I had not thought of her in weeks.

Then, together, Peter and I experienced a final resignation to the situation. We could not force the Church, these women and priests, to accept us. Secretly, I hoped that it would soon be over.

"I don't think I'm ever going to be a priest, Mary," Peter said to me as we were driving home from Sunday Mass.

"Nonsense. Of course you'll be a priest," I assured him. "If the bishop doesn't want you, he'll tell you."

"No. They're just playing games. It's Archbishop Hunthausen all over again."

I put my hand on his arm. I hoped he would feel in my touch an understanding and a composure that I could not express in words. My eyes filled with tears as I fumbled with my gloves and purse, pretending to look out the car window. It seemed with each passing day our dreams had faded to nearly nothing.

I thought of that yellowed piece of newsprint I had brought from Vashon Island and taped to the refrigerator door in our new home in Tulsa.

The seedling. In God's all powerful hand.

New growth.

Expectation.

"Whatever God has in mind for us, Peter, we'll know when the time comes. It's not time yet or we'd know for certain, wouldn't we?" I turned to him and smiled through my tears. "I still believe that God has a plan; that in his wisdom he is going to give us something wonderful. It may not be exactly the way we think we want it, or in our time, but it will be completely his, and it will be far more wonderful than anything we plan. We must try to give ourselves over to him even more completely than we have."

"I won't dump it. But I don't expect them to ordain me. They would have by now, if they were going to. We've been here sixteen months. If they don't know me by now, they never will." His voice was filled with anger and bitterness. "I know you don't agree with me, but I've always felt it's not too important that I become a priest. Oh, I know I should be, but for me the important thing is that I've tried. We've done our part." He held his breath momentarily, then sighed. "That's the most important thing. So what if we fail."

Peter's attitude upset me, yet I knew in my heart that he was right. It seemed now that they probably wouldn't ordain him, and I knew too that the important thing was that we had tried. That the Lord had called and we had answered yes, to the best of our ability. I had to ask myself, why was it so easy for some and so hard for others. When we left the Episcopal Church we wanted to become Catholics first. Priesthood, if it was God's will for us and for the Catholic Church, would follow.

Now, it seemed, we were suspect for that reason.

Like Peter, I could never feel that those men who waited for Vatican approval and an ordination date before leaving the security of employment in the Episcopal ministry did the right thing. If we are called, then we must give ourselves unconditionally. For us, anyway, there could be no bargains with God to see if things would work out before we made our commitment.

Still, we had given up everything.

Everything.

Our friends.

Our home and security.

Even our furniture and appliances.

Well, it was done, and I had to admit that I was glad we did it this way, no matter what the outcome.

"There's just one thing I ask of you, Peter."

"Yes. What's that?"

"That you make them tell you they don't want you. For my sake and in the name of God, don't make it easy for them."

The following week, Michelle, a personal friend and one of the Sunday school teachers, asked Peter to substitute for her eighth grade class. When the Director of Religious Education learned that Peter had set aside the material on Thoreau's *Walden Pond* to talk about teen suicide at the students' request, she came to his office. She was furious. Michelle had not asked her if Peter could substitute, which appeared to be part of the problem.

"If you're ever involved again, stay with the material," she said angrily.

"I set aside the assigned material because I thought

the discussion of suicide was more important." Peter sputtered. "You should be grateful."

"You're offending me," she retorted and abruptly turned to leave. Her next stop was Father Dorney's office.

There was no effort to help the two reach an understanding. No reconciliation.

Later that week Father Dorney warned Peter, "You lost your temper again. You've just about burned your bridges behind you."

35

Bishop Law, now Bernard Cardinal Law of Boston, announced that there would be a meeting of the men and women of the Pastoral Provision in November, 1984. Peter and I felt reluctant to attend the meeting, because Peter had been one of the first to apply and now, more than four years later, he was still not sure that Bishop Beltran intended to ordain him. However, with the bishop's encouragement we decided to go, though the cost of the airfare was a sacrifice for us in light of our uncertain future. I'm not really sure why we went to Boston, all things considered. It just seemed something we should do.

When I met the others, I can only say that I was touched beyond words that Peter and I were a part of that group of intrepid men and women. They were fine people of great courage, and each of them had a story to tell. I felt stronger myself for being a member of this tiny band.

I didn't meet one person who had left the Episcopal Church to run away from something. They had come, like Peter and me, to be Catholics, to experience the full faith in the church that Jesus Christ had established. Without exception, they had come with no promise of material gain, and many came without even minimum financial support. Wives talked of holding down two jobs to keep children in college. Others talked of selling homes, leaving families behind. Not one person complained because they were forced to live on less income or had less status. Again and again I heard them say how much they had given up, and yet how much it meant to be Catholic, to have come home to their roots.

The morning we said good-bye, Cardinal Law, a giant

white haired man with dancing blue eyes, put his arms around Peter and me together, gave us a big bear hug, and said, "Hang in there, you two. Bishop Beltran loves you and needs you. *I* need you."

We returned to Tulsa feeling that our lives had been touched by God. These were people like us, living out their faith in the power of the Holy Spirit. We were not alone. Others had walked this path with us and ahead of us, and by God's grace there would be still others to follow. We felt humble and grateful indeed.

Within the week we flew to Washington state where our oldest child, John, married Sherry Evans in her home town of Sequim. Not only would it be a Catholic wedding in which Peter would not be allowed to participate, except to read a lesson, but we were going to see all our old friends. We knew there would be many questions, and an equal amount of speculation as to why Peter had not yet been ordained. No doubt a few bets on the final outcome would be exchanged, with a good many I told you so's after we left. It would not be easy. We would again have to summon every ounce of love and dignity we had left. Though the situation was painful for me, it was most difficult for Peter, for it required that he answer questions honestly and with love, and by now we were both feeling a great deal of anger as well as pain.

Our family and friends were clearly delighted to see us. And, as predicted, they wanted to know everything. In our openness, we felt cleansed and supported in an even more loving way than when we had left them over a year before. We didn't have to tell them of the struggle. They knew. They were still with us, praying for us and cheering us on. They knew Peter well. They knew his vocation to the priesthood. Even our Catholic friends on the island didn't need a Catholic bishop to tell them he had a vocation.

When we left them behind, as we had left Cardinal Law and the other couples in the Pastoral Provision two weeks earlier, we felt stronger and more supported by their friendship and prayers than we could ever have expected.

Though I didn't speak of it, it seemed clear to me that we were a problem only to those priests and sisters with whom we would serve. I began to understand that even this tiny handful of married priests seemed to be viewed as an undermining influence to the structure of a celibate-only ministry.

Why, I wondered?

In my mind, I heard their words echo again and again, "It isn't fair . . . isn't fair . . . isn't fair . . ."

A few days before Christmas we received a rather large, mysterious-looking package in the mail. We recognized the return address as that of a member of the charismatic prayer group in our former congregation on Vashon Island. We hardly knew what to expect as our daughter Monica opened the elaborately bound box. As the newspapers and stryofoam pebbles fell away, we saw the statue of the Blessed Mother, the one from the back of the little church, and we recognized the gesture of healing that it symbolized. The small statue remained securely attached to the shelf that had held it in the church. Tears rolled freely down my face, and I thought of the wisp of a girl, hardly older than the Blessed Mother, who had thought to send it to us.

> I don't have much time. The baby's crying. This statue of Mary was in the church attic, and they were going to throw it out. I wanted you to have it, knowing how much you loved it.
>
> *Debbie*

I looked at the Blessed Mother. Her pastel robes draped softly around her feminine body. The soft blue cape and veil I remembered so well framed her delicate features. In her arms she gracefully cuddled the baby Jesus, his hand raised in blessing. It was a lovely work of art, and we were deeply touched by Debbie's sensitive caring. Now it was more a symbol of Debbie, her crying infant and two other toddlers and our life on Vashon Island, than anything else.

As I studied the statue, it occurred to me that no longer did I think of Mary as the Mother of Jesus the infant. In these years of change and challenge in my own life, I had come to think of her as the Bearer, living out her life as the Mother of God, of Jesus the Man.

In his ministry.

In his derision, his humiliation, his suffering.

And finally, in his triumphant resurrection and ascension.

A presence and example in her earthly life, and with us now for all eternity in heaven.

Almost for the first time, I think, I understood the symbolism of Mary standing alone.

For me.

For each of us.

In January we settled into a routine. It gave me a chance to think of all that our lives meant to each other and to God, and I felt more at peace than I had for a long time. I stopped thinking of our great losses if Peter were not to be ordained. I began to understand that it is enough simply to be called. To try. To answer yes to the Lord beside Peter. The growth I had experienced. The richness in my life that I had never dreamed possible. Neither of us would ever be the same as when we first began. Simply because we had *tried* we were forever changed. God in his gentle mercy and love had received us. He had accepted the offering of our frail human sinfulness. If we were now rejected by other human persons, it would be no less than what they had done to Our Lord.

In my sadness, I found a greater joy.

That same prayer, seemingly so benign, so harmless: Lord, help me to know you, to love you, and to serve you.

Somewhere in it was the key to everything else.

For I, Mary Dally, child of God, wife of Peter, had finally begun to really give my life to God, without any deals. Without condition, and with love. In doing that I gave my life more completely to Peter, my husband. It was as though I stopped struggling to be free, and when I stopped, I experienced a freedom that was more complete than I ever could have dreamed possible.

I remembered that in one of Alexander Solzhenitsyn's stories he tells how a prison train on its way to Siberia stops at a remote outpost. The prisoners have been without water for days. In their misery, they cry out for relief from their thirst. An old woman from the tiny village bravely makes her way past the guards with a cup of water. As the train begins to move again, tears come to her eyes, and she makes the sign of the cross over the prisoners. Through her bravery and dignity, the prisoners receive the courage to recognize their own dignity. They demand that the guards address them with respect, treat them like human beings. A remarkable thing happens. Those who are the prisoners realize that only they, not the guards, are free.

Peter and I realized that in having given completely of ourselves to God and his Holy Church, we had won. We were called, and in our brokenness we had freely answered yes without condition, without cause. The rest was up to the Church. To human persons in all their imperfection. They would be the instruments by which we would be received if that were to pass.

I thought of the other Mary now. She was free from sin, but she was also free to turn away from God's plan for her life. She chose to be faithful. She could have said no, but her humble response was simply, "Thy will be done." She is the perfect example of how we are to live, for she met each day living out the details of her life, meeting the challenges and the adversities, embracing the blessings and joys, totally in the power of God's plan for her. Truly, she is "the woman" for all of us. For me. I felt warmly, mystically close to her life. Mother of God. My mother. My sister. Myself.

When we had been in the second parish six months, Peter made an appointment to see Bishop Beltran. Again, they did not discuss anything definite with regard to ordination.

In referring to the incident between Peter and the

Director of Religious Education, Bishop Beltran said, "You lost your temper again. I would like to see more self-control. I'd like you continue at St. Pius."

Again we forced aside thoughts that this might be their way of saying they really didn't want us here in the Diocese of Tulsa.

Peter stood at the window with his back to me. He seemed mesmerized by the dead plants we had set in the ground the spring before. "Don't you see? This really settles it. They're not going to ordain me. They don't want us. We have to face the fact that it's over for us, Mary."

"Not yet," I said. "They'll have to tell us. Remember, you promised me."

In mid-afternoon the same day, Peter received a phone call from Carol, Bishop Beltran's secretary. He would like both of us to come to the airport to talk with him before he left town on business. Carol explained that this was the only time available for the bishop to see us.

As we drove in silence toward the Tulsa International Airport in the congested late afternoon traffic, I could not help but wonder what the next hour would bring. If this were the end, I would be relieved. At least we could get on with our lives in the secular world. But, Peter. His vocation. How could a man who felt so strongly as he did, live with . . . And then we were there, walking toward the bishop, as we had on that first visit three years earlier.

"Peter, when you left my office this afternoon, you looked so sad and dejected. I felt I could not leave town without talking to you again," Bishop Beltran began.

"Well, I guess I just thought that six months have passed since you assigned us to St. Pius, and you said you would have something definite to say after six months," Peter said. "Maybe I expected too much." He looked away, thinking of the Bishop's words: "You lost your temper again."

"No. I just don't have a date for you at this time. I fully intend to ordain you as things stand now, but I can't ordain you alone. It's expensive, and if I have ordinations too frequently, people just don't turn out for them."

"I see."

"You probably don't even realize it, Bishop, but you've not actually said, until now, that you are going to ordain Peter," I said. "We haven't known what to expect." My voice faded with sudden embarrassment.

"That's why I wanted you to meet me here. I apologize for this kind of meeting, but it's the only thing I could arrange since I must be on this flight. I didn't want to leave without knowing that you understand the situation."

"Thank you, Bishop," Peter said quietly.

Now as the weeks grew into a month . . . two months . . . it seemed there wasn't anything we couldn't handle. We stopped feeling that we were on trial, that we had to somehow prove ourselves. We no longer mentally tabulated the minor rejections we experienced with the staff. They were no longer important. Nor were we plagued with the feelings of doubt and uncertainty about Peter's role and others' acceptance of us in the Catholic Church. We did all that we could to keep a low profile, to try not to call attention to ourselves, as we quietly waited on our bishop.

Then, quite suddenly it seemed, Bishop Beltran called to say that the Congregation for the Doctrine of the Faith had approved Gary Sherman's petition. Peter and Gary would be ordained together. It was an historic moment, for Gary would be the first married former Lutheran minister to be ordained a Catholic priest in the United States. Technically not a part of the Pastoral Provision, his was a special case which had been considered and approved at Bishop Beltran's request.

Peter and Gary were quietly ordained deacon at the Church of the Immaculate Conception on March 15, 1985.

Bishop Beltran presented Peter with the same Bible he had received when he was ordained a deacon in the Episcopal Church in 1953. It was a Ronald Knox Roman Catholic Bible. I sewed a quilted cover for the well-worn book and embroidered a red and white Jerusalem Cross on the front. That was in thanksgiving for the prayers of Sister Elsbeth and the sisters of the Carmel du Pater and for our pilgrimage to the Holy Land.

Our daughter Monica was with us, and our son John and his new wife Sherry came from Chicago. Mary Sherman and I sat together in the pew. I held our godson, baby Zachary Sherman. There were three other Sherman children beside us.

I thought of my father that night. His words, "I thought you would be the one to be a Catholic." His hurt and bewilderment then. I wondered how my dad would feel now. An Irishman, I felt sure he'd say things had gone too far. I thought of my great-grandparents too, Brigid McGuinness and Martin O'Hearn. And after them, Mary Jane O'Hearn and George Vincent. Their son, my father, James. It's a big day for an Irish Catholic family! How many generations—I smiled to myself as I thought of them—have they waited, and it's the daughter's husband who becomes a priest?

Inside, I hoped they'd find it an honor.

And my mother. I thought of my beautiful, sacrificing mother. If she had received the love and healing compassion of the Church as it is today, might she not rejoice also?

Peter and Gary would be ordained priests with Timothy Davison at Holy Family Cathedral on the Feast of the Visitation, May 31st, 1985.

For more than two months I held my breath. I could hardly believe it was happening; so long had we waited. We had wanted priesthood, but in his infinite wisdom God had given us so much more.

That sometimes when he says no, it's an ever better yes.

We had been changed and molded in a far more

powerful way than if we had walked out the door of the Episcopal Church and into the priesthood of the Roman Catholic Church. As the wounds began to heal even then, we found ourselves thanking God that he had allowed our suffering which had brought us into a more loving relationship with him and with our brothers and sisters.

We had talked of fulfillment.

Fulfillment indeed!

"My dear brothers and sisters in Christ, these men, your relatives and friends, are now to be raised to the order of priests," Bishop Beltran's words began.

I am touched by this bishop and his openness, his love for the Church. I realize that none of us, not even a bishop, has the right to expect perfection in himself or in others.

The love and grace to carry out the Lord's will for his Church is enough.

None can claim this mystery, this gift of priesthood for his own. God alone calls, and a man answers in his own human unworthiness; each one arrives here from a different background in a separate pilgrimage in faith.

Still, each has been validly called by the Lord.

In the Old Testament, the Prophet Jeremiah proclaims:

> The word of the LORD came to me thus:
> Before I formed you in the womb
> I knew you,
> before you were born I dedicated you,
> a prophet to the nations
> I appointed you.
> "Ah, Lord God!" I said,
> "I know not how to speak;
> I am too young."
> But the LORD answered me,
> Say not, "I am too young."
> To whomever I send you, you shall go;

whatever I command you,
you shall speak.
Have no fear before them,
because I am with you to deliver you,
says the LORD.

Jeremiah 1:4-8

The ancient Litany of the Saints moves slowly and majestically forward. The drama has begun, and I forget everything else as the cantor leads the congregation in a single voice of exhortation and petition. It is like a wave that moves over me, catching my body. Now covering me. Then holding me until I am caught in the next wave. Again. In unrelenting motion.

"Holy Mary, mother of God"

"Pray for us."

The warm air in the cathedral is heavy with Oklahoma humidity, and I am aware of the nearness of so many others. I breathe deeply and the pungent incense fills my head. The aromatic scent and the shadowed figures in the veiled haze reinforce the illusion that I've been a part of this scene for more than my lifetime. My head reels and spins with the mystery of the moment as the ancient odor fills my lungs, to find its way to the tips of my fingers and toes. Still, my body speaks only of calm and poise, as I stand undistinguished in the crowd of cathedral worshipers. My thoughts turn inward to the recurrent loneliness, always a mysterious emotion in a lifetime filled with others. It seems a strange emotion tonight, surrounded as I am.

Yet it has always been so.

My adult children kneel beside me. I turn my head slightly to see that their unblinking eyes are held by the robed figure of the man prostrate before the altar. It is their father. Peter. My husband.

Even now I want someone to tell me that tonight is not a dream, to assure me that my mind has not created a mirage of this Camelot scene. I look down at my body for the assurance that I am really there, and my rose-white silk dress creates all the more of an illusion, the lace modestly touches the contour of my neck and shoulders, then drapes easily down the front, held by silk again, and lost in the shadowy layers of skirt lengths.

Here in the cathedral I want this magic to seep into every part of me. I want to be present to each moment. Every move. Every word. Help me to realize that the hands that I have loved will be the healing hands of Peter, the priest. These hands that will now begin the daily devotion and privilege of the consecration of the bread and the wine into the Body and Blood of our Lord in the Mass are the same hands that have dried my tears and embraced me. Hands that have held our babies.

Our lives will never be the same again.

Still, nothing will be changed.

I will rest beside him and feel the warmth of his body as I have always. And then I'll smile to myself because I know that the strength of our love and the grace of a good marriage are the ironic conditions to his Catholic priesthood.

A blanket of calm and peace lightly embraces my shoulders as Bishop Beltran places his hands on Peter's head in the traditional way that the priesthood has been transmitted since the time of Christ. The choir softly chants the ancient hymn, *Come Holy Ghost*. I am spellbound as each priest in his turn moves slowly, deliberately across the sanctuary to place his hands on Peter's head in the same manner as the bishop, and my heart is overcome by the depth of this simple sacramental act.

Now it's time for me. In front of the altar, I take the deacon's stole from Peter's shoulder and place around his neck the stole of the priest. I lift the chasuble over his head. Not the one I have sewn for him, but it doesn't matter now.

It carelessly musses his hair.

The choir sings *You Are A Priest!*, the medieval Latin fills the air.

With our backs turned to the people, we wait, stilled by the moment. Peter takes my hand in his. It seems that a long time passes before we turn to face the congregation. When we do, he smiles and lightly kisses me on the mouth.

Once again I am his bride.

The applause reaches me, and I turn my head to face a sea of happy faces. A woman bites her lip to hold back her tears. Her fingers curl around the arm of the tall man next to her, and she shyly leans into him in a gesture of intimacy.

Our children smile big smiles amid gently elbowed comments to each other.

I smile to myself.

Once again I think of the other Mary . . .

And tomorrow?

What will tomorrow and the next day bring?

I turn to look up into the face of my husband.

We have waited long. Ours souls, as one, have been touched by the breath of God.

Could it have been any other way?

And now, bishop, priests, people. Together we enter God's great mystery.